HORN
of
PLENTY

Also by John Baird:
A Leap of Faith
The Whole Gospel for the Whole World
All Things Are Thine
Profile of a Hero
The Shining Fire

HORN

of

PLENTY

THE STORY OF THE
PRESBYTERIAN MINISTERS' FUND

John Baird

Tyndale House Publishers, Inc., Wheaton, Illinois

Permission to quote material from *The Presbyterian Enterprise: Sources of American Presbyterian History*, edited by Maurice W. Armstrong, Lefferts A. Loetscher, and Charles A. Anderson, is gratefully acknowledged. Copyright MCMLVI, by W. L. Jenkins. Used by permission of The Westminster Press.

First printing, February 1982

Library of Congress Catalog Card Number 81-53035
ISBN 0-8423-1452-0, cloth
ISBN 0-8423-1451-2, paper

To

MILLARD E. GLADFELTER

Chairman of the Board

1968-1978

with appreciation and respect

ACKNOWLEDGMENTS

Work on this book began in 1978 with conversations between Arthur M. Adams, Robert J. Lamont, and the author. From the start their enthusiasm for a story about the Fund proved of incalculable aid.

Many persons have helped me along the way. Without exception, company officers have furnished facts and made suggestions which have been of great value. Particular mention must be made of Miss Mary P. Capuzzi, Corporate Secretary with a genius for discovery and memory.

PMF made available its official records and historical papers, granted me access to employees and policy holders, and permitted me complete freedom of thought and expression.

Important information was provided by staff members of The American College, American Council of Life Insurance, Eastern Baptist Theological Seminary Library, Genealogical Society of Pennsylvania, Historical Society of Pennsylvania, Lower Merion Library Association, Million Dollar Round Table, Philadelphia Free Library, and Presbyterian Historical Society.

Special thanks go to these persons for their generous counsel: Miss Agnes Allen, Horace T. Allen, Mrs. Edward S. Buckley, 3rd., John M. Cookenbach, Paul J. Cupp, Miss Julia Dulles, Miss Vivian Fenstamacher, Miss Esther George, Anthony A. Geyelin, Mrs. Mary Virginia Geyelin, Millard E. Gladfelter, Donald L. Helfferich, Raymond I. Lindquist, Mrs. Helen Mackie, Samuel R. Moore, Jr., M.D., Hamilton R. Redman, Mr. and Mrs. Orvel Seabring, Mrs. Alice Mackie Smullen, J. B. Millard Tyson, Mrs. Lilly Dulles VanPelt, Mrs. Elizabeth E. Wasson, and Samuel C. Wasson, Jr.

CONTENTS

LIST OF ILLUSTRATIONS

FOREWORD

"To whom much is given much is required" seems to be not only a Biblical principle; its truth is also built into the moral fabric of history's unfolding story. It has seemed to me and to the Board of Directors of Presbyterian Ministers' Fund that the story of the world's oldest life insurance company and one of America's oldest corporations should be shared with the larger educational, financial, and religious community of our land.

Over 250 years ago, a small group of dedicated Presbyterians, filled with compassion for their fellows and convinced of the Biblical mandate "to provide for the household of faith," created something entirely new in the world — contract life insurance.

The results of this creative act became the heritage of Presbyterian Ministers' Fund. It is this heritage that we desire to share. The Board of Directors looked to only one man to tell this story in his own unique style. John A. Baird, Jr., a fellow corporator and director, comes from a family dedicated to the service of our nation over a period of 200 years. Beginning with a Scottish immigrant, John Baird, who fought and died in the French and Indian Wars near Pittsburgh, Pennsylvania, the history of this amazing family parallels the history of Presbyterian Ministers' Fund.

We are indebted to John A. Baird, Jr., for his dedicated leadership as a director, his incredible feel for history, his sensitive insight into the dynamics of leadership; and we are grateful for his facile pen, which makes this book fascinating reading.

In a day that seems to have a growing appreciation for the past in the hope that a pattern for the future may be discerned, John Baird offers whatever insight our corporate history has to share.

Robert J. Lamont, President
Presbyterian Ministers' Fund

13

PREFACE

Four flags fly over Rittenhouse Square, Philadelphia, each business day. They dominate the red brick facade of a modest office building near the northeast corner of that historic place in the City of Brotherly Love.

This is 1809 Walnut Street, the Home Office of Presbyterian Ministers' Fund, the nation's oldest life insurance company, organized in 1717 and incorporated, 1759. Red, white, blue, and gold bunting confirm the commitments of this American, Christian, Pennsylvania enterprise through the colors of Old Glory, the Protestant Church, 1776 America, and the Keystone State.

Horn of Plenty tells the story of this insurance company which may truly be described as, *sui generis*, unique and one of a kind. Presbyterian-founded and Presbyterian-guided for 220 years, the firm has skillfully combined a Biblical stance with financial acumen, providing for the security of religious professionals and their families from the beginning of this country to the present day.

Not a business history in the usual sense, *Horn of Plenty* concentrates upon four periods in the life of the corporation rather than recording an exhaustive, total account of all that has happened. Response to challenge, resulting in consistent growth and expanding influence, is presented through an emphasis upon the years when selected presidents held office.

Despite Ralph Waldo Emerson's observation, "There is properly no history; only biography,"[1] this book is not a series of mini-biographies; but, rather, the story of a company told through the events which took place when fourteen of these men guided the enterprise. Policies are presented as well as personalities.

Millard E. Gladfelter, Chairman of the Board of Directors, 1968-1978, and now a corporator, puts it this way:

"The company is built around the presidents rather than the presidents being so dominant they eclipse the company. Each president has made a particular contribution conditioned by the time in which he served."[2]

Presidents, however, are seldom ordinary persons. For the most part, those selected for focus in this account confirm the opinion of William Breiby, vice-president of Pacific Mutual Life, Los Angeles, in a talk entitled "The Spirit of Life Insurance Company Management." Breiby declared, "The president's spirit, character and personality shape those of his company."[3]

Horn of Plenty describes my perception of this shaping as through more than twenty-two decades PMF refines a passion for service to those who serve God.

Beyond the growth of this specific corporate cachet, larger relationships develop: to the city where the company has had its being; to the state and nation; with the Presbyterian Church and other communions; indeed, to far places where its policyholders have taken the gospel of Christ.

Throughout lives the spirit of reward from thrift, bounty from wise investment, prosperity for those who save now for liberality later—qualities summarized in the credo of this extraordinary enterprise found in II Corinthians 6:9 "He that soweth bountifully shall reap bountifully."

Books have been described as windows of the soul, and it is my hope that this volume provides that perspective for the Presbyterian Ministers' Fund.

John Baird
Villanova, Pennsylvania

PART ONE

Early
Adventures

CHAPTER ONE

A Cleric Forms a Company
(1759-1766)
Rev. Robert Cross, President

God moves in a mysterious way
His wonders to perform;
He plants his footsteps in the sea,
And rides upon the storm.

William Cowper

On a winter day long ago two Presbyterian preachers from Ireland and a local judge started a business in Philadelphia which had twenty-three words in the name of their company.

Francis Alison, Robert Cross, and the Honorable William Allen secured a charter signed by Pennsylvania Lieutenant Governor William Denny for "The Corporation for the Relief of Poor and Distressed Presbyterian Ministers and of the Poor and Distressed Widows and Children of Presbyterian Ministers." It was January 11, 1759.

The enterprise not only survived this inauspicious beginning, but became a remarkable life insurance success story for more than 220 years.

The world moved from carriages to cars, from ponies to planes, and from lanterns to lasers. The company moved with it, kept up to date, proved flexible in meeting fresh challenge and ingenious in adapting to changing needs. Under God, this primitive endeavor earned a position of leadership and respect by providing distinctive financial security for generations of full-time Christians and their families as it shortened its name to three words, Presbyterian Ministers' Fund.

The year 1759 was significant for the British Empire and the American Colonies. It marked the predominance of English influence in North America as General James Wolfe captured Quebec by defeating the French on the Plains of Abraham. Britain had recently adopted the Gregorian Calendar, and Samuel Johnson published his first novel, *Rassalas*, as the successful reign of King George I neared its end.

Presbyterians, Episcopalians, Methodists, and Christians of other denominations were laying foundations for future missionary work.[1]

While George Washington and Robert Morris were still in their mid-twenties, Thomas Jefferson a teenager, and

James Madison a boy of eight, Benjamin Franklin at 53 had already established himself as one of Philadelphia's leading citizens.

This is not the place to retell the history of that city named for the Greek word "brotherly love" by William Penn in 1682. By 1759 it had gone far beyond the "greene countrie towne"[2] of its founder; and, although younger than Boston or New York, had become "the second English-speaking city in the world."[3]

For more than thirty years an influx of Scotch and Irish immigrants had crossed the Atlantic, boosting the population until, by 1753, the first official count revealed 14,563 people in the community.[4] In addition to several thousand houses, Philadelphia had by this time 120 licensed taverns and thirty-seven persons who owned a four-wheel chaise.[5] John Bartram's House, 1731; the Pennsylvania Hospital, 1751; and Woodford Mansion, 1756 (in Fairmount Park near 33rd and York Streets) survive today as architecture of the time.

Philadelphia, the "Holy Experiment,"[6] was a city of cobblestone streets and red brick houses with a mixture of Quaker, Catholic, and Protestant activists which produced a vitality unmatched by any other American colonial city.

Education flourished. The William Penn Charter School and Friends Select School date from 1689. Benjamin Franklin founded The Library Company in 1731. The American Philosophical Society first met in 1743; and the Pennsylvania Academy, which later became the University of Pennsylvania, in 1749.

It was as a commercial center, however, that Philadelphia merits particular recognition. A river town between the Delaware and the Schuylkill, it thrived as a port city. Merchants were the leading citizens. Business practices reflected religious teaching which stressed the Puritan ethic of hard work, keeping out of debt, and thrift. Pioneer firms including the Perot Malting Company (1687), J. E. Rhoads

& Sons (1702), and Franklin Printing Company (1728) confirmed the early character of the community. The Philadelphia Contributionship, America's oldest fire insurance company, began in 1752 and continues in business today.

Thomas C. Cochran, more than two hundred years later, in his book *Pennsylvania, A Bicentennial History*, puts it this way:

"From the early 1750's until the Revolution the city enjoyed an almost continuous boom broken only by a few years of recession in the mid-1760's. . . . In 1774 Philadelphia shipped flour worth £720,000 and maintained a favorable over-all trade balance of £100,000."[7]

This climate nourished the coming together in 1759 of two historical developments which made possible that year the creation of the company which is the subject of this book. Primitive life insurance stirrings of a century or more in both Europe and America, combined with a growing Presbyterian determination to do something about the financial insecurity of their clergymen, produced at that particular time the nation's first business of this kind. Not unlike a nuclear reaction of today, these two forces in the proper setting reached a "critical mass" with dramatic results! Each deserves to be examined in some detail.

"The principles of life insurance seem to have been first applied in Europe in the sixteenth century," according to corporator of the Fund, George H. Stuart, Jr.[8] This application had limited significance "in view of the high premium rate charged," because "there were not sufficient data upon which to base risks, and there were not sufficient risks taken which would constitute an average."

Stuart may have been aware of a policy issued June 15, 1583, by the office of Insurance within the British Royal Exchange for 383 pounds 6s 9d on the life of William Gybbons for a term of twelve months. Thirteen citizens underwrote the contract, but refused to pay when the insured died within the year. The heirs recovered after taking the matter to the Court of Admiralty.[9]

Life insurance, it may safely be said, did not develop in the modern sense "until the capitalistic corporate device gained acceptance and the mathematicians developed the theory of probability and actuarial science."[10]

Blaise Pascal, the precocious French philosopher and mathematician, formulated such a theory as early as 1654. His work, and that of the Dutch scientist, Christian Huygens, were first applied in 1671 by Jan DeWitt of Holland, to life contingencies, "for the sole purpose, however, of determining the value of life annuities and reversions, to aid that government in the raising of loans."[11]

Another seventeenth-century intellectual who contributed to the basic knowledge upon which life insurance came to be based was Edmund Halley who later became an Oxford University geometry professor. In 1682 he first saw the comet which bears his name, and finally deduced it was the same heavenly phenomenon previously observed in 1607 and 1531. Halley predicted its return in approximately seventy-five years, and was proved correct when the comet reappeared in 1759. This brilliant man did more than stare at the nocturnal sky. He constructed a mortality table in 1693, based on the registers of Breslau. Halley's table, imperfect as it may have been, "is said to have been the first which recognized the two factors essential to all mathematical calculations as to life insurance values, namely, mortality and compound interest."[12]

Between 1698 and 1706 three life insurance ventures began in London, but none of these British companies survived. Mercer's Widows' Fund, the Society of Assurance of Widows and Orphans, and the Amicable Society for a Perpetual Insurance Office failed for a variety of reasons, including the assuming of bad risks.[13]

"Presbyterian" comes from the Greek word for elder. Christians by this name trace their beginnings to the 1500's when John Calvin organized the Reformed Church in Geneva, Switzerland. Within a hundred years Presbyterian churches appeared in North America and their members took an active part in the life of the times.

Meyer M. Hostetter, a modern writer, declares, "The story of Presbyterianism in the United States is inseparably bound up with colonial history."[14]

The focus of this activity sharpened in 1701 when Jedediah Andrews became the original pastor of Philadelphia's First Presbyterian Church located on the south side of High Street between 2nd and 3rd. The formation of other churches brought about the creation of the first Presbytery, in 1706, which later came under the first General Assembly. Convener and moderator of this initial Presbytery was Francis Makemie, who had served a number of churches in Maryland and Virginia.[15]

On March 26, 1707, the Presbytery noted, "It be recommended to every minister to set on foot and encourage private Christian societies."[16]

Three years later minutes of the Presbytery record "an interest in these American plantations."[17]

In 1714 the Presbytery took into consideration "the desolate condition of the people in Kent County," and "appointed our brother, Mr. James Anderson, that he supply them with preaching."[18]

The dynamics of Pennsylvania colonial life found Presbyterian ministers not only in the population centers but also on the Western frontier. The clerics went through the wilderness with the settlers, trying to meet their spiritual needs, and those of the Indians, too. These preachers met challenge and experienced hardship. Worst of all, they and their families knew poverty.[19] The new Presbytery recognized their plight and soon urged steps to alleviate it. In a

September 23, 1715, letter of thanks for past help and request for continuation of gifts to Mr. Thomas Reynolds in London, Jedediah Andrews and Daniel Magill wrote:

"We accept your Christian bounty in good part and make it as a mark of our common Lord's goodness and care to the support of his servants in narrow circumstances."

Reynolds was urged to ask his "public-spirited friends to go into ye same good design for supporting our ministers."[20]

In 1716 a further organizational step was taken with the formation of the first American Synod in Philadelphia. It comprised the four Presbyteries which emerged from the 1706 original. The Synod made possible a broad effort across the burgeoning denomination, and within a year it created a "Fund for Pious Uses."[21]

The venture got off to a brisk start, and minutes of the very next meeting record, "That this day . . . was weighed and delivered into the hands of Mr. Jedediah Andrews, Treasurer for the time being, the just sum of eighteen pounds, one shilling, and six pence, for which he obliges himself, his heirs Executors, and Administrators to be accountable to the Synod, unavoidable emergencies only excepted."[22]

Andrews, the minister of the First Presbyterian Church, who had acted as moderator of the Synod's first meeting, was continued as "treasurer of the fund till the next Synod."[23] He was to serve a total of thirty years and thereby contributed significantly to the stability and continuity of the Fund.

Contributions from cooperating churches were administered by a committee "appointed each year by the Synod."[24] In 1719 this committee included Treasurer Andrews and five others. They were to consider "some proper methods of disposing of it to the best advantage."[25]

It should be noted that, in addition to accumulating money to aid ministers and their families in financial distress, the Synod used these resources "to build new churches and to support missionaries in frontier settlements, especially among the Indians."[26]

In this same year it had become apparent that local contributions were inadequate for these two purposes, and the Synod looked across the seas for additional support. On September 18 "a number of persons" were "empowered to receive the collection of the Synod of Glasgow and Ayr if it arrives in safe goods, and put them into the hands of some substantial persons, to be sold to the best advantage for money."[27]

The widow of the Rev. John Wilson was the first person to receive benefits from the Fund. She was given four pounds, initially, and the treasurer granted "if he sees necessity requires, to give her some further supply . . . not exceeding three pounds."[28]

Before long others were helped and it soon became obvious that constant efforts were needed to assure the inward flow of contributions. Synod minutes of the early 1720's reflect this concern at every meeting. Typical references include:

"Ordered, that every minister of this Synod do their diligence to obtain what collection they can from their respective congregation toward the fund."

"That the members of the Synod be inquired of tomorrow morning, what collection they have made toward the fund."

"It was found that Masters Andrews, McNish, Webb, Orme, Conn, Thomson, and Gelston have brought collections . . . and the remaining ministers having given their reasons why they obtained no collections, they were sustained."[29]

As eleemosynary requests increased and missionary opportunities multiplied, a number who sought assistance were denied. For example, in 1724 the records disclose this terse statement: "Mr. Tennent, having written to the Synod for some supply out of the Fund, his request was denied."[30]

Two years later a clergyman named Robert Laing received forty shillings "in testimony of the compassion of the Synod," but the unfortunate individual was advised to leave the ministry, as his witness had become "a detriment to the interest of religion, and rather a scandal than a help to the gospel."[31]

The Fund for Pious Uses ended its first twelve years with a record of experience gained and accomplishment recorded. Yet the lack of assets persisted. This impecunious circumstance continued to be the greatest problem facing the infant insurance endeavor. Money for missions, money for ministers and their dependents, and money for Synod administrative expenses remained ever in the minds of the committee. Three pounds per annum, for example, were needed for the salary of the treasurer.[32] The minutes of the Synod meeting held September 18, 1729, say:

"Inquiry being made who had brought collections for the Fund, it was found that members have been generally defective in that matter, and it was recommended that the appointment in reference to the raising collections for the Fund, be carefully observed for the future."[33]

Proper perspective for this undertaking comes from a realization of the broader Presbyterian picture in the three decades which followed. Earlier mention has been made of the eighteenth-century immigration from the British Isles. An estimated 200,000 Scotch-Irish came to America during this period. "Poor, land-hungry, boisterous and contentious, these people were also tenaciously Presbyterian."[34]

A theological upheaval called "The Great Awakening" marked this contention, and its life vividly confirms the tenacity of those on both the "New Side" and the "Old Side" of this religious convulsion.

Rev. Gilbert "Hell-fire" Tennent, a disciple of the famous revivalist, Charles Whitfield, led the "New Lights" with a sermon he preached in Nottingham, Maryland: "The Danger of an Unconverted Ministry."[35] Tennent was described by a contemporary as "impudent and saucy," one who caused people to wallow in the winter snow day and night "for the benefit of his beastly brayings."[36]

Tennent, however, represented more than noise in the pulpit. He and his sons achieved spiritual and intellectual leadership because they were alert to the perils of a somnolent orthodoxy in the churches, and possessed the capacity to articulate this concern to high degree. They founded the "Log College" in 1727, to train young men for the ministry, and about them gathered "a strong body of earnest, devout and zealous ministers and laymen."[37]

As the reformers gained strength, they also developed an unfortunate arrogance of spirit. "They became critical and censorious of those who could not follow them. They excited opposition and complaint."[38] Those in opposition included the minister of Philadelphia's First Presbyterian Church, Rev. Robert Cross. Cross protested the "Log College" in particular and the disruptive attitude of the "New Lights" in the work of the denomination.

At the Synod meeting in 1741, Cross charged the "New Side" with denying the power of Synod, being "guilty of schism, and preaching so as to cause men to cry out, or fall in convulsion fits."[39] Standing with Cross in this counterattack was another local religious leader, Rev. Francis Alison. These two men were the leaders of the "Old Lights" in the struggle with their former clerical colleagues.

Both sides went beyond name-calling. Each faction possessed a certain educational audacity. To match the "New Light" Log College, Alison began a Presbyterian Academy at New London, Pennsylvania, November 16, 1743. It later became the University of Delaware.[40] Not to be outdone, the Tennents and other "New Side" men secured a charter for The College of New Jersey in 1746. This school grew into Princeton University.

Moving into the 1750's, both groups seemed to solidify their positions. Compromise seemed unlikely. The "New

Side" organized "their church," Second Presbyterian at 3rd and Arch Streets.

In 1752 Francis Alison came to Philadelphia as assistant pastor of the First Church. Alison had more on his mind than doctrinal dissent. Within two years he proposed to the Synod a plan of real life insurance to benefit ministers' widows.[41] By May 30, 1755, the plan was complete and adopted by Synod. It provided for the formation of a company, appointed trustees to guide it, and empowered those trustees "to take our fund into their hands."[42]

Alison, his "Old Side" compatriot, Robert Cross, five businessmen, and the Honorable William Allen received this designation. Allen, the Chief Justice of Pennsylvania, was nominated in absentia. Alison and another member of Synod were successful in enlisting Allen, and this good news appeared in the minutes of the May 27, 1756, meeting.[43]

As it had already become apparent, however, the "Widows' Fund" could not be operated effectively. Members were not bound by contract to make annual payments, and supplementary income from voluntary contributions proved uncertain. Recognizing the need for a more formal structure, the Synod authorized Alison, Cross, and three others to seek a corporate charter for the new fund from the governor.

One year later this document of request was sent by the Presbyterian Synod of Philadelphia to:

"The Honorable Thomas Penn and Richard Penn, Esqs., true and absolute Proprietaries of the Province of Pennsylvania and the Counties of New Castle, Kent and Sussex on Delaware."[44]

The petition contained two signatures, that of Francis Alison and Robert Cross, and it was dated May 27, 1756.

More than twenty-seven months elapsed before the petition was granted, but during this time the "Old Side" and "New Side" factions of the Church agreed to a reconciliation. It became official at the May, 1758, meeting of the Synod, making "the securing of the charter for the new insurance corporation coincident with the reunion of the two early divisions of American Presbyterianism."[45]

The original twelve members of the corporation who signed the charter February 6, 1759, reflect this new spirit, as leaders of both factions joined together to formalize this crucial new step in the operation of the Fund. "Old Siders" Alison, Cross, and like-minded merchants served with "New Siders" Gilbert Tennent, Samuel Finley, Richard Treat, and community leader and businessman, Andrew Reed.

May 2, 1759, the charter was "recorded in the office for recording of deeds for the City and County of Philadelphia," and the struggling corporation was in business.[46]

Events moved swiftly in the succeeding months, but they will be better understood if we briefly review the background of the three men who took the most active part in the beginning days of America's first life insurance company.

Francis Alison, born 1705 in County Donegal, Ireland, seemed an unlikely life insurance company founder. A classical scholar, he was an original member of the American Philosophical Society, and served as rector of Benjamin Franklin's Philadelphia Academy in addition to holding ministerial duties at First Presbyterian Church. Alison, a man of many talents, combined spiritual perception, religious activity, and intellectual acumen. He has been described as "a leading educator in the middle colonies."[47] In 1758 the University of Glasgow, his alma mater, made him a Doctor of Divinity.

William Allen, born 1704 in Philadelphia, studied law as a youth, inherited money at an early age, achieved success in business, and became a public servant, being elected Councilman (1727), Member of the Assembly (1731), Mayor of Philadelphia (1735), Recorder of Deeds (1741), and Pennsylvania Chief Justice (1751). As a philanthropist he sponsored an Arctic expedition, supported many charities, and became a patron of the famous artist Benjamin West.

Judge Allen's horses were among the finest in the city, and his equestrian panache survives today in this doggerel:

"Judge Allen drove a coach and four
of handsome dappled grays;
Shippens, Penns, Pembertons, and Morrises,
Powels, Cadwaladers, and Norrises
Drove only pairs of blacks and bays."[48]

Robert Cross, born 1689 in Bally Kelly, Ireland, came to this country in 1706, was received by Philadelphia Synod in 1717, ordained to the Presbyterian ministry two years later, and arrived in Philadelphia in 1737 as assistant pastor at First Church.

Two centuries after the 1759 incorporation of the company, a later president writes:

"In Cross, Alison and Allen were not merely symbolized but definitely exemplified the three essentials to the successful management of a life insurance company—religion and the acute consciousness of human need, scholarship, especially in the area of mathematics, and sound common sense in finance and the management and investment of money."[49]

A 1759 chronology of the nascent company includes these dates:

May 22—
  Synod accepts charter and fixes rates of contributors.
June 14—
  Approval given for "Fund to be laid before the different Presbyteries for their approbation."
October 4—
  Fund raising methods considered.
November 21—
  Cross, Tennent and Alison to prepare proposal to General Assembly of the Church of Scotland "to obtain one day's collection in all their churches."

December 17—
  Robert Cross elected first president; Francis Alison, Secretary;
  William Allen, Treasurer. Elected Members (Corporators) "the
  following Ministers and Gentlemen": John Redmond, M.D.,
  Hon. George Bryan, Rev. Charles Beatty, Rev. John Blair, Rev.
  John Ewing, Rev. John Rodgers, Rev. Sampson Smith, Rev.
  Robert Smith, Messrs. Andrew Elliot, William Humphreys,
  John McMichael, John Rea, Samuel Smith, and John Wallace.
  Appointed a Corporate Seal Committee composed of Robert
  Cross, Gilbert Tennent, Francis Alison, Richard Treat, and
  Thomas Bourne.

This last-named quintet was instructed to "think of, and
be provided with a suitable Device, Inscription, and Motto
for the Seal, and that every other member employ his
thoughts for the same purpose."[50]

1760 maintained this momentum with the Rev. Charles
Beatty going to Great Britain in search of venture capital.
He wrote the Board, June 10, he had "succeeded as far in
Scotland . . . a collection to be made in all their Parishes the
second Sabbath of February next."[51]

Philadelphians subscribed, too. Before long a list of
forty-three contributors appeared; and, at the same time,
the first twenty-one policies were issued.[52]

While the first policies provided for some premiums to be
paid by the ministers, most of the money came from the
churches. Physical examinations were not required, and two
of the insured made their applications by proxy.[53]

These contracts involved two life contingencies, provided
for premiums at a fixed level until death, and were without
restriction as to residence or travel—an unusual feature at
that early date.[54]

At the end of the following year company records reveal
the success of Charles Beatty's mercantile missionary endeavor. £ 3,827 had been collected in addition to donations
for the capital of the Fund.[55]

By 1766, company assets rose to 9,837 pounds sterling.
The Board of (in)corporators grew from twelve charter

members to thirty-seven, with fifteen ministers, eighteen merchants, two judges and a physician serving at that time—thus strengthening the initial pattern of combined ordained and lay leadership for the Fund, which continues to the present day.

The Corporate Seal had been designed and rendered in silver by Philadelphia goldsmith, William Hollingshead, at a cost of two pounds, one shilling and eleven pence.[56] The seal portrayed a farmer planting seed encircled by the words, "He that soweth bountifully shall reap bountifully" from II Corinthians 9:6.

In the outside world the Treaty of Paris ended the French and Indian War, but the British passed the Stamp Act, pushing the colonists toward revolution which would come in the next decade.

Robert Cross died in August, ending seven years as the first president of the Fund. Almost seventy when elected, and in poor health, he let the secretary and treasurer do the work.[57] Cross and his wife, Mary, who died the same year, were buried beside the First Presbyterian Church. His grave marker contained this epitaph:

"Excelled in prudence, and gravity and genteel deportment."[58]

Cross scarcely fits the modern concept of a chief executive officer; yet, during his term of office, the Fund began as a corporate entity and became the base upon which his successors would build one of America's most successful life insurance companies.

CHAPTER TWO

More than Mathematics (1767-1779)
Rev. John Ewing, President

My country! 'tis of thee, Sweet land of liberty,
Of thee I sing: Land where my father died! Land of the
pilgrims' pride! From every mountain side let freedom ring!

Samuel F. Smith

A terse entry in the minutes of a July 3, 1767, meeting of the corporation reveals "Mr. Ewing was chosen president."[1] This laconic understatement conceals three important facts: the dramatic contrast between the head of the company and his predecessor; their common purpose; and the challenges faced by the enterprise during the months which separated their terms of office.

John Ewing, born June 22, 1732, in Nottingham, Maryland, attended New London Academy and became a tutor there. He graduated from the College of New Jersey in 1755, studied theology under Francis Alison, and taught philosophy at the College of Philadelphia. Ordained by the New Castle Presbytery in 1758, he became assistant to Alison at Philadelphia's First Church the following year, as well as a corporator of the embryonic insurance fund.[2]

In good health, age thirty-five, and a skilled mathematician, Ewing, as the new president, seemed the opposite of the aged invalid Robert Cross whom he succeeded. Yet these differences were somewhat deceiving. Both men were "Old Light" preachers, both served the same church, and both sought to advance the fortunes of the annuity company they were selected to lead.

Cross died in office and Ewing assumed the post as the company committed itself anew to missionary work on the Western frontier. Corporation meetings of the early 1760's involved action on reports of Indian atrocities and assistance to surviving victims.[3]

The savages scalped and murdered the husband of a certain Catherine Crow who, herself, later escaped from captivity. The Board voted her money to pay for a "warrant for land not exceeding two hundred acres."[4]

Other colonials were kidnapped and held for ransom. Thomas Smiley received fifteen pounds to redeem his daughter, who had been a prisoner for eight years![5]

Despite these depredations, both Synod and company

continued to feel the tug of evangelism. Charles Beatty and John Brainerd were commissioned in 1763 to take the gospel to the Indians. The corporation agreed to pay their expenses, but tribal warfare cancelled the expedition.[6] Blocked in this attempt, the corporation decided to "help the distressed frontier in another way," and appointed a special committee with ₤150 "to provide the necessaries of life for those poor families who are in greatest distress . . . driven from their habitations by ye savage Indians."[7]

On July 29, 1766, the Fund tried again, and this time appointed Beatty and George Duffield to go among the Redmen for the cause of Christ. They were ordered not to preach to white people living on former Indian land if it had not been purchased.[8]

This venture cost seventy-seven pounds, two shillings, two pence, including traveling expenses for the two missionaries and the Indian interpreter who accompanied them, as well as an allowance for Duffield's horse, which was lost.[9]

Rev. Richard Treat, elected president "pro tempore" at the end of 1766, and Captain Thomas Bourne, given that title the following May, guided the corporation as it dealt with the frontier crises, in addition to the routine insurance business of annuity contracts, delinquent payments by the insured, death claims of the survivors, and regular examinations of the treasurer's books.

These were also days of asking questions—both by the Philadelphia Synod and by the corporation. The former asked the company for an accounting of money granted by the church of Scotland. The latter asked an elusive individual for a similar measurement of money advanced for frontier Indian work.

On May 27, Synod posed four queries:

"1. What power has the committee of the Synod in the distribution of this money?
   2. What was the total put into the hands of said corporation by ye

general assembly of that church to be distributed in conjunction with a committee of synod?

3. What part of said money said committee are to have any concern with?

4. Whether there is any part of said money to be distributed this year. . . ?"[10]

The company response to the first question contained a trace of starch: "A corporate body may not in the management of their affairs legally associate with persons not in membership."[11]

The company agreed, however, to consult with such a committee when and if appointed; but indicated that it would not be hindered in the conduct of its business. Despite this vigorous declaration of independence, the Fund indicated that interest income from 700 pounds was available for yearly use.

At the July 3 meeting, when John Ewing became president, the corporation appointed Francis Alison, George Bryan, and William Humphreys as a special committee of its own to "bring Mr. Josiah F. Davenport to give an account of our money."[12]

This action reflected a five-year effort to trace the use of 500 pounds given in 1762 to the provincial governor to "reward" the Indians for releasing some 400 white captives. Governor Hamilton placed Davenport in charge of this campaign, but a satisfactory accounting had not been received.[13] This and future efforts were to prove as inconclusive as previous attempts to trace the money. There is no record of satisfactory report ever being received.

The year 1767 passed without further incident. The final corporation meeting was held December 16. Cold weather kept many men home, but eight new members were elected as Rev. Richard Taite, Drs. James Bayard and Hugh Williamson, and merchants Samuel Caldwell, William Hodge, Samuel Purveyance, William Rush, and Jonathan Smith joined the thirty-seven corporators already serving.[14]

While these developments took place within the Fund, the colonies reverberated with resentment against the mother country. *First Families*, a modern book by Nathaniel Burt, summarizes the reaction of many to a series of British provocations, including a renewal of the Writs of Assistance (1760); the revisions of the Sugar Act (1764); and the short-lived Stamp Act (1765) which:

"Made Americans realize two things: that the English government intended to govern America, but that Americans had no voice in and no control over that English government."[15]

John Adams, later President of the United States, writing in 1765, mentioned "a love of universal liberty that projected, conducted, and accomplished the settlement of America, with a plan both of ecclesiastical and civil government in direct opposition to the cannon and feudal system. The leading men among them, both of the clergy and the laity, were men of sense and learning."[16]

These men included John Ewing, his mentor, Francis Alison, and many of their ministerial colleagues. While the Quakers professed to be neutral, and the Church of England favored the King, Presbyterian ministers were identified with the patriot cause in word and deed. Alison, continuing his able service as secretary of the Fund, "was aggressively on the side of independence."[17]

For the first two years of Ewing's presidency of the Fund, Alison and the Rhode Island Congregational pastor, Ezra Stiles, organized a General Convention of the churches in their respective denominations "To form a firm union against Episcopal [Church of England] encroachments." Alison called the Stamp Act "an insult to common sense" and got the Presbyterian Synod to proclaim its repeal as "the joyful occasion . . . a confirmation of our liberties."[18]

The Church of England in America organized its own widows' and children's relief fund in 1769, with the new company closely patterned on the Presbyterian enterprise now in its eleventh year. It was chartered in Pennsylvania, New York, and New Jersey.[19]

These developments in politics and business were accompanied by scientific advances, including the invention of the steam engine by James Watt, and astronomical observations such as those conducted by the American Philosophical Society June 3. At that time John Ewing, as a mathematician and faculty member of the College of Philadelphia, gathered with five companions and four telescopes in the State House yard to record the transit of Venus. A cloudless sky made the event a total success, and Ewing wrote a forty-eight-page report for the Philosophical Society.[20] At Presbyterian Ministers' Fund headquarters today Dr. Ewing's portrait shows the company president with clerical collar around his neck and a telescope by his side — scarcely the anticipated pose of a business leader.

Ewing, however, did more than stare at the sky. He strengthened the company. That very year John Witherspoon became a contributor to the Fund; and total assets increased from £ 10,614, at the time of his elevation to the presidency, to £ 11,914.[21]

Witherspoon, the newly-arrived president of the College of New Jersey, was admitted in recognition of his services in obtaining Scottish contributions for the Fund before his coming to America. Until December 9, 1770, the Fund had no provision for accepting ministers from Europe or from neighboring Colonies.[22]

The early 1770's also brought a decision to equally divide all Scottish money given the company between the Widows' Fund and frontier gospel work. An initial 642 pounds, two shillings, five pence, halfpenny Sterling was designated for each purpose.[23]

The Committee of the Synod, which worked with the corporation, brooded over these figures; and, on May 23, 1771, "experienced a want of satisfaction with some parts of the account." The Board voted to "end all disputes" by giving the Synod Committee an extra thirty pounds annually for missionary work. In return that body gave "its assent and approbation of the distribution of all Scotch money in times past." The Synod Committee also agreed to forgo any future claim on the capital earning the thirty pounds yearly interest.[24]

Corporation meetings, since the initial session at First Church, had been held at various Philadelphia locations. The Board followed a general practice of alternating the May meeting each year between the First and Second Presbyterian Churches. Lengthy agendas sometimes required the Board to assemble on consecutive days. At times meetings were held in private homes, including those of George Bryan and Robert Harris. On other occasions, after morning deliberations at one of the churches, the corporation adjourned to a tavern on South Fourth Street known as The Indian Queen. It was one of many famous inns and taverns in the city of those days, including the Wigwam, the Pewter Platter, and the Crooked Billet, which was patronized by Benjamin Franklin.[25]

Company progress under president Ewing combined stiff requirements for an individual's participation in the Fund with a corporate willingness to ask the Synod for help in developing business. At one meeting of the Board it was decided that a minister from another location moving into the Synod of New York and Philadelphia had "one whole year . . . and no longer to deliberate whether he will become a contributor or not." If over forty years of age he would not be admitted under any circumstances.[26]

However, on another occasion, the secretary of the corporation was ordered:

"To give a copy of the membership regulations to the moderator of the Synod and to request the Synod in the name of the corporation to take such measures as they think that every minister belonging to any of their presbyteries may know these rules so that no young man may be deprived of the benefit of this Fund."[27]

Business in Colonial America was conducted at a leisurely pace with long waits between trading transactions. The Fund realized a steady growth in assets, but the amounts involved were modest in terms of the things to be done and actually done.

Ewing's own life illustrates this particular tempo. During his years as president of the Fund, the energetic cleric not only assisted Francis Alison at First Church, but also maintained his position as a faculty member at the College of Philadelphia. This relationship led to his later (1779) appointment as the first provost of the University of the State of Pennsylvania. Ewing, it has been said:

"was fortunate in possessing both scholarship and an unusual personality. He knew several languages, including Hebrew; and in scientific fields he was an original and critical thinker. In the pulpit or on the lecture platform he needed and used no flourishes of rhetoric; his tall, handsome figure, powdered hair brushed back from a high forehead, and keen eyes made a striking and impressive appearance. In private life he was a genial host and an easy conversationalist."[28]

Married to Hanna Sergeant at the time he came to Philadelphia, Ewing fathered eleven children beginning in 1759. Daughter Elizabeth, born 1772, was to marry Robert Harris, a president of the corporation of whom we shall hear more later.

The dynamic clergyman found it possible to leave the affairs of business the following year and take a trip to England and Scotland for the purpose of raising money for his alma mater, the New London Academy, now located at Newark, Delaware. While abroad he received an honorary Doctor of Divinity degree from the University of Edinburgh, and later interviewed one of the most famous literary figures of the time, Dr. Samuel Johnson.[29]

Minutes of corporation meetings during his absence[30] record the members' continuing preoccupation with complexities of annuity payments to survivors. This had been a genuine concern for some time. When Charles Tennent died February 5, 1771, his widow, Jane, applied for her annuity; but the Board could not decide on the proper division of the money between her and the children. It was not until December 20, 1773, that payment was finally approved to their attorney, Isaac Snowden.

Mention is made of a Mrs. Bostwick who received her whole annuity at this time; but, more often than not, money to the bereaved went through a man with proper power of attorney. The Fund took care to be sure these individuals possessed legal authority for their position. When satisfied, it paid Mrs. Nancy McCracken's stipend to Mr. John McCalla, and Mrs. Jane Henry's annual income to Rev. James Caldwell.

Another widow, a certain Mrs. Blair, received her payment without benefit of an intermediary. Her case holds special interest because the annuity was paid in full although her deceased husband owed twenty-nine shillings and six pence. The Fund, however, deducted his amount from the figure remitted. The Board went on to "maturely consider that this may be the state of many of our annuitants," and agreed "that in any case, where a widow or family may have so nearly paid up the sum demanded, they shall be allowed the full annuity, the small sum being deducted still due, provided always, that such a small outstanding sum does not exceed one third of the rate paid by the deceased minister."[31]

Eighteen new corporators were added during John Ewing's presidency. In addition to eight elected in his first year and already mentioned, James Mease joined the group in 1768 and Ebeneezer Hazard, 1772. Eight others were approved October 1773, including: Andrew Allen and James Allen (both sons of charter member Chief Justice Allen); Andrew Caldwell; Peter Chevalier; James Craig; George Fullerton; Robert Smith (a hatter); and Rev. James Sproat.

These men brought to fifty-five the total elected since the beginning of the Fund in 1759.

The fires of liberty burned brighter in the early 1770's as the Boston Massacre (1770) and the Boston Tea Party (1773) warmed the colonial fervor for freedom. These events were accentuated by articulate men who spoke and wrote the rationale for revolt. Samuel Adams, for example, declared:

"As neither reason requires, nor religion permits the contrary, every man living in or out of a state of civil society has a right peaceably and quietly to worship God according to the dictates of his conscience. . . .

It is utterly irreconcileable to these principles, and to many other maxims of the common law, common sense and reason, that a British house of commons, should have a right, at pleasure, to give and grant the property of the colonists."[32]

In 1774, when assets of the fledgling insurance company reached 16,161 pounds, a group of audacious men organized the First Troop, Philadelphia City Cavalry. More than 200 years later it could rightly claim the title of the oldest military organization in the United States in continuous service. The "City Troop" would see action in the coming revolution. More than once it would serve as General Washington's bodyguard.

Simultaneously another group of men came to Philadelphia from each American colony except Georgia. They met September 5 in Carpenter's Hall, located on a narrow court off Chestnut Street between 3rd and 4th Streets, as the First Continental Congress; and composed a proud "Declaration of Rights and Grievances" to be sent to King George III.

This document contained more hubris than humility and the monarch responded with 10,000 troops dispatched to America as the war became a certainty. In less than two years the Congress declared the independence of the United States with those famous July 4, 1776, words learned by generations of school children which begin:

"When, in the course of human events, it becomes necessary for one people to dissolve the political bands which have connected them with another. . . ."[33]

Horace Walpole is reputed to have explained the Revolution in this way: "Cousin America has run off with a Presbyterian parson."[34]

Company policyholder John Witherspoon signed the Declaration as did a number of other Presbyterian leaders. The execution of this landmark testament of liberty emphasizes again the persistent influence of Francis Alison who, in 1776, had been serving as secretary of the Fund since its inception in 1759. A later president of the company wrote:

"Three signers of the Declaration of Independence—Thomas McKean, George Read, and James Smith—went to school at Alison's New London Academy . . . Charles Thomson, Secretary of the Continental Congress, and Dr. Hugh Williamson, serving at different times as professor at both the College, Academy and Charitable School of Philadelphia and at the College of New Jersey, were both, together with a great host of unreconstructed and eternal rebels, pupils of Francis Alison at New London."[35]

Other things were happening in the colonies and across the sea. The Phi Beta Kappa Society was founded at the College of William and Mary, Williamsburg, Virginia. The famous Scottish economist, Adam Smith, published *The Wealth of Nations*. Smith's emphasis upon free trade and opposition to government interference with the laws of supply and demand made it a timely book for 1776; and his factual basis perpetuated its influence for generations. Smith "recognized the function of insurance in a mercantile system among free men." He found insurance morally sound and explained the distinction between it and gambling.[36]

Within the Fund itself a new treasurer took office. His name was John Ewing, the president of the company. Here is how it came about. At the May 2 meeting of the corporation William Humphreys resigned for reasons of age and health, although the records of the time fail to disclose the details. Humphreys, a Philadelphia merchant, became the second treasurer of the Fund June 25, 1760, as Justice William Allen, the initial incumbent, resigned after only a year in office. Humphreys served almost sixteen years. He took no salary and "bestowed his labor to promote ye good and charitable designs of the corporation."[37]

The Board examined Humphreys' books and discovered the assets came to 344 pounds, twelve shillings, eleven pence in cash plus 16,806 pounds, eight shillings, eleven pence in investments for a total of more than 17,151 pounds.[38]

Is it any wonder the Board responded with profuse thanks for his long and exceptional service? His compatriots wished him "all kinds of happiness for his disinterested friendship to the widows and children of our deceased minister."[39]

Not being able or willing to appoint a successor on such notice, the men turned to one of their number who had already proved his competence, John Ewing. He was "appointed to receive the books, the cash, and to pay off the widows."

At a subsequent session, three days later, it was decided the new treasurer should be paid sixty pounds per year for his trouble and be required to post bond for 10,000 pounds. Alexander Stewart was elected, in absentia; and a committee of Messrs. Ewing, Alison, Rodgers, and Miller asked to "wait in him and let him know that he is appointed."[40]

The following day, at a continued meeting, word came from Mr. Stewart that he would not accept the position. Faced with the need for continuity of operations, Dr. Ewing, Captain William Alison, and William Rush were made joint treasurers to take care of the Fund. Alison and Rush are not mentioned again in this capacity, as Ewing assumed the responsibility himself.

As both president and treasurer, the dauntless clergyman faced one of the most demanding periods in the history of the company up to that time. As the war pressed closer the colonial capital was moved to Baltimore in December, and the following year the British occupied Philadelphia.

Company investments until this time had been concentrated in bonds and mortgages. With the coming of the Revolution everything was put in jeopardy. Rampant inflation, a weakening currency, lapsed policies, and uncertain investments made these dangerous days for the struggling corporation. It was at this juncture that the prevailing Presbyterian endorsement of the war came to fruition in a particularly appropriate manner.

The Board voted, May 7, 1777, to supply money to help finance the Revolution by loaning to the Continental Congress 5000 pounds through the purchase of Loan Certificates. This candid investment in freedom confirmed the company motto: "He that soweth bountifully shall reap bountifully." In the future the growth of the young insurance company paralleled the development of the Republic as both contributed to far-reaching changes for the individual citizen. For nearly two years, however, there were no further meetings of the Fund.

The treasurer was directed to "remove our strong chest, books and bonds to some place out of this city,"[41] and the corporation was "dispersed by the English army" until May 24, 1779.[42]

The British left Philadelphia June 17, 1778, as the French entered the war and Philadelphia became the capital again July 2. The resilient insurance Fund met at the Second Presbyterian Church the following May with the first recorded order of business the selection of another man to be president, Rev. James Sproat.

John Ewing, age forty-seven, had resigned as head of the company; but he continued as treasurer and would hold that office another twenty-two years! Ewing's reasons for selecting the subordinate role remain at least partly conjectural, but several assumptions seem safe. The treasurership outranked the presidency in responsibility and ultimate importance; and the energetic minister had been appointed provost of the University of the State of Pennsylvania, chartered that very year by the legislature.[43]

In contrast to later years and modern business practice, the president at this time served as a volunteer, while the treasurer, beginning with Ewing three years earlier, now held a remunerative position. The compensation of the financial officer defined the juxtaposition of the titles. Need more be said?

Ewing's academic advancement coincided with the reorganization of the new University formed by what historian E. Digby Baltzell calls: "the revolutionary forces led by Presbyterians."[44]

This man of many talents continued, in his twelve years as president of the Fund, the tradition of his predecessor, Robert Cross. Both men regarded this unusual company as a sacred trust, and managed its affairs (in the words of the Charter acceptance to Thomas Penn and Richard Penn, Esqs.) "that the pious and benevolent design thereof may be answered to your satisfaction, and the benefit for those whom it is intended."

Dr. Ewing later experienced controversy and opposition as the lengthening of life shortened his temper and accentuated his dogmatic disposition. His leadership of the Fund, however, remains unquestionably effective.

CHAPTER THREE

364 Days in Office
(1779-1780)
Rev. James Sproat, President

All Things are Thine; no gift have we,

Lord of all gifts, to offer Thee,

And hence with grateful hearts today

Thine own before Thy feet we lay.

John Greenleaf Whittier

On the twenty-fourth day of May, 1779, the corporation elected another Presbyterian minister, Rev. James Sproat, its third president. He was fifty-eight.

Sproat, born in Scituate, Massachusetts, lost his father at the age of four. His mother saw to his religious education and it is said at an early age he could recite from memory the entire shorter catechism. As a youth he worked on a farm with an Indian friend, Tom Flex; but later he "determined to go to college and be a gentleman."[1]

At Yale he initially succumbed to the temptations of good-time living to the detriment of his upbringing. When Rev. Gilbert Tennent came to the campus during a religious revival, Sproat and his friends tried to harass the noted evangelist. Tennent preached Matthew 5:20 with such vigor and persuasiveness that the spirited rebel left the service, "returned to his room, locked the door, and in great distress threw himself on the floor."[2] The next day Sproat went to Tennent, confessed his predicament, and committed himself to Christ.

Graduating from Yale in 1741, the future insurance company president earned a masters degree, and studied theology with the great Jonathan Edwards in Northampton, Massachusetts. Two years later he was ordained to the ministry and served as pastor of a new Presbyterian church in Guilford, Connecticut, until 1768 when he moved to Philadelphia.

In the Quaker city he became the minister of the Second Church, then located at 3rd and Arch Streets, where he would remain until his death from yellow fever in 1793. His twenty-four years in that pastorate were summarized in these words:

"During his ministry there a change was made in the psalmody of the church from Rouse to Watts, and a mission was established at the corner of Coates and Second Streets."[3]

The unfair bias of this brevity comes into focus when we learn of the leadership he provided and the company he kept in denominational affairs. Received by the Synod of New York and Philadelphia, May 17, 1769, he was named to a committee with Francis Alison, Richard Treat, and John Ewing "to examine credentials of ministers from New England or other parts who volunteered to be missionaries to the Southward."[4] Sproat proved regular in attendance at Synod meetings through the next two decades and would assume additional responsibilities with the passing of time.

What about his short tenure as president of the Fund? How did he compare with Cross and Ewing? How did this "Newside" preacher differ from his two "Oldside" predecessors? Elected a corporator 1773, the minister from Massachusetts became president in a year which clearly was not the best of times.

The year 1779 found that pecuniary Frenchman Stephen Girard in Philadelphia and embracing American citizenship as Benjamin Franklin, the doyen of the Colonial government, pressed its cause in Paris. Franklin's "Political, Miscellaneous, and Philosophical Pieces" was published that year in London by Benjamin Vaughn.[5]

The Continentals achieved a brilliant military victory, July 15, when General Anthony Wayne captured Stony Point, New York, in a battle which raised the morale of the patriots as the war stretched into its fifth year.

The corporation lost its founder and secretary of twenty years, October 28, with the death of Francis Alison. Alison's incalculable contribution to the early success of the Fund was completely ignored in this laconic statement which appeared in the minutes of the next meeting of the company:

"The corporation did not meet according to last adjournment, which was occasioned by their having no urgent business to transact, and by the indisposition of the Rev. Dr. Francis Alison the late Secretary who died."[6]

Other than a few sermons, Sproat's company colleague left little in writing, which partially accounts for his present obscurity, but "there is no doubt about his greatness," a successor president wrote more than 150 years later.[7] Alison left a good library, a large family, but died with a modest estate. His Fund policy, which cost him a premium total over the years of $336.00, paid his widow and children $1,213.33. Alison not only carried the responsibilities of the secretaryship, but he helped the treasurer (William Humphreys and later John Ewing) keep a running record of all transactions in a volume called the "Waste Book." A perceptive modern writer affirms: "during its early years . . . the guiding and controlling hands in the management of the Fund were those of Francis Alison and John Ewing."[8]

With Alison gone, Sproat and the Board turned their attention to the chaotic financial circumstances of that Revolutionary winter. Runaway inflation caused by under-assessment of property, breakdown of revenue, floods of paper money, and flagrant non-payment of taxes made management of any business difficult. Collapsing currency had not been fatal to the Fund because of two things recently done by the Board.

The corporation loaned the American government $35,600 and made substantial investments in real estate. "466 acres were purchased [in one location] and 3300 acres were purchased on the waters of the north branch of the Susquehanna."[9]

In 1779 assets of the corporation had grown to 21,534 pounds,[10] but income from annuitants fell below expectation as ominously noted by the secretary:

"As many ministers fail in paying their yearly rates—ordered, that the treasurer write to every Session of their respective congregations, informing them, that their ministers are in arrears, requesting to lay before them the disgrace of being sued, or the distress of their families after they are dead, which must be very disagreeable to this corporation and to the congregations."[11]

The delinquent clergymen were given six months to pay up.

Sproat developed a familiarity with the problem, for he encountered it in different form at Synod, where by this time he served as Stated Clerk.

In 1778, for example, that body noted "the lamentable decay of vital piety still continues; that gross immoralities are increasing to an awful degree." The Synod called for all congregations "to spend the last Thursday of every month in fervent prayer to God."[12]

The unsettled times affected all citizens, Christian or otherwise; and among the Presbyterian faithful, laymen and ministers alike frequently failed to do that which they ought to have done. The corporation also suffered from a reduced number of eligible ministers who sensed the investment opportunity in this pioneer form of financial protection for their families. Many who could have participated failed to act.

Despite these internal operating problems, and the vexations of a turbulent community, Sproat had the satisfaction of seeing the Fund's corporate charter confirmed by the new American government. An Act of the Commonwealth for Vesting the Estates of the Late Proprietaries of Pennsylvania in this Commonwealth became law November 27, 1779. It provided:

"That all and every the rights, titles, estates claimes and demands which were granted by or derived from the said proprietaries . . . before the said 4th day of July, 1776, shall be and they are hereby confirmed, ratified and established power . . . are directed and appointed."[13]

Important in itself, this action must have seemed particularly sweet to the corporation which had earlier shown such tangible faith in the struggling infant government.

The following year began badly for the Colonial cause. Benedict Arnold's treason and the loss of several battles in the South made war news grim in early 1780. Financial uncertainty increased. Colonial currency was now "essentially worthless with overuse."[14] Even Synod had problems, with absenteeism at meetings! Records of those days confirm "the non attendance of many of our members . . . it appears there is a criminal neglect in this matter."[15]

As black is balanced by white in the achromatic color spectrum, these patriot setbacks were soon ameliorated by certain victories and the promise of others. March 1, slavery was abolished in Pennsylvania through the efforts of George Bryan, a Presbyterian elder, Supreme Court Justice, and corporator of the Fund, thus resolving a troublesome dilemma which had burgeoned in the minds of many Christians since the Declaration of Independence.

Dr. Benjamin Rush, the father of American medicine, and other Presbyterian abolitionists had already condemned the practice accepted by many church-going and God-fearing Christians before the Revolution. Rush "was appalled by the inconsistency of Americans struggling for their liberties against England while enslaving Africans."[16]

The practice had persisted, however, until it became unlawful. Even preachers held slaves, including the extraordinary Francis Alison. He freed his by last will and testament.

Military morale rose as a French fleet with 5,500 troops under the Compte de Rochambeau sailed from Brest to America. They would make things hot for the Redcoats in days to come.

Colonial independence from Britain, personal freedom for slaves, the conduct of Synod affairs, and the successful operation of the Fund were in these ways related. "Capitalism as the social counterpart of Calvinist theology"[17] furnished the intellectual and spiritual background for this intermingling. The character and personality of individuals including John Ewing, Francis Alison, and James Sproat provided the dynamic for specific accomplishment.

Sproat may be said to have been among the others but not

of them in the matter of personal leadership. Clearly he ranks below Ewing, Alison, and even Cross, as an executive. His strengths were legislative rather than authoritarian. His role at Synod illustrates an apparent penchant for record-keeping, in contrast to conceptual thought and forthright action.

It is not surprising, therefore, to find Sproat being elected Secretary of the corporation May 22, 1780, with the presidency going to another member of the Board, George Bryan. The minister of the Second Presbyterian Church enjoyed a term of office lasting 364 days; but he would continue his new relationship to the Fund for another thirteen years.

The assertive Ewing traded the Fund presidency for the treasurer's post as he assumed the responsibility of provost at the University of the State of Pennsylvania. The benign Sproat accepted transfer to the secretaryship as a position better suited to his administrative temperament. In addition to the factor of these distinguishing personal traits we must remember the volunteer status of the presidency in those days as compared to the paid role of the other officers. Sproat, as president, served without compensation. As Secretary he earned £ 25 per year.

Sproat held the Fund presidency a shorter time than any man in the history of the corporation. He not only avoided serious mistakes; he led the company safely through a terribly difficult time when bankruptcy threatened every business venture.

When he died a victim of the 1793 yellow fever epidemic, a marble tablet was placed in the nave of his church. It contained these words of evaluation:

"Whatever is guiltless
Candid and benevolent
In the human character
Was conspicuous in him.
Amiable in domestic life,

Fervent in piety,
Mighty in the Scriptures
Plain, practical and evangelical
  In preaching,
Eminent in tenderness and charity for others,
Humble in his views of himself,
He was beloved and respected as a man,
Useful and venerable as a minister of Christ."[18]

CHAPTER FOUR

Desk and Bench
(1780-1791)
Judge George Bryan, President

O God, in whom we live and move

Thy love is law, Thy law is love;

Thy present spirit wants to fill

The soul which comes to do thy will.

Samuel Longfellow

The twelve charter (in) corporators of the Fund increased in number to thirty-seven during the tenure of Rev. Robert Cross. Further growth in Rev. John Ewing's time raised the total to 55; and, with no additions in Rev. James Sproat's short term, the May 22, 1780, Board included seventeen ministers, thirty-two merchants, and six professional men. This alliance of laymen and clergy proved effective from the start and would continue to be a wise combination through the years to come.

With ordained men comprising only 30 percent of the total when Sproat resigned as president, however, the election of a successor from the laity is not surprising. The choice of George Bryan seems even less surprising. Although once described by a vituperative newspaperman as "the tallow-faced chronologer, otherwise Judge Grinner,"[1] Justice Bryan had already earned a reputation as "Pennsylvania's leading Presbyterian."[2] He possessed both community prestige and company experience.

Bryan began his life, August, 1731, in Dublin, Ireland. He came to Philadelphia in 1752, entered the importing business, and soon formed a partnership with a local entrepreneur, James Wallace. The Wallace and Bryan firm lasted only three years, but in 1755 the energetic young immigrant started a business of his own at Market and Water Streets.

These were times for not only the gaining of commercial experience, but for spiritual development as well. Converted to Christianity by the preaching of the persuasive Gilbert Tennent, George Bryan joined the Second Presbyterian Church at 3rd and Arch Streets. Before long he became an elder. On April 21, 1757, he married Elizabeth Smith and Rev. Tennent performed the ceremony.

As a man of varied inclinations and great capacity, Bryan sought other experiences beyond the importing business. He studied law and showed interest in public life. In 1760 he joined the Board of the Presbyterian Fund, and contributed 15 pounds to strengthen the cause.[3]

His first political success came two years later when he defeated Benjamin Franklin for a Philadelphia seat in the Pennsylvania Assembly, and began his career of public service as a champion of the people. After a period of legislative apprenticeship the Assembly sent him, John Dickinson, and John Morton on a mission to meet with New England committees "to seek redress for the colonies from Great Britain, and draw up a memorial to the King and the House of Common, setting forth their grievances."[4]

In 1764 George Bryan became a judge of the Common Pleas and Orphans' Court; and, with his growing prominence, soon found himself elected a trustee of the College of New Jersey.

Soon after the July 23, 1764, death of Gilbert Tennent, the dynamic young patriot transferred his church membership to First Presbyterian. Rev. George Alison, his new pastor, baptized the Bryans' fifth child, Mary, December 2 of the following year.

Judge Bryan gradually became more involved with the annuity company. In July 1767, as noted earlier, Bryan served with Francis Alison and William Humphreys as members of a special committee to obtain a satisfactory accounting of the 500 pounds previously advanced by the Fund, through Governor James Hamilton, to a certain Josiah Davenport for frontier Indian work. At the December 16 meeting that year Bryan was named to a new committee, with John Bayard and John Wallace, and directed to confer with lawyers Benjamin Chew and John Dickinson about the matter. The trio was authorized, if necessary, to take legal action to secure the desired information about the missing money.[5]

The 1770's found this gifted and zealous man appointed to the Synod Commission, elected a University of the State of Pennsylvania trustee; but, primarily, attaining greater political influence and governmental power. Credited with a large part in the enactment of the first Pennsylvania Constitution, and elected vice-president of the Supreme Executive Council in 1776, Judge Bryan assumed the presidency of that body after two years. By 1780 he became a judge of the Pennsylvania Supreme Court as well as president of the Presbyterian insurance corporation.

The myriad nature of these duties affected Bryan's role at the Fund. His presidency began on a casual note. After his election, May 22, the Judge did not attend a meeting of the company for two years! By May 18, 1786, he had been present only twice in twelve meetings, and during his eleven years in office missed eighteen of twenty-six sessions for an absenteeism rate of 69 percent. Despite this startling record of apparent nonparticipation, the Fund successfully faced financial challenges which threatened its very existence during the 80's, and ended the decade stronger than ever. Bryan undoubtedly took a more prominent part than his roll-call responses would indicate. Then, too, his associates included two former presidents: Rev. John Ewing, then the treasurer; and Rev. James Sproat, secretary. William Rush, vice-president, presided in the Judge's absence and proved a capable "second in command."

Corporation meetings in those years were held "according to the notifications given in the public papers."[6] At the November 29, 1780, gathering of the Board, the effects of war-time financial fluctuations and a depreciated currency brought crisis to the struggling enterprise. Income was reported insufficient "to pay the full annuities to the widows and children."[7]

The men decided to pay half the annuity sums due "to those families that may apply," and to place a paid notice in the press inviting all contributors to meet the corporation at the next Synod meeting "to consult with them upon some method of paying the annuities and preserving the Fund."[8]

A few contributors accepted the opportunity with the

result, the following May, that an agreement was reached with the Synod committee to use the thirty pounds annual interest from the Scottish Fund of that entity for payment of widows' annuities that year.

Shrinking currency values crystalized a second problem arising from pre-payment of a principal sum by certain participants. The income from these amounts now fell below the figure needed to cover their annual rates and were "by no means equal to the sums they ought to have paid."[9]

The treasurer was ordered to return the money to these contributors or "demand an additional sum; so the whole may be equal to what they should have paid in Specie." Rev. Ewing was also directed to follow this principle regarding payment by these persons of their annual annuity rates.

The pecuniary creakiness of the company was thus temporarily alleviated by these forthright decisions, but the total situation extended far beyond the specific perplexities faced and countered by these courageous insurance precursors. A fortunate event for the corporation and the colonies took place the last day of that year.

On December 31, 1781, Congress incorporated the Bank of North America, and within a week the institution opened for business. The bank was located on Chestnut Street near 3rd; and it represented the fulfillment of a plan developed by the famous Revolutionary War financier, Robert Morris, to place the monetary structure of the colonies on a firm basis.

Imagination helped assure the institution's success from the start, as this revelation confirms:

"Many devices were used for keeping silver in the bank and for reassuring the depositors. Whenever silver was removed, secret agents of the bank were sent to persuade those withdrawing it to deposit it again. This practice was continued for six weeks until the bank was well established. A clever device was the endless chain or belt with silver coins in boxes attached to it, which ran from the vaults into the bank behind the cashier's cage. The silver was hoisted, lowered, hoisted again, and finally strewn in glittering heaps upon the counters. Reflectors multiplied the coins, dazzling the eyes of the spectators. The public was properly impressed; the depositors, satisfied."[10]

Despite this and other measures which improved the financial stability in Pennsylvania and the other colonies, the corporation's duress continued. In 1782 the Scottish Fund principal of 600 pounds was taken to help meet annuity payments for ministers' eligible survivors.[11]

Company history was also made in 1782 by the commutation of the annuity owed the survivor of Rev. Alexander McDowell, who died January 12. From the beginning the Fund declined to commute for cash the annuities payable to widows and minor children of deceased ministers enrolled in the corporation. The Board practiced a sense of ongoing protection for the helpless through this policy, despite frequent pleas for lump-sum settlements.

McDowell's sole survivor, Rev. John McDowell, also a policyholder and later a director of the Fund, requested his due at once. President Bryan, Treasurer Ewing, and John Bayard reviewed the adult son's request and settled the matter for $674. Premiums amounted to $496.[12]

In the late spring of the next year the president did not attend the annual meeting of the corporation. He and Chief Justice Thomas McKean "comprised the bench" for the April term of the Pennsylvania Supreme Court when many cases were heard.[13] On April 19, General George Washington declared the North American war for independence at an end; and the air age began at Annonay, France, with the Montgolfier brothers' first balloon ascent. Within a decade a balloon would rise over Philadelphia and Washington would observe the event.

The year 1783 concluded with the election of a minister, two lawyers, an Army officer, and a businessman as corporators when Rev. Robert Davidson, Joseph Read, Esq., Jonathan D. Sergeant, Esq. (Pennsylvania's Attorney General), Colonel Ephraim Blaine, and Hugh Lennox joined the Board.

Judge Bryan presided at the May 22, 1784, meeting at which time members of the Synod were advised that, owing to the few eligible ministers buying annuities to protect their loved ones, "the corporation have it in contemplation to receive a number of gentlemen of the laity" as policyholders to strengthen the Fund.[14]

This warning produced a Synod promise to urge annuitants in arrears to pay their obligations, as well as an agreement by that body to promote the Fund among other clergy not already embracing the opportunity to secure survivor benefits for their families.

When not in court or at the Assembly, Bryan enjoyed his home on Vine Street between Second and Third. He had famous neighbors: Drs. John Redman and Benjamin Rush on Second Street; Robert Morris at Front and Market; and Charles Wilson Peale at Third and Lombard.[15]

The middle years of the decade brought the founding of several Philadelphia business firms which have survived to the present day: Lea and Febiger, publishers; and The Mutual Assurance Company for fire protection. The Episcopal Academy, originally on Fourth Street, and now in the suburbs, also dates from this period. This country day school is the largest of its kind in the United States.

Rev. Ashbel Green, who came to Philadelphia in April 1787, and soon assumed the duties of assistant to Dr. James Sproat at the Second Presbyterian Church, had this to say about the city that year:

"On Independence Square there was no building but the State House, with perhaps one or two of the offices that are now attached to it.

The market house in High Street, if I recollect rightly, did not extend farther westward than to Fourth Street. There was a floating bridge over the Schuylkill, opposite Market Street; but there was then no other way known to me of passing that river but by boat.

Washington Square is a quite recent improvement. For many years . . . it was the Potter's field, the burial place of strangers and the friendless. There were vacant lots in every square in the city, and its general extension westward was not much beyond Fourth Street."[16]

The Fund continued to threaten Synod with the possibility of insuring laymen if the clergy did not respond with increased dependability and in great numbers. Yet the company kept going, building its strength upon a blend of confidence in the annuitants, a concern for their dependents, and a kind of management toughness in financial decisions. The case of Rev. Alexander Houston, deceased, illustrates this mercy tempered with justice.

Houston died five years in arrears to the Fund, leaving a widow and children who needed the annuity for which the departed cleric originally contracted. After much deliberation the Board resolved "not to allow the payment."[17]

That year six additional men were elected members of the corporation. Several had names with a familiar ring: Rev. Patrick Alison, and Rev. William Tennent. Others would later gain national prominence: William Bradford, Jr., Esq., had a distinguished war record including service at Valley Forge and White Plains, and would become Attorney General of the United States; Rev. Samuel Stanhope Smith achieved the College of New Jersey presidency. A final pair began family traditions of continued service to the Fund: Robert Patterson, a Second Presbyterian Church elder and former City of Philadelphia treasurer, would soon assume that title with the company; Isaac Snowden would be followed as a corporator by his son as well as a third person to bear that name who subsequently was elected president.

Judge Bryan's attendance record at the Fund improved in May, 1787, when he presided at two of four meetings held that month at the First and Second Churches. It was an important time to be present.

The Board reviewed an appeal from William Hunter, the

Executor of the late Rev. John Carmichael, to pay an annuity to his widow and children although that clergyman's policy had lapsed prior to his death.

The Board had previously decided not to pay the annuity, but considered the matter anew in response to a petition presented by the Session of Carmichael's "Forks of Brandywine" Church between Downingtown and Harrisburg. This time the corporation resolved "the petitioners have misunderstood and misrepresented the facts; and that, on reconsidering the matter fully, this Board cannot rescind the former determination."[18]

Treasurer Ewing was instructed to draw up and lay before the Synod "a true and accurate state of the facts relative to the family of the late Rev. John Carmichael, together with the state of the Fund and some observations thereon."[19]

To demonstrate their conviction that this represented the proper course, the men also agreed, "if the Executor of Mr. Carmichael shall enter a suit against the corporation," that the treasurer "employ counsel and be authorized to defend it."[20]

While no actual suit was brought, the affair would not be finally settled for another six years.

The Board, on this date, also adopted a new plan to increase future business. It encouraged congregations to pay their pastors' premiums, and provided for moves, successors, and other contingencies inherent in such a relationship—with special arrangements for ministers not otherwise eligible to participate.

With the Carmichael embroilment vivid in their minds, the corporators did one more thing before adjournment. They told Secretary Short to send a letter to all financially-delinquent contributors "informing them if their arrears be not paid up before the 22 day of May, 1788, the corporation will consider them contributors no longer."[21]

The leaders of the Fund were neither harsh nor capricious. They acted to preserve the corporation from sentimentality and keenly felt responsible for its solvency. Financial uncertainty persisted throughout the colonies. As Dr. Benjamin Rush noted:

"In the year 1788 there were 1000 empty houses in Philadelphia. The value of property in and near the city was two-thirds less than before the year 1774. Bankruptcies were numerous and beggars were to be seen at the doors of the opulent in every street in our city."[22]

Economic distress of this kind had led to a revision of the Articles of Confederation by which the colonies had been governed for ten years. In May, 1787, as the Fund struggled with its problems of careless annuitants, and made plans for greater future income, another group of men met in Independence Hall with George Washington presiding. After three and a half months these statesmen produced the Constitution of the United States, which became law the following June. This unique document made possible a new relationship between all sections of the country, as the states experienced business improvement and greater monetary stability.

Robert Smith, a local merchant, was elected to the corporation as the twelfth and last man to join the Board while Judge Bryan occupied the president's chair. Smith was the sixty-seventh person so recognized since the start of the company and the sixth with that particular name.

The reorganization of the government found a Presbyterian counterpart in the creation of the first General Assembly which held its initial meeting in Philadelphia's Second Church at 3rd and Arch Streets. Four Synods, representing fourteen Presbyteries, took part. Owing to the national scope of the denomination in the colonies, a modern scholar terms this 1789 event "a matter of natural inevitability."[23]

As George Bryan's leadership at the Fund neared its end, Americans counted themselves for the first time. The census was taken by "enumerators," paid between one-third cent and two cents for every inhabitant tallied. "The effort required 18 months and revealed a population of just under four million."[24]

The judge died January 27, 1791, and Rev. John Ewing preached the funeral sermon. He described the fallen president in these words:

"Formed by nature for a close application to study, animated with an ardent thirst for knowledge, and blessed with a memory surprisingly tenacious, and the uncommon attendant, a clear, penetrating and decisive judgement, his mind was the storehouse of extensive information on a great variety of subjects."[25]

CHAPTER FIVE
New Medicine
(1791-1796)
John Redman, M.D., President

O bless the Lord, my soul!

Let all within me join

and aid my tongue to bless his name,

Whose favors are devine.

Isaac Watts

In the year that Judge Bryan died, Christianity also lost one of its most ardent advocates, John Wesley, the founder of Methodism. The Aldersgate reformer left an economic credo as influential as his gospel proclamation. Unlike certain twentieth-century clerics who, in their financial ignorance, attack the concept of capitalism, Wesley helped define it as a Christian commitment to "the earth is the Lord's and the fullness thereof."[1]

Wesley's declaration, "We must exhort all Christians to gain all they can, and to save all they can,"[2] as recorded by Robert Southey in his life of the great evangelical leader, helped provide the intellectual and spiritual climate for the growth of the Widows' Fund as the corporation of Presbyterian ministers and laymen labored to build a business based upon Biblical ideas of stewardship as interpreted by the Oracle of Geneva, John Calvin: "Do the works of him who sent him, as long as it is yet day."[3]

One such layman, John Redman, deserves particular mention at this time, for he was elected president of the Fund at the 1791 annual meeting, May 25.

Redman, the first native Philadelphian to hold this office, was born February 27, 1722. His early education came from Rev. Gilbert Tennent's famous "Log College," Neshaminy. He was one of its few graduates who did not enter the ministry. Instead he became a doctor.

In the days before American medical schools, entrance to the profession came through apprenticeship to an established practitioner. Young Redman worked and studied with Dr. James Kearsley. After a few years' experience, in Bermuda, Redman went abroad for further study. This opportunity was financed by Justice William Allen, one of the three founders of the Fund.[4]

The ambitious colonial physician spent 1746 in Edinburgh, and received his M.D. July 15, 1748, from the University of Leyden. His European experience also included advanced study in Paris, and a stint at Guy's Hospital, London.[5]

1751 found John Redman back in Philadelphia beginning both a medical and community career. He served as a consulting physician at the Pennsylvania Hospital as well as a City Common Council member. His medical capacity met its first severe test with the smallpox epidemic which ravaged the population in 1756. Redman did more than struggle to save the sick. In a paper, "A Defense of Innoculation," published three years later, the well-trained medico made a cogent argument for that treatment of the disease.[6]

Dr. Redman's Christian convictions matured in these years as he joined the Second Presbyterian Church and became a trustee. This led to his interest in the Widows' Fund as a charter (in)corporator, 1759.

A few years later the capable doctor faced an even greater challenge to his professional skill when the dreaded yellow fever struck the City of Brotherly Love. Redman described the local source of the disease in these words:

"It was found to have originated in a number of small, back tenements, forming a kind of court, the entrance to which was by two narrow alleys from Front and Pine Streets, and where sailors often had their lodgings, to which a sick sailor from on board a vessel from Havanna(h) [where it then raged] was brought privately after night, before the vessel had come up to town, to the house of one Leadbetter, where he soon died, and was secretly buried. . . . Leadbetter, with most of his family and many others in that court soon fell a sacrifice to the distemper; and from thence it spread rapidly."[7]

More than 140 years before Drs. William Gorgas and Walter Reed, who solved its deadly puzzle as part of building the Panama Canal, Redman and his medical compatriots had to depend upon primitive methods of hygiene in their struggle with yellow fever in 1762:

"A bowl of vinegar in the chamber with a hot iron sometimes put therein, which served for the benefit of both patient and physician, and attendants; and indeed was useful for dipping the hand therein and rubbing one's face before approaching the bed and feeling the pulse. This was the chief preventative or preservative I used, besides great temperance, avoiding to visit patients fasting if possible, and keeping tobacco in my mouth while in the sickroom, not from any expectation of benefit from any quality in the tobacco, except that of preventing my swallowing my saliva."[8]

In the early 1760's Dr. Redman's reputation made him mentor to a number of young doctors-in-training, including Benjamin Rush.[9] The future insurance fund leader became a College of Philadelphia trustee; and, in 1786, he helped establish the College of Physicians and Surgeons, serving as its first president. This, then, was the man selected to succeed Judge Bryan at the corporation.

Sixty-nine years old when he took the president's chair, Redman found corporation assets stood at $118,885. There were forty-seven ministerial contributors, and families of twenty deceased pastors received annuities amounting to $10,615. Despite the progress, these figures reflect the fact that the Fund had experienced slow growth since its incorporation thirty-two years earlier.

For one thing, its benefits were available only to the small group of clergymen from the Synod of Philadelphia. For another, the forfeiture feature of its contracts caused great dissatisfaction. In a sense, the rule enforced a financial discipline which helped carry the company through the perilous days of the Revolutionary War. However, the rule provoked genuine resentment. We have noted the Houston and Carmichael cases; and the continuing efforts of the Board to persuade more eligible ministers to become contributors. Until the formation of the General Assembly nothing seemed to work. The new ecclesiastical entity led to important changes in the operation of the Fund; and as the aging medical man began his administration the first of these new rules were adopted.[10]

While the forfeiture bug-a-boo remained, all General Assembly ministers were now eligible for insurance. Adjustments were made for those over twenty-eight years of age, and a single payment could be made by the contributor instead of annual amounts during the lifetime. These initial reforms provided a prelude for the greater changes to be adopted the following year.

Mid-1792 Widows' Fund minutes confirm the rationale for these progressive management decisions "to encourage delinquent contributors to pay up their arrears upon easier terms than formerly, and to induce others to become subscribers."[11]

Company, and, indeed, insurance history was made at the October Board meeting when the "Plan of 1792" was formally adopted and 500 copies ordered printed for distribution among the Presbyteries. Twenty-eight articles comprised the new basis for operation, introduced by the phrase, "That is to say."

Article I mentioned annual rates from the insured from "five dollars and one third to twenty-four dollars," with annuities paid to survivors to be "respectively five times the yearly rates."[12]

Articles II through VII spelled out the details whereby any minister under the jurisdiction of the General Assembly could be insured to protect his surviving widow and children. Article VII eliminated non-forfeiture, provided the contributor exchange his old bond (contract) for a new one.

Articles VII through XIV made it possible for Presbyterian congregations to insure their pastors.

Articles XV through XIX defined the methods of annuity payments to survivors, with an ominous warning that benefits to a widow would be "no more than half" upon her remarriage.

Articles XX through XXIV concentrated upon the rights of dependent children.

Articles XXV and XXVI were devoted to procedures for preserving corporation capital if difficulties should arise regarding payment of annual benefits.

Article XXVII described the death records to be maintained "in the corporation book."

Article XXVIII permitted further changes in the plan.

The new rules seem entirely logical to the modern mind, but they were advanced and quite liberal for those days. They were promulgated with a sample form of contract as well as a table of premiums according to age.

The insurance rates were prepared by Dr. Robert Patterson, a member of the Board since 1785, President of the American Philosophical Society, and a noted mathematician. Patterson, who would be elected treasurer of the Fund, 1798, furnished "the first actuarially-supported premiums for American life insurance."[13]

Somber mortality figures of the time underscore the crucial importance of his computations as the company prepared to broaden the scope of its operations and enter a period of more rapid growth. Miscalculations could be fatal.

Records of Christ Church and St. Peter's for 1792 illustrate the longevity pattern of Christians in Philadelphia as the new plan began:

"Buried under 3 years (of age)	39	From 40 to 50 years	16
From 3 to 10 years	7	50 to 60 years	11
10 to 20 years	8	60 to 70 years	9
20 to 30 years	12	70 to 80 years	5
30 to 40 years	14	80 to 90 years	5"[14]

Concurrent with adoption of an improved actuarial base by the company came greater financial stability of another kind. For years the Fund suffered from the chaotic Colonial monetary system. "In April, 1791, Congress passed a National Coinage Act which provided for a decimal system based on the dollar."[15] The Act authorized a United States

Mint, whose cornerstone was laid July 31, 1792, at 7th and Filbert Streets. The first coins were minted by October.

It's interesting to note close relationship between the Mint and the Fund. "Five of its directors including Robert Patterson served the Fund in various capacities and were active in its management during the period 1792-1861."[16]

Seven new corporators joined the Board the year of the new plan, including: Rev. Ashbel Green, Rev. Andrew Hunter, Rev. Alexander McWhorter, John Bleakley, Jr., Ebeneezer Hazard, David Jackson, and Hon. Charles Pettit.

Two meetings in May 1793 dramatize the complexities of the new relationship between the Fund and the General Assembly. The company convened at Jonathan B. Smith's house because the denominational gathering occupied Second Church. The insurance board listened to a further plea from the executor of the improvident deceased, John Carmichael. The brethren at the General Assembly decided to use their "influence with the corporation of the Widows' Fund in favour of the petitioners."[17]

Wearied with six years of harassment for adherence to principle, the company finally capitulated to this additional pressure and voted the widow Carmichael $93.33 per year for life. It would amount to $1,680 by the time of her death. Five directors, including Robert Patterson and former president, John Ewing, voted "nay."[18] As a later president put it: "While the Fund did a charitable deed in taking care of the widow of the redoubtable John Carmichael, it had no business to take other people's money to make good John's carelessness."[19]

As president, John Redman coped with this kind of pious sentiment. As doctor, that year, he faced a new epidemic of yellow fever which killed some 3,500 people in and around Philadelphia, including his predecessor, Rev. James Sproat, who had served capably as secretary of the company for thirteen years.

Sproat's successor as secretary, Rev. Ashbel Green, had been a member of the Board less than twenty-four months when he took office May 7, 1794. Green, a controversial figure in later life, would retain the position more than twice as long as any of the sixteen secretaries in company history, fifty-four years.

The final period of Dr. Redman's Fund leadership brought an important new name to the underwriters' world. The first proprietary corporate insurer founded after the Revolutionary War obtained its charter April 14, as the Insurance Company of North America began operations at 107 South Front Street. The new firm possessed life insurance powers, but made limited use of them at the time. INA issued primarily term contracts "purchased to cover the hazards of a sea voyage."[20]

Within the Widows' corporation seven additional members were elected to the Board, bringing to fourteen the number added during Redman's tenure: Hon. Gunning Bedford, John Nicholson, Rev. James F. Armstrong, Rev. James Boyd, Rev. John B. Smith, Joseph Nourse, and Robert Ralston. One of these men would soon plunge the company into crisis.

John Nicholson, a Presbyterian active in religion, politics, and business, engaged in land speculation. This circumstance brought tribulation to the Fund, embroiled John Ewing, as treasurer, in controversy and scandal, and placed the new corporator in debtor's prison, where he died December 5, 1800.

Nicholson, a partner of the financier Robert Morris in real estate development, was more careless, it would seem, than criminal. His actions, however, brought anguish to his friends at the Fund who were forced to place the good of the corporation ahead of personal feelings. The origins of the countretemps went back to earliest days of the company. From the beginning loans to Board members were made without hesitation.

When the Widows' Fund, in the early 1790's, sought to liquidate its extensive investments in land, John Nicholson offered to help. He bought the properties along the Susquehanna and in Northern Pennsylvania, but the mortgages were not recorded. Dr. Ewing compounded the problem by making additional "mortgage investments in properties in which Nicholson was interested — and had acted apparently without authorization from the board."[21]

Dr. Redman and the corporation faced this unpleasant situation in a series of 1795 meetings starting May 28 when the treasurer's reports raised doubts about the handling of these loans. The appointment of several committees that summer to examine Dr. Ewing's accounts and confer with lawyer Jared Ingersoll revealed "some of the titles to the property pledged by him [Nicholson] to the corporation are not satisfactory."[22]

These difficult days for all concerned led to Redman's resignation "for age and health" at the next annual meeting, May 26, 1796. He did not attend that session, but sent a letter requesting to be relieved. At seventy-three his wish is easy to understand; but, free from the burdens of office and retired from the active practice of medicine, he lived another twelve years.

This vivid description of the intrepid doctor speaks to his striking appearance and colorful personality. According to a noted nineteenth-century historian, Dr. Redman:

"Was known to the public eye as an antiquated looking old gentleman, usually habited in a broad-skirted dark coat, with long pocket flaps, buttoned across under his under dress; wearing in strict conformity with the cut of the coat, a pair of Baron Steuben's military shaped boots, coming above the knees, for riding; his hat flopped before, and cocked up smartly behind, covering a full bottomed powdered wig — in front of which might be seen an eagle-pointed nose, separating a pair of piercing black eyes — his lips, exhibiting (but only now and then) a quick motion, as though at the moment he was endeavoring to extract the essence of a small quid. As thus described, in habit and in person, he was to be seen almost daily, in fair weather, mounted on a short, fat, black, switch-tailed horse, and riding for his amusement and exercise, in a brisk racking canter, about the streets and suburbs of the city."[23]

Company assets climbed to $129,000 the year Redman resigned.

PART TWO

Consistent Growth

CHAPTER SIX

A Stronger Prescription
(1850-1856) (1858-1862)
Alexander Mitchell, M.D., President

Forward through the ages, in unbroken line,
Move the faithful spirits at the call divine:
Gifts in differing measure, hearts of one accord,
Manifold the service, one the sure reward.

Frederick L. Hosmer

Alexander W. Mitchell was the third doctor to serve as president of the Widows' Fund, and the only man in the history of the corporation to be elected twice. Despite the importance of his leadership years to the growth of the company, little is known about the man as a person. We not only lack a physical description, but are without details of his birth, education, and family life.

Dr. Mitchell became a director of the Princeton Theological Seminary, 1837; and was elected a corporator of the Fund three years later. Ashbel Green, then seventy-seven, misspelled his name in the minutes of the corporation.[1] Mitchell lived on Walnut Street, west of Broad.[2]

Beginning 1846, the Philadelphia physician took an active part in the work of the General Assembly, serving as trustee, treasurer, and member of the Executive Committee of the Board of Publication. As of February 13, 1847, he continued to hold these posts and also assumed the title "President of the Trustees of the Board of Publication."[3]

That year Mitchell attended his first Widows' Fund Finance Committee meeting, May 26. It was held at the United States Mint. Robert M. Patterson, company treasurer and secretary of the committee, spelled the doctor's name correctly.[4]

In the late 1840's Matthew L. Bevan, a banker-merchant, headed the company; and soon after his death, December 11, 1849,[5] Dr. Mitchell was named president. Before describing the significant developments of his years in office, however, a brief review of the previous half-century will prove worthwhile. World, national, and Philadelphia events had varying effects on the Fund. Within the corporation itself, interesting personalities acquired and lost influence as the business continued to grow and modify its methods of providing ministerial peace of mind through financial security for loved ones.

Early 1797 saw John Adams elected President of the

United States, and Dr. Robert Harris succeeded John Redman to that office at the Fund. In the next fifty-four years twelve men would lead the nation while only four would guide the annuity company. The capital moved to Washington as the century drew to a close; and, across the seas, Rev. Robert Malthus published his famous theory of population. The English clergyman-economist's work reflects the increased attention being given at this time to the complexities of human longevity.

As the centuries changed, Philadelphia maintained its financial supremacy.[6] Site of the First Bank of the United States, and the approximate geographical center of the nation, the Pennsylvania city experienced agricultural and commercial growth of many kinds. Shipbuilding, turnpike construction to other cities, and brokerage flourished. "New banks were springing up everywhere."[7]

Fire and marine insurance burgeoned in the early decades of the new era, but life insurance languished. By 1800 only four American companies were authorized to handle it; and, of these, only one would survive. On September 2, 1812, The Pennsylvania Company "for insurances on lives and granting annuities" began operations at 72 South 2nd Street.[8] This distinguished firm eventually became a bank and is among the leaders in that field today. Robert M. Patterson, treasurer of the Widows' Fund for twenty years, served as an early president of this new insurance company.

1812 also brought war once again to America. England and Napoleon, in a desperate struggle for control of Europe, caught the young country in their net of naval blockades. Hopelessly outclassed at sea, the United States won a number of land battles, and after two years both sides claimed victory. Trade diminished, but American manufacturing rose rapidly.[9]

This strange war had little effect on the Fund. The year it began, Rev. Ashbel Green, secretary since 1794, was made president of the College of New Jersey, where he promptly started the Princeton Theological Seminary with nine students.[10] The Fund soon insured its first professor, Rev. Archibald Alexander.

In 1813, four years beyond its fiftieth anniversary, the corporation rejoiced in these substantial figures:

"The productive capital is	$37,360.75
Which yields an annual interest of	2,241.04
The amount of annuities payable is	1,013.31
Leaving an annual surplus of	628.33
Besides which, there are contributions due	1,073.80

The present number of contributors is 18."[11]

No wonder the men "contemplated the situation with pleasure." They took the occasion to review the investment experience of the first thirty-six contributors to the Fund which had by that time "become extinct":

"Those 36 contributors paid into the Fund $9,746.67 and their families received $46,337.75, nearly five times the amount the contributors paid."

"The families of 16 contributors still in the fund have received $15,719.42, the contributors having paid $8,030.37."

"The total paid to the families of deceased contributors— $62,057.17."

The annuity company felt so good about this record, it decided to share its enthusiasm with the General Assembly, noting "so large a sum of $62,000 could not have been distributed for these purposes without producing very sensible effects." President Robert Harris and the Board mentioned "gladdening the hearts of 50 widows, and wiping away the tears of many an orphan," as they tried to expand the scope of the Fund. "How much more useful might the institution be."[12]

Earlier efforts to serve more Presbyterian clergymen had brought little success. So few had the vision and sense of thrift to participate. Some may have held back from doubt about the future of the Fund; but, with fifty-four years of successful survivor protection, that could no longer be the case.

This time the corporation stressed the voluntary nature of the Board's service. It included typical cases of rich reward enjoyed by the families of selected insured, believing these examples "will be sufficient to satisfy the most incredulous." Here are the startling statistics:

"A contributor paid to the fund $112—
his family received $3658.61

Another contributed 336.00	his family received 1114.00
Another contributed 354.67	his family received 2146.67
Another contributed 261.33	his family received 1821.33
Another contributed 336.00	his family received 1213.33
Another contributed 32.00	his family received 3072.00
Another contributed 354.67	his family received 2520.00
Another contributed 130.67	his family received 2370.67"[13]

The campaign seemed to produce few additional insured; but the corporation continued to prosper by making wise investments, taking in more than it paid out. Dr. Robert Harris died, 1815, and Robert Ralston took the president's chair. Eight new corporators were added in the first two years of his term; and by 1818 the company sent another glowing report to the General Assembly.

Despite the record of steady accomplishment, one member of the company felt far from satisfied. A University of Pennsylvania mathematics professor, he had served as treasurer of the Fund twenty-two years, since the resignation of John Ewing. His name was Robert Patterson.

Patterson, born 1743 in Ireland, led three generations of his family in distinguished service as treasurer of the Fund. His stature is measured by a stone tablet originally erected in Scots Church (located in Dr. Patterson's time on Spruce Street between 3rd and 4th, Philadelphia) and displayed today in the lower hallway of the Alison building on Rittenhouse Square.

"In memory of Robert Patterson, LL.D., late president of the American Philosophical Society, Vice-Provost of the University of Pennsylvania, Director of the Mint of the United States, and for nearly fifty years an Elder of this church. Distinguished among Philosophers for profound Science; beloved among Christians for his liberal Spirit and sincere piety; a Patriot of the Revolution, and constant to its principles; a Friend to the Humble and Oppressed, in social intercourse, cheerful, condescending, and instructive; in domestic relations, kind and affectionate."[14]

It was Patterson who guided the finances of the Fund through the trying times after the Revolutionary War. It was Patterson who computed the premiums for the Plan of 1792. He died July 22, 1824, age eighty-two; and was succeeded as treasurer by his son, Robert Maskell Patterson.

The second generation proved equal in accomplishment to the first. The son, born 1787 in Philadelphia, had joined the corporation 1816 after studying medicine at the University of Pennsylvania and serving as United States Consul-General at Paris. He then became a professor and vice-provost at the University, Director of the Mint, and president of the Philosophical Society.

Robert M. Patterson held the treasurer's post at the Fund four years, resigned briefly for a sojourn as professor at the University of Virginia, resumed the treasurership in 1836, and retained it until 1852. Combined service for the two men reached a total of forty-six years. The father received $200 per annum for expenses of the responsibility. The son started at this figure but was raised to $300 for the last sixteen years of his incumbency.

In this brief review of the fifty-four years of the Fund between the presidencies of Dr. John Redman and Dr. Alexander M. Mitchell, further attention must be given to 1824. It marks the second policy shift of the corporation since the 1759 beginning. In 1792 came the non-forfeiture provision and certain other changes. Now, thirty-two years later, the time had come for an even larger forward step:

insurance for aged preachers. The first two Pattersons were totally involved.

The elder Patterson, as teasurer, thought more and more about those Presbyterian ministers who "instead of dying and thereby providing for their families through the Fund, cling to life as helplessly infirm for various periods, resulting in suffering to both themselves and their family."[15]

As early as 1820, Dr. Patterson began work on a method to provide insurance protection for ministers to go with the Widows' Fund, now firmly established for their surviving dependents. He brought to fruition the original intent of the founders expressed in the 1759 twenty-three-word corporate title. A move of this kind could not be taken without careful preparation. The treasurer teamed with a special committee, appointed by president Robert Ralston, composed of his son, also Dr. Archibald Alexander, Rev. J. Jones Janeway, and Rev. Ashbel Green to develop the idea. When it was adopted by the Board on June 8, 1824, father Patterson resigned. Mission accomplished.

The plan consisted of a separate "Ministers' Fund" announced by an "Address to the ministers and congregations of the Presbyterian Church in the United States of America." This printed document, written by Secretary Ashbel Green, contained some 3000 words. After several verbose introductory paragraphs, the offer was made to furnish "an annuity for life, to commence at a certain age, by the payment of a single premium, at some previous period, never to be withdrawn."[16]

Illustrations of benefits were given. A twenty-five-year-old minister who paid $103 into the new fund would receive an annuity of one hundred dollars at age sixty-five. Premiums could be increased fourfold to yield a maximum retirement income of $400. Congregations, as well as parsons themselves, were invited to provide for their clergymen "when grown old." The opportunity, it was stated, "will tend to the prosperity of congregations by enabling them to call a colleague, or to obtain an able successor to a superannuated minister."[17]

In answer to the anticipated objection that many ministers might not expect to reach retirement age, it was suggested that longer life might be brought about by this guarantee of future financial security.

It also suggested to young ministers experiencing difficulty raising the premium money that they "fairly present the subject to pious females of the congregation." Such individuals, "there is good reason to believe," will be happy to provide it. The Address concluded with a table of premium rates for ages twenty to sixty-four.

With the new Ministers' Fund a reality, the corporation found itself in an awkward position with the established Widows' Fund. Gyrations in the nation's financial system between 1811, when the First Bank of the United States closed, and 1821, when President James Monroe named Nicholas Biddle a government director of the Second Bank, brought investment complications to the Presbyterian annuity venture. By the annual meeting the following year, total obligations exceeded available assets by $1,592.22.[18] Changes were necessary to attract more contributors, and these changes were adopted in 1826 as defined in another "Address" composed by corporation secretary, Ashbel Green.

The "New Plan of Agreement" offered more generous terms of insurance. The old requirement that men over twenty-eight pay a substantial first premium penalty no longer prevailed. Age compensation would henceforth be made by larger annual premiums. In the future, also, benefits to survivors would begin at death of the insured; and be continued through the life of the annuitant, other conditions notwithstanding.

The Board's optimistic expectations for the new plan ultimately brought results, but this would take time. Furthermore, in 1826, two years after the announcing of the

Ministers' Fund, not a single new cleric had taken advantage of the opportunity!

Outside the Fund these were the years of the Monroe Doctrine (1823); the opening of the Erie Canal—which did Philadelphia commerce no good (1825); and the establishment of new insurance companies, including New York Life (1830) and New England Mutual (1835).[19]

Inside the Fund little took place to season slow, steady, growth. Hon. John Kintzing Kane served as treasurer for the eight years Dr. Patterson spent in Virginia (1828-1836). Judge Kane would hold higher office in the corporation at a later date. President Robert Ralston, a successful shipping merchant, died August 11, 1836. He was succeeded by the Philadelphia lawyer, John McMullin, May 19, 1837. Ralston's last twelve years in the president's chair changed the $1,592.22 balance against the company in 1825 to $5,768.04 "in favour of the Fund" at McMullin's election.[20]

John McMullin appreciated this sound beginning, for the start of his presidential tenure coincided with two historic convulsions which threatened the future of the ministerial insurance company: the financial panic of 1837; and a theological controversy splitting the Presbyterian denomination. Too few dollars and too much doctrine presented corporation survival problems to the attorney and his Board associates. Both crises had been developing for some time.

By 1843 the Fund had survived the first danger and fashioned a formula to cope with the second.

The first is identified with Andrew Jackson's populist attack on the Second Bank of the United States. He vetoed its 1831 recharter application, and then ordered government deposits withdrawn and placed in a number of politically favored wildcat banks.[21] This led to its later demise—an event which aggravated the existing financial speculation of the times. In 1836, when interest rate fluctuations caused the pet banks to tighten credit, Jackson compounded the situation by demanding "payment in specie for government land."[22] The combination of these factors brought genuine panic to business interests. In May 1837, "banks in New York, Philadelphia, Baltimore, Albany, Hartford, New Haven, and Providence suspended specie payment."[23] The depression became nationwide, and many companies failed.

With this financial fiasco came a religious row over doctrine, dividing the Fund's clientele into antagonistic factions. In a sense the argument represented a reprise of those earlier Presbyterian differences reconciled at the incorporation of the Fund, 1759. The eighteenth-century words used were "New Lights" and "Old Lights," while the counterpart terms were "New School" and "Old School." Regardless of language, each conflict flung innovators against traditionalists, liberals in collision with conservatives.

Rev. Gilbert Tennent's preaching started the first quarrel. Rev. Albert Barnes sparked the nineteenth-century version. Barnes preached a sermon on February 8, 1829, in Morristown, New Jersey. It was based on Titus 3:4-7 and called "The Way of Salvation." The Princeton Seminary revivalist's title caused trouble when Philadelphia's First Church called Barnes to be its minister. Despite some opposition, he was installed as pastor, but in 1836 faced a charge of heresy brought by Dr. George Junkin, president of Lafayette College. "Back of Junkin were Ashbel Green and his cohorts," claims a later Presbyterian historian.[24]

This person was the same Ashbel Green who founded Princeton Seminary, served as trustee of the College of New Jersey, became president of Jefferson Medical College, was elected moderator of the General Assembly, and had served as secretary of the Presbyterian insurance Fund since 1794!

The identification should not surprise us. The Fund leaders at that time were primarily "Old School" men: Green, Robert Ralston, John McMullin, and Jacon J. Janeway. Green, described by Dr. Alexander Mackie as the "old pope,"[25] and by his son-in-law, Rev. Joseph H. Jones, as a

person of "strength, boldness, and decision,"[26] first pub-
licized the "Old School" and "New School" labels, in his
magazine *The Christian Advocate*, as early as 1824. It is easy
to imagine Ashbel Green nodding in vigorous assent to this
"Old School" credo:

"The voice of history is the voice of God speaking by his providence; and let him beware who refuses to listen and heed."[27]

To Green this meant strict adherence to Calvin and the
Westminster Confession of Faith, with particular emphasis
upon the doctrine of imputation that all man's sins were
attributable to Adam. Barnes and the New Schoolers stood
for fresh thought on the subject, greater knowledge, and
loving interpretation.

Deeds soon took the place of discussion. Philadelphia
Synod agreed to the heresy charge against Barnes. The
General Assembly reversed the stand, but the damage had
been done. In 1837, actual church separation came when
the Barnes group walked out of the General Assembly.[28]

Aside from doctrinal dissimilarity, the groups felt differ-
ently about the Congregational Church. Presbyterian
ministers from the New England seminaries often expressed
more enthusiasm for the Congregational viewpoint of
congregational independence than they did for General Assembly government. The Old School declared "all our
troubles come from Congregationalism."[29]

Matter prevailed over mind, however. The Fund, "free of
ecclesiastical control" and related to the Presbyterian
Church only "on the basis of history, sentiment, and courtesy,"[30] discontinued its annual reports to the General Assembly.[31] It proceeded to do business with each school.

At the corporation meeting held May 17, 1839, the Board
voted to receive as a contributor "any minister of the Presbyterian Church in the United States."[32]

Three years later the Fund had definitely survived the
financial crisis which came to focus in the previous decade;

and had managed a method to counter the religious rumpus. It was an occasion for thanksgiving. President McMullin asked Dr. Archibald Alexander to open the annual meeting of the company with prayer. It was the first time in eighty-three years!

On the world scene the mid-1840's brought Charles Dickens's *A Christmas Carol*. Florida, Texas, Iowa, and Wisconsin joined the union as the nation grew to thirty states. It was also a time of growth for the personal underwriting industry. New companies came into being: New England Mutual Life, Mutual Benefit Life of New Jersey, Philadelphia's Penn Mutual Life, and Mutual of New York.[33] The last-named began business with modern selling methods in a novel kind of competition with the earlier firms, including the Presbyterian Fund.

Matthew L. Bevan, a banker-merchant, became president of the Widows' and Ministers' corporation, replacing John McMullin, now deceased.[34] Bevan's five-year term of office brought little excitement. The doughty Ashbel Green died May 19, 1848, after fifty-four years as secretary—a record of service not to be equaled in the entire history of the company. Dr. Robert M. Patterson assumed this position in addition to his duties as treasurer.

Dr. Green was accorded one of the few memorial minutes in the corporate records up to that time. Nevertheless, when his family subsequently requested their annuity be commuted to a single payment, the matter was referred to a committee with instructions to adjust the claim "in such manner as shall not be prejudicial to the pecuniary interests of the corporation."[35]

The company now stood at the middle of the nineteenth century, and elected as president the mysterious Dr. Alexander M. Mitchell, May 17, 1850. In literature, Nathaniel Hawthorne published *The Scarlet Letter*. In business, a number of new insurance companies were being formed at this time including: Manhattan Life, U.S. Life, Phoenix

Mutual, Berkshire Life, and Massachusetts Mutual. 1848 brought the first policy loans in the industry; and, the following year, New York passed its first general insurance law.[36]

Paul Johnson, the English writer, describes Christianity as a "time religion" and quotes Andrew Marvell in confirmation:

"But at my back I always hear
Time's winged charriot hurrying near."[37]

Rev. Archibald Alexander, a few months before he died in 1851, may not have felt the approaching apocalypse; but he sensed the urgent need for action by the board of directors. In May he proposed the appointment of an agent to tell church congregations about the Fund. In July he "earnestly pressed the importance of making changes in the plan of the corporation with a view to the increase of its usefulness."[38]

A special committee, chaired by Judge John Kintzing Kane, studied the matter, and within four months recommended changes to conform "more closely to the terms of ordinary insurance companies."[39] The Fund was on the march.

1852 marked the appearance of *Uncle Tom's Cabin* by Harriet Beecher Stowe, as the Civil War loomed nearer. *The New York Times* survived its first year as a fledgling newspaper, and the Presbyterian insurance enterprise made one change after the other. The year began as Dr. Mitchell appointed a committee to consider a new name for the company. Dr. Patterson, age seventy-five, resigned his duties as secretary and treasurer. The "New Plan" was announced.

Rev. Joseph H. Jones succeeded the venerable Patterson as secretary. His son, Robert Patterson II, was elected treasurer. Although young Patterson was also the nephew of Judge Kane, nepotism need not be imagined. The new financial officer of the company continued the high standards established by other members of his family. He soon proved to be an outstanding choice for the job.

As 1792 introduced non-forfeiture of benefits; 1824 brought the separate Ministers' Fund; 1826 saw more attractive provisions for the Widows' Fund; 1852 provided for cash surrender values and a broadening of the market to include "all Presbyterially-governed bodies such as German Reformed, Dutch Reformed, Associate Reformed, Lutheran, Reformed Presbyterian, and Cumberland Presbyterian."[40]

President Mitchell and Secretary Jones signed the twenty-three-page "Address" which contained plenty of the fine print which has become associated with insurance policies in the mind of the public. Here are some of the highlights.

The "Address" began with a historical summary of the Fund which admitted only fifty-five ministers were insured, of the thousands in the Presbyterian churches.

Three plans were offered: The long-standing annuity for widows and children; an ordinary life policy (for an amount not to exceed $3,000); the ministers' retirement annuity. Payments could be made in three ways: fixed sum at one time; annual premium; by church or institutional permanent deposit with benefits for successive incumbents of pulpits or teaching chairs.

Despite the formation of new companies and significant growth of the industry, life insurance had not reached the level of general public acceptance. *The New York Times*, 1853, declared:

"He who insures his own life or health must indeed be a victim of his own folly or other's knavery."[41]

The new plan brought additional business to the Fund. The years 1851-1854 raised the number of insured ministers from fifty-five to seventy-six, as corporation assets climbed to $62,454 from $57,699. The seventy-six contributors included seven admitted before 1825; twenty-three under the

1825 plan; and forty-six as a result of the 1852 program. In addition there were thirteen life depositors, nine church and seminary subscribers, but only two participants in the Ministers' Retirement Fund. The Board felt the need for further action.

On May 19, 1854, plans were made "to bring the claims of this corporation before the two General Assemblies." The treasurer was authorized to "pay such persons as may interest themselves to obtain assurers"; and a certain Rev. A. B. Quay was engaged for this purpose "at a commission equal to ten percent on the 1st year's premium demandable for such insurance."[42]

Quay's career as the Fund's first paid salesman soon ended. He died September 22, 1857, but left his family a $1,000 policy.

The Delaware River froze over in 1854, but life at the Fund was far from that condition. May 16, two years later, the Board approved the action taken by the Court of Quarter Sessions, County of Philadelphia to change the name of the corporation from its original cumbersome designation to Presbyterian Annuity Corporation. With the stroke of a pen, twenty-three words were reduced to three![43]

At the same meeting Dr. Mitchell's initial service as president came to an end when the doctor resigned to go to St. Louis. Mitchell could find satisfaction in continued, albeit gradual, company growth during his time in office to eighty-seven insured ministers of record, and company assets of $66,244.82.

Two years later he returned to Philadelphia and was promptly reelected president of the company—Hon. John Kintzing Kane, who served in his absence, having died February 21. Mitchell's second term of leadership coincided with a notable event in the industry. Massachusetts appointed Elizur Wright the State Insurance Commissioner, 1858.

Since 1847, forty-two life insurance companies had

appeared on the scene; twenty-four failed from poor management. High expenses, liberal dividends, and low premiums reflected the low standards which then characterized the underwriting world. Restoration of public confidence demanded dramatic action, and Wright's appointment provided it. Known later as "the father of life insurance," he pioneered industry standards for sounder mathematical calculations for actuarial success; fought for legislation to require companies to follow these standards; and brought about greater policyholder protection. The beginning of modern state insurance regulations is usually associated with Wright.[44]

In a sense Elizur Wright brought other companies in line with the conservative practices which the Presbyterian Fund had followed for 100 years. When the corporation began its second century of service in 1859, Dr. Mitchell and his associates could, in all modesty, take pride in the essentially conservative approach to underwriting which had carried the Fund safely through repeated wars, panics, and frequent human indifference to the protection proffered. Mitchell would have echoed Wright's perceptive comments:

"Life insurance is the standing together, shoulder to shoulder, of hosts of manly men to defend each other's home from that enemy that shoots on the sly and in the dark."

"Life insurance is the first concern of the thoughtful young man."

"It is the realization of fraternity without destruction of independence and individuality. It is charity without cant which enriches the giver and does not humiliate the receiver."[45]

When war came between the states in 1861, the Fund remained intact. It resolved not to let "the political circumstances of our country impair the contract between the contributors and the company."[46]

The Philadelphia physician remained as president until the next year, when at the June 13 meeting of the Board he was recorded as deceased. His twofold leadership years saw the election of twelve new corporators: Robert S. Clark, James N. Dickson, and Benjamin W. Tingley (1851); Rev. Thomas Brainerd, Charles W. Shields, and George H. Stuart (1853); Rev. Henry Darling, George W. Forbes, and Rev. C. P. Rogers (1856); and Joseph P. Engles, Rev. P. B. Westbrook, and Rev. Theodore W. J. Wylie (1858). The period also brought the company a new name, and broader insurance protection for Presbyterian ministers and their families.

The legacy of Alexander Mitchell's service to the Fund finds expression in Julia Ward Howe's famous hymn, written that very year:

"He has sounded forth the trumpet that shall never call retreat
He is sifting out the hearts of men before his judgment seat;
O, be swift, my soul, to answer him! Be jubilant my feet!
Our God is marching on!"

CHAPTER SEVEN

The Judicial Executive (1856-1858)
Judge John Kintzing Kane, President

O for a thousand tongues to sing,
My great Redeemer's praise,
The glories of my God and King,
The triumphs of his grace.

Charles Wesley

The second of two judges to serve as president of the Fund took office on his sixty-first birthday, May 16, 1856. This date also marked the first use of the new corporate name, Presbyterian Annuity Company. Neither the new face nor the new name had much initial effect on the fortunes of the insurance enterprise.

Judge Kane enjoyed community prominence as jurist of the United States District Court,[1] but his administration spanned only six board meetings of the corporation: three were adjourned without a quorum; and two others were held for the sole purpose of approving the satisfaction of a single mortgage.

Kane's lasting contribution to the business came from his thirty-one years as a conscientious corporator; his eight years as treasurer (1825-1836); his skillful handling of a difficult property dispute; and his leadership as a member of two board committees to change the company (1825, 1851). He was not alone in achieving other Fund positions of rank.

John Ewing and James Sproat, as we have noted, held the offices of treasurer and secretary, respectively; but these appointments in each case came after the presidency. With Kane it was just the opposite. His years as treasurer began at age thirty. When elected president he had completed his autobiography eight years earlier! With two men resigning the presidency to accept lower positions, and a third reaching it after making his principal contributions to the firm; the locus of company leadership during the first 100 years of the enterprise clearly differed from the later pattern of a powerful chief executive officer which emerged toward the close of the century.

Born in Albany, New York, in 1795, the subject of this chapter lost his mother when he was only three. His father, a lawyer, was active in the political life of that community.

In 1801 the family moved to Philadelphia. Years later the Judge described the journey in these words:

"I came in the sloop 'Fox,' a five, or as I think it was, a seven days' voyage, with the family of Uncle Elias, memorable because I scaled my shin by knocking over the teakettle in playing with the andirons; and from New York, a long two days' ride in the Swift-Sure stage, under the charge of my father's clerk."[2]

Baptized John, the future judge soon took Elisha as a middle name to distinguish himself from several cousins. When the elder Kane married again, his son, then twelve, substituted his stepmother's maiden name for his assumed cognomen, and thereafter became John Kintzing Kane. What a compliment to a woman cast in a usually unpopular role! Kane "loved her very sincerely."[3]

As early as 1812 the youth began courting Jean Duval Leiper, daughter of Thomas Leiper, a successful Philadelphia tobacconist and friend of Thomas Jefferson, who later owned valuable quarries in Delaware County. They were married April 20, 1819, after Kane graduated from Yale, studied law, and began his career as a lawyer in a modest office at 7th Street facing Samson.

The struggling attorney got to know Dr. Robert M. Patterson, at that time a University of Pennsylvania mathematics professor. Patterson and Kane helped form The Musical Fund Society (1820). Both men belonged to a group which "had the habit of meeting in each others' houses to listen to string quartets." Soon the society had a board of twelve managers and a membership of eighty-five persons.[4]

Thomas Sully painted the portraits of John and Jean Kane in 1824 after the artist noticed her beauty at a costume ball given by the City of Philadelphia for the Marquis de Lafayette. Judge Kane's "serious, sensitive, strong portrait" survives today in the Princeton University Museum.[5]

Within a year the ambitious lawyer, by now a member of

the Pennsylvania legislature, had been admitted to the Philosophical Society and joined the Board of the Presbyterian insurance corporation. He would rise to the presidency of each organization, but his start at the Fund immediately tested his mettle.

As noted earlier, Dr. Redman and the Board struggled with the complexities of company real estate investment in 1795 as they came to focus in the questionable actions of John Ewing, as treasurer, and John Nicholson, the corporator whose offer to help the Fund liquidate unproductive land resulted in a dispute over unrecorded mortgages and unclear titles. President Redman's committee to investigate the matter brought some clarification; but, in 1825, as John Kintzing Kane came on the Board, the issue remained unresolved owing to the later involvement of another Philadelphia lawyer, John B. Wallace.

Wallace, like Nicholson before him, offered to help the Fund by purchasing certain company lands. For fifteen years Wallace paid interest on a mortgage securing the purchase price; but the final settlement proved elusive. Once again faulty title to land conveyed gave a mortgagor reason to refuse payment. A later president writes:

"Suit was brought and judgment secured against Mr. Wallace but because of flaws in the title never pressed to a final issue. John Kintzing Kane, Esq., and, later, Ashbel Green, Jr., Esq., were entrusted with the complicated task of straightening out the matter."[6]

Kane also found himself on another special committee with Patterson and Green to propose changes in the Widows' Fund which had not been amended since 1792.[7] Their proposals were incorporated in a "New Plan of Agreement" circulated among the ministers and churches. Lower premiums for an annuity of one hundred dollars were dramatized by this comparative chart in the "Address":

Age	Old Rates	New Rates
30	$317.96	$357.61
40	407.78	421.35
50	519.80	502.21
60	651.88	599.23
70	801.26	721.51
Means	$559.73	$520.38[8]

The friendship between Kane and Patterson found further expression, 1827, when the lawyer and his wife named their fourth child for his mentor at the Fund. Robert Patterson Kane grew to manhood and became a noted admiralty lawyer.

Patterson's interests extended beyond musicales, philosophy, and the financial operations of the insurance corporation. These endeavors were avocations in contrast to his academic career at the University, which paid his salary. Greater professional opportunity beckoned at the end of 1828, with the offer of a faculty position at the University of Virginia.

Patterson resigned as treasurer of the Fund, December 30, and John Kintzing Kane succeeded him in that position at the established salary of $200 per annum. As Kane's term in office represents the only break in fifty-four consecutive years of a three-generation incumbency of the treasurership (1798-1852) by the Patterson family, we should note his particular contribution.

The first two Pattersons brought business experience and mathematical training to the job. They carefully studied financial details, and combined this knowledge with actual longevity experience to develop a statistical basis for the sound operation of the Fund.

Kane, a lawyer with political ambition, took a different approach. He had the ability to know what should be done in a given situation, and the vigor to do it. He showed little interest in actuarial calculation.[9] He was a man of affairs rather than a man of figures, but "discharged his duties as interim treasurer of the Fund with great satisfaction to everyone."[10]

While serving in this capacity John Kane secured appointment as Philadelphia City Solicitor under Mayor Dallas. Kane campaigned for Andrew Jackson; and, in 1832, the President appointed him to a commission to settle claims with France arising for the Treaty of July 4, 1831.

In the late 1830's Kane supported President Jackson's attack on the Second Bank of the United States. This may have been good politics, but it worked against the Fund, which thereby lost the advantages of doing business in the nation's banking center.

The energetic Democrat joined Governor Shunk's cabinet as Attorney General, 1845; and eighteen months later President James Polk named him to the Federal Bench of the Eastern District of Pennsylvania. The judge described his installation in this manner:

"I had not expected a ceremony. Hurrying into the Courtroom, I was surprised to find it filled, and by all the best members of the bar. Judge King swore me in, and I simply announced the order of the business for the rest of the term. At this moment the whole Bar rose, and Mr. William Rawle addressed me on their behalf, . . . and expressing their united judgment of my qualifications for the post to which I had been raised . . . I know I must have floundered sadly in my reply of acknowledgements."[11]

Judge Kane's continuing service on the Finance Committee of the Fund kept him close to the fortunes of the corporation. He was well aware of the slow growth in number of insured ministers, and the potential competition from other companies being formed in these mid-century years. He represented a natural choice to head a new committee appointed in response to the Archibald Alexander proposal for Fund changes to increase its usefulness.

The distinguished jurist embraced the opportunity; and,

with Rev. Albert Barnes, Rev. Joseph H. Jones, W. J. B. Mitchell, and Robert Patterson II, produced a plan which went into effect in early 1852 to make "more generally known the existence of the corporation and the terms of its contracts."[12]

Kane requested the treasurer to prepare tables of premiums for use at this time. On February 10, Patterson included these in a long letter to Kane in which he noted that the Fund insured a small number of a special segment of society. The treasurer anticipated a mortality experience rate no worse than other insurance companies because "the clergy . . . being, from their very profession, separated from the dissipations and excitements most prejudicial to health, must enjoy longer lives than the average of the community."[13]

Within the Fund, Kane enjoyed a record of accomplishment and acclaim from his associates. As a public figure the judge provoked occasional controversy. His attitude toward slavery seemed ambivalent. In one case he ruled against an agent for the Abolition Society, Pasmore Williamson, and sent him to jail for helping a slave and her children escape to freedom. Yet, in 1851, he decided in favor of a certain Euphemia Williams and her seven children, who were claimed by a Maryland man.[14]

As the jurist declared in his *Autobiography*, "I never spoke what I did not think,"[15] we are left with his reputation for integrity and knowledge of the law in these two incidents of apparent contradiction.

His short presidential years coincided on the national scene with the famous Dred Scott decision; the invention of the Bessamer Converter in steel manufacturing; and the financial panic of 1857 during which the Girard Bank suspended specie payments and the Bank of Pennsylvania failed.

The Fund survived this economic turmoil, but some tempers were short, as noted in this comment about "the swindling, rotten, robbing banks of Philadelphia," which railed against:

"The thieves at the head of these concerns [who] ride in their carriages, go with their lazy sons and daughters to the opera, flourish at fashionable watering places, despise honest working men, and yet steal like beggars, bring honest people to penury, and after all escape the State Prison."[16]

John Kintzing Kane's Christian conviction made him a trustee of the Second Presbyterian Church; a trustee of the General Assembly; a trustee of Girard College; and vice president of the Institution for the Instruction of the Blind. It also made him sensitive to the Biblical basis of life insurance found in I Timothy 5:8, "If any provide not for his own and specially for those of his own house, he hath denied the faith."

Judge Kane, insured by the Fund as a lay contributor, left his widow an annuity of $120, when he died February 21, 1858.

CHAPTER EIGHT
War and Peace
(1862-1873)
Charles Macalester, President

Living for Jesus a life that is true,

Striving to please Him in all that I do;

Yielding allegiance, glad-hearted and free,

This is the pathway of blessing for me.

Thomas O. Chisholm

E. Gordon Alderfer, a twentieth-century writer, observed: "The movement of the human spirit in time, which we try to categorize with the word 'History,' is far more than a series of scientifically measurable facts."[1]

Charles Macalester, the twelfth man elected president of the Presbyterian Annuity Company, personified this element of experience which goes beyond a given sequence of events. The Philadelphia banker headed the corporation during the Civil War and the "Gilded Age" which followed. These were years of slow growth for the company. While assets inched up an average of 2.7 percent per year for more than a decade ($81,061.91, 1862, to $106,480.13, 1873); "persons interested in the Fund" actually declined from a modest 160 to a paltry 125 — a 33 percent drop in people paying insurance premiums accounting for most of this decline.

Yet through it all the corporation redefined its structure, simplified its protection offerings, reasserted its independence from denominational control, and avoided the mistakes made by numerous other life insurance companies which failed in the 60's and 70's.

Much of the credit for these achievements belongs to Charles Macalester, known to his St. Andrew's Society associates for "his sterling integrity and force of character."[2] The financier demonstrated an effective way with both money and men early in life. He came to the leadership of the Fund after decades of banking success and community experience.

Born in Philadelphia, February 17, 1798, Macalester was educated at Grey and Wylie's school and the University of Pennsylvania. At an early age he became a director of the Pennsylvania Company for Insurances on Lives and Granting Annuities.[3] Moving to Cincinnati at age twenty-three, he went into business there and married Eliza Ann Lytle, 1824. Three years later the capable young man returned to Philadelphia and soon secured his first appointment as a government director of the Second Bank of the United States. In 1835 he organized his own firm of Gaw, Macalester & Company, bankers.[4]

Macalester spent the 1840's accumulating a fortune in real estate through astute investments in Philadelphia and Chicago. He acquired a new wife, Susan Bradford Wallace, niece of Hon. Horace Binney; and lived in London, where he became a friend of the American banker-philanthropist, George Peabody. While the Presbyterian financier enjoyed the British capital, Charles Dickens came to Philadelphia and found it lugubrious. The famous author looked out his Chestnut Street hotel window and described the Second Bank of the United States in these words:

". . . a handsome building of white marble, which had a mournful ghost-like aspect, dreary to behold. . . . It was the Tomb of many fortunes; the great Catacomb of investment."[5]

Returning to America, Macalester continued his relationship with Peabody as a trustee of that individual's Educational Fund. In 1849 the Philadelphia banker retired from business, but began a new phase of his life through election to the Presbyterian insurance corporation and prompt appointment to its finance committee.

Living until 1873, the altruistic layman would spend almost as many years as a full-time, non-paid participant in Christian activities and community affairs as he did earlier as a banker and businessman. In a sense, he exemplified the spirit of voluntarism which, since the Revolutionary War, played "a role in the religious lives of Presbyterian Americans . . ." whose activities and organizations "mirrored the fundamental characteristics of the American way." The former financier, and others like him, found voluntaryism the best way to express what a modern history professor calls: "The legitimate concerns of men trying to understand and to adjust to the changing patterns of religion and society in America."[6]

Before long the Second Presbyterian Church trustee found himself caught up in the maelstrom of the 1857 financial panic which struck Philadelphia, September 25.

"Business men were thrown into a fever of excitement, and the managers of some banking institutions called for detachments of police to protect them from the clamorous importunities of creditors. Many of the leading business men insisted that the State legislature would give relief to them by legalizing the suspension of specie payments. On the 8th of October they held a mass meeting in Independence Square, at which Charles Macalester presided, urging the General Assembly to do something that would relieve the 'suffering community' in its monetary distress."[7]

The year before his assumption of the Presbyterian Annuity Company presidency, June 13, 1862, Macalester spoke at another mass meeting of the citizenry. In National Hall, where a crowd of pre-Civil War anti-coercionists swarmed, the good-hearted former banker declared: "The South should have remained loyal to the Union . . . but as they seem determined to go, let them go in peace . . . for we be brethren."[8]

Macalester, a Jacksonian Democrat at one time, but "never a politician, always a patriot," would vote for Lincoln's reelection three years later as well as for Ulysses S. Grant in 1868.[9]

Presbyterian Annuity Company finances provide a fascinating frame of reference for the start of Charles Macalester's tenure as president. Celebrating its first century of service to the ministers of that denomination and their families, the Fund found opportunities to emphasize again the often startling benefits of insurance protection. On one such occasion, treasurer Robert Patterson II told this story of rewarded thrift and wise investment:

"During the present year we have paid assurances to the estates of three ministers, Viz. Rev. Jos. M. Quarterman of Pitatka, Florida, Rev. E. D. Mackey, of Princess Anne, Maryland and Rev. Thomas B. Wilson, of Xenia, Ohio; Mr. Quarterman had paid for $9.03, and died one month after securing his covenant; which amounted to $1,290. Mr. Mackey died within 4 months of the date of his covenant; he had paid but $53.80 and secured reversion of $2,000. Mr. Wilson died within sixteen months of his assurance; he had paid but $42.67 and secured $1,000."[10]

Despite this particular outgo of $4,295 for only $105.50 taken in, Fund assets had reached a substantial level for those days. President Macalester learned that the corporation resources at his installation totaled $130,443.94 against liabilities of $108,680.37 for a favorable balance of $21,763.07. One hundred years of conservative investment policy made the difference.

These computations involved more than simple arithmetic. The third Patterson to hold the company treasurership went beyond the primitive efforts of his predecessors in their efforts to predict mortality experience and its effect on the operations of the business. Robert II made "a laborious calculation based upon life insurance principles." The basis being "a comparison of our risks, according to the received probabilities of life assuming a moderate interest for money, with our means either invested or probably derived from premiums."[11] Patterson assumed a 5 percent interest rate, and used the general mortality experience from the English village of Carlisle. In other words, these mid-century reckonings involved the element of contingency in the growing sophistication of life insurance accounting.

Before the end of 1862, the Fund bought $25,000 U.S. Bonds to help the Union Cause, thus repeating the Revolutionary War pattern of extending financial help to the government in time of peril.[12] The investment was kept secret until the bonds were sold eight years later.

Strangely enough, the corporation seems to have existed more than 100 years without formal by-laws. Minutes of annual meetings refer to procedures followed as "required by charter." From time to time duties of the treasurer or activities of the finance committee were defined; but a comprehensive plan of operation did not exist until June 19, 1863, when a special committee composed of Charles Macalester, Robert Patterson II, and Joseph H. Jones presented such a document "suitable for the government of the corporation." The new by-laws provided for the election of corporators; the dates of the annual meetings (the Friday succeeding the third Thursday each May); the duties of the officers (the president was to affix the seal to all contracts — except for covenants for annuities or assurances, where the treasurer is empowered to act); the functions of the finance committee; and the order of business for each annual meeting. In contrast to prevailing contemporary practice, where minutes of many organizations are routinely accepted as previously distributed, these 1863 Fund by-laws specified all minutes were to be read.

Macalester's second presidential year also brought two other important decisions. One reflected the traditional conservatism of company management. The other confirmed a consistent record of independence from outside control.

The Civil War notwithstanding, "ministers employed in the military or naval service, or in foreign countries, or in districts where contracts depending on life are more than usually hazardous" would not be insured.[13]

The Presbyterian Board of Publication insured its secretaries with the Fund to secure annuities for their survivors. The General Assembly, meeting in Peoria, Illinois, decreed this was a mistake, and demanded a refund of the deposit. The Fund convened a special meeting to review the matter. After "due deliberation" and several paragraphs beginning with "whereas," the company resolved:

"That while the Presbyterian Annuity Company entertains the highest respect for the General Assembly, yet it is the unanimous opinion that this corporation have no authority to restore to the Board of Publication the fund deposited for their secretaries."[14]

121

Macalester's gregarious nature found further expression the following year with his election as president of the St. Andrew's Society. He had been "constant in attendance at meetings and generous in his contributions" to its activities.[15]

These mid-1860 years brought the end of the Civil War and the abolition of slavery in the United States. The life insurance industry acquired a further dimension as Connecticut General pioneered substandard risk coverage which had been unknown prior to this time. Within the Fund itself, the Board began the practice (which is continued to the present day) of recording in its official minutes the names of the insured at their decease — a policy emphasizing the almost-family nature of the enterprise which distinguished it from purely commercial competitors. The first name so recorded was that of Dr. John McDowell. He died February 13, 1863.

Also recorded in the minutes of almost every meeting were dramatic cases of annuity benefits paid to survivors. These invariably reinforced the company credo of bounty for the loved ones of those ministers thrifty enough to buy insurance from the Fund:

"Rev. Philip Lindsley, D.D., of Nashville, Tennessee, for example, left a widow and children who shared his $400 life desposit and individual annuities of $120 each;

"Mrs. Margaret Riddell, to name another beneficiary, died April 23, 1863, age 90, after receiving $80 per annum since 1830;

"The widow of Rev. John B. Smith benefited from his policy for 44 years."[16]

The Fund survived payment of these substantial benefits and modest growth in size because of selected insurance risks and the shrewd investment policies of a century. Newer companies, without these advantages, moved with greater dispatch and less caution. A case in point is the Equitable Life Assurance Society of New York. Founded, 1859, by Presbyterian layman Henry Baldwin Hyde, the

Equitable soon adopted an extremely aggressive sales policy which was to reverberate through the industry.

Hyde rediscovered Dr. Lorenze Tonti, a seventeenth-century Neopolitan banker, who devised a scheme to raise money for the state.[17] This speculative plan was adapted to life insurance by the Equitable, which featured the tontine method for paying dividends.

Tontine insurance provided for dividend periods. If a policyholder died before the end of his contract period, the face value was paid, but no dividends. If he paid premiums to the end of the specified period, he shared in both his dividends and the forfeited reserves of those who had died earlier or who had allowed their policy to lapse. Although actuarily sound, tontine insurance "produced a bitter rift in the insurance business."[18] Some considered it "an invention of the devil." It was denounced as "life insurance cannibalism whose sole function is to make the rich part of the company richer by making the poorer part poorer."[19]

Regardless of the turmoil engendered, within twenty years most United States companies followed the Equitable. Within less than another twenty years, however, all tontines were banned after an investigation of life insurance misman-agement conducted by the New York legislature.

The Fund kept to its course during these vicissitudes of its increasing number of competitors, untouched by the ton-tine phenomenon. In a sense it actually benefited, for, "in retrospect, the tontines made America life insurance con-scious."[20]

1868 brought the American literary scene *Little Women* by Louisa May Alcott. It brought the Christian hymnody "O Little Town of Bethlehem." The words of this popular Christmas carol were written by Phillips Brooks, the famous rector of Holy Trinity Episcopal Church on Philadelphia's Rittenhouse Square, within a city block of the present headquarters of the Fund. Brooks completed the carol the third week of December. The church organist, Lewis H.

Redner, in an experience which surely stands unique in the romance of the faith, set the words to music Christmas Eve, and the hymn was sung for the first time the following day.[21]

The Fund secretary since 1852, Rev. Joseph H. Jones, died that very week. He was the fifth man to hold that office since its first incumbent, Francis Alison; and the son-in-law of one of his predecessors in office, the illustrious Rev. Ashbel Green, who served as secretary, 1794-1847. Jones's successor would be Thomas L. Janeway, whose father had been a corporator fifty-eight years. Without a trace of self-consciousness about nepotism, continuing family interest in and succeeding generations of service to the Fund were in this way affirmed anew. Finding good men for the task at hand prevailed over genealogical introspection with genuine benefit to the company.

As previously noted, more than a few men who took an active part in the operation of the Fund held responsible positions elsewhere in the city. Robert Patterson II, the treasurer at this time, helped organize the Fidelity Trust, Safe Deposit and Insurance Company, becoming its first secretary and treasurer.[22]

Charles Macalester fitted this pattern to perfection. In addition to holding the presidency of the Presbyterian Annuity Company, he also served as a director of the Camden & Amboy Railroad, the Insurance Company of the State of Pennsylvania, Jefferson Medical College, and Patterson's Fidelity Trust.

The crowded decade of the 60's neared its end. In the world of affairs, men laid the Atlantic Cable, completed the transcontinental railroad (at Promentory, Utah), and opened the Suez Canal. Christian developments included the founding of Charles Spurgeon's Metropolitan Tabernacle in London and William Booth's beginning the Salvation Army in the same city. United States life insurance matured with the introduction of the American Experience Table of Mortality published as a part of New York law.[23]

In a sense the Presbyterian Fund's Robert Patterson had been this country's first life insurance actuary as early as 1792 when he prepared a primitive table of premiums for the corporation plan of that year. His son and grandson added to the science with their successive computations in 1825 and 1851.

Concurrent with these later Fund developments came the work of Mutual Life of New York's Charles Gill. He produced a new mortality table, first used in 1853, to supplement the Carlisle and Northampton projections based on general population records of those English towns. Gill had trouble with the management of his company. A certain ambiguity existed regarding his role. The early resistance of executive leadership to actuarial advice is compared by a modern writer to "hiring a dog and doing your own barking,"[24] but it was very real in these years of the profession's infancy.

By 1858, however, Sheppard Homans, who succeeded Gill as Mutual Life's actuary, compiled the first generally-accepted mortality table, christened "American Experience" by the New York legislature.[25] Although based on the operations of only two firms, the new table was now required by statute to be used throughout the industry to determine company reserves against future contingencies.

A further step for the life insurance business came in 1869. The United States Supreme Court ruled, in the case of Paul vs Virginia, insurance not to be a transaction in commerce and therefore not subject to Federal law.[26] These events would affect the Fund's future as they marked a steadily-increasing sophistication and experience on the part of a growing number of competitors.

Charles Macalester's presidency of the Fund reached its climax in 1871. That year a new "Address" went to the ministers and laymen of the denomination describing "the objects and advantages of contracting with the corporation."[27]

This announcement emphasized two forms of insurance: ordinary life with annual premium; and a deferred annuity at age fifty-five, sixty, or sixty-five years of age—a Widows' Fund policy, and a Ministers' Fund policy. Permanent deposits by churches or other organizations were suggested once again; but a previous provision for securing a deferred annuity by single premium was discontinued because the company "did not deem that plan a judicious one for the minister."[28] This meant the Fund no longer offered (the actuarily unsound) annuity payable to a deceased minister's family.

In addition to specific policy details and illustrations of their benefits, "arguments" were also advanced on behalf of the "venerable" Presbyterian corporation. The message concluded with this statement signed by Macalester, the rest of the Finance Committee, and the treasurer:

"Feeling that we unite safety, economy, and liberality of management with an organization entirely under Presbyterian control, we should rejoice if, through the sympathy and patronage of the church, its ministers and laymen, our objects could become more widely known and our sphere of usefulness enlarged."[29]

Propitious timing marked the new address. It came soon after the historic reunion of the "Old School" and "New School" factions of the denomination which had been divided since 1837 when the Presbyterians formed two General Assemblies in a dispute over the status of theological seminaries, the approval of publications, and the qualifications of ministers. "Old Schoolers" limited expression to the Bible and the Westminster Confession of Faith; justified slavery; and had little enthusiasm for evangelism. The "New School" men urged cooperation with the Congregationalists, fought against slavery, and found room for a social gospel emphasis.

The corporation served both sides, but the controversy did little to strengthen the denomination or encourage the growth of the Fund. By 1870 only 120 ministers out of 4,238 Presbyterian clergy were insured! The Annuity Company welcomed the 1866 overtures for rapprochement when the General Assembly noted its "fraternal affection for the other branch of the Presbyterian Church."[30] As the Civil War forged union for the nation, its aftermath brought a coming together of the bickering church factions which had formed almost thirty years before.

The "Old School" took the initiative and eventually compromised. The "New School" would not accept surrender as the basis for reconciliation. Eventually a modified proposal was approved endorsing the Westminster Confession but permitting "various methods of viewing, stating, explaining, and illustrating the doctrines of the Church, which do not impair the integrity of the Reformed or Calvinistic system."[31]

Reunion came May 19, 1870, at the First Church, Pittsburgh. Rev. Philemon H. Fowler, former moderator of the "New School" General Assembly, preached a sermon on Ephesians 4:4 and the Presbyterians were united again![32] These flowery phrases reflected the flavor of the occasion:

"While fears for orthodoxy and apprehensions of commotion from the mingling of discordant elements and surviving antipathies disinclined many of the Old School Brethren to the Reunion, it was repugnant to a few of the New School Brethren as likely to restrain the Christian liberty of thought and to destroy or impair the pleasantness of their ecclesiastical associations, and as calling off their church from a course of bold and successful enterprise which it was pursuing.

A better acquaintance with each other allayed suspicions and anxiety on both sides."[33]

With the nation at peace, with the denomination restored, and with a fresh insurance program for its constituency, the fortunes of the Fund began to improve. Despite the financial panic of 1873, the number of insured ministers increased and corporate assets grew from $101,466.20 in 1870 to $104,492.50 in 1872. There was nothing automatic about this progress. "Speculation and financial corruption plagued the nation. Business scandal was rampant," records a modern historian.[34] Between 1868-1870, twenty-three life insurance companies failed; from 1870-1872, thirty-three others went out of business. Once again the Fund survived a time of peril to emerge stronger than before. Careful investments, prompt payment of claims, and integrity of its leadership provided a corporate mystique equal to the challenge.

Nearing the end of his time in office, Macalester, 1873, counted twenty-two corporators elected during his tenure:

1863—Abraham R. Perkins, Col. J. Ross Snowden
1864—Rev. J. W. Dulles, James Dunlap, Winthrop Sargent
1869—Rev. William Pratt Breed, Thomas M. Freeland, Rev. Daniel March, Thomas Marshall, Morris Patterson.
1870—Rev. R. H. Allen, Rev. Herrick Johnson, Alfred Martien, William J. McElroy, Joseph E. Mitchell, William E. Tenbrook
1871—William L. DuBois, Hon. William S. Pierce
1872—Gustavus S. Benson, Samuel C. Perkins
1873—John C. Farr, George W. Mears.

James Dunlap's name appeared in the company minutes, but is missing from present records. Three others (Snowden, Dulles, and Tenbrook) became president of the Fund. Board turnover proved brisk. Of twenty-two members listed in the 1871 "Address," fifteen were elected during Macalester's presidency, which means they had served less than eight years.

This same year Charles Macalester made a gift of land to start a college in Minnesota. The grateful trustees named the institution for its Philadelphia benefactor, as property at St. Anthony's Falls, near St. Paul, became the campus of this Presbyterian institution which opened two years later.

The insurance leader-philanthropist died suddenly of a

heart attack December 9, 1873. He lived at 1016 Spruce Street, Philadelphia, where his last will and testament was written and signed only fifty-five days before. Article sixth of this will left $5,000 to start a new Presbyterian church "anywhere on Grant Avenue, in Torresdale" (where he owned a second home). Another $5,000 was bequeathed to provide annual income toward the support of the pastor "for the time being, and of said church and congregation forever."[35]

Three local newspapers noted his passing in these words:

"A benevolent giver from his means, but not an undiscriminating bestower of unmerited charities."

> Public Ledger, Philadelphia
> December 10, 1873

"He left one descendent, Mrs. Lily Macalester, widow."

> Public Record, Philadelphia
> December 10, 1873

"For many years a trustee of Second Church, he died a member of First Presbyterian on Washington Square. He was interred at Laurel Hill Cemetery, with pall bearers from the St. Andrew's Society."

> Evening Telegraph, Philadelphia
> December 13, 1873

These terse announcements, together with many tributes, appeared in a memorial volume which began with a poem by S. M. Remak:

"A form fondly cherished is with us no more,
A voice well beloved is still;
A generous heart's true pulsations are o'er,
His place he no longer can fill . . .

Such a beautiful life is not ended, though here
No longer its presence we see,
'Tis immortal! — its virtues are dear,
And blest shall his memory be!"[36]

CHAPTER NINE

A Flair for the Dramatic (1874-1878)
Colonel J. Ross Snowden, President

Once to every man and nation
  Comes the moment to decide,
In the strife of truth with falsehood,
  For the good or evil side;
Some great cause, God's new Messiah,
  Offering each the bloom or blight,
And the choice goes by forever
  'Twixt that darkness and that light.

James Russell Lowell

The first Fund president born in the nineteenth century, and the fourth lawyer to head the company, achieved primary prominence as an expert in coins and medals. He also held the military rank of colonel.

J. Ross Snowden began life December 9, 1809, and grew to continue the pattern of legal corporation leadership established by George Bryan (1780-1791); John McMullin (1837-1844); and John Kintzing Kane (1856-1858). *The Dictionary of American Biography*[1] lists him first as a numismatist, and during the Civil War he served as an officer in the First Regiment, Philadelphia Home Guard.

Snowden's father, Rev. Nathaniel Randolph Snowden, curator of Dickinson College, descended from John Snowden, who came to this country from Nottingham, England, in the late 1670's. John Snowden is believed to have welcomed William Penn when that individual first visited his province.[2]

James Ross Snowden attended Dickinson College, studied law in Carlisle, Pennsylvania, gained admission to the bar at age nineteen, and began his legal practice in Franklin, Venango County, 1830. He soon secured an appointment as district attorney of the community, and within a few years, was elected to the Pennsylvania legislature (1838-1844). He served as speaker of the House of Representatives for the last two years of that time. An early interest in military matters found fulfillment in his election as colonel of a local militia regiment. In 1845 "he presided at the state military convention in Harrisburg."[3]

Public service for the young lawyer also involved the treasurership of Pennsylvania, where his activities were somewhat controversial.[4] A twentieth-century writer, Neil Carothers, in his book, *Fractional Money*, notes:

"Apparently he was a man of great force of character, ignorant of monetary principles and but little hampered by any regard for laws that did not accord with his views."[5]

Snowden's next achievement came as treasurer of the United States Mint then located at Chestnut and Juniper Streets, Philadelphia. He assumed the position March 24, 1847.[6] Benjamin Rush held the post 1797-1813, but Snowden would keep it only three years. September 13, 1848, he married Susan Engle Patterson, the daughter of General Robert Patterson[7] and soon thereafter moved to Pittsburgh, where he resumed the practice of law. Two sons and three daughters would be born of this marriage.

In 1853 the Snowdens returned to Philadelphia, as the energetic lawyer went back to the United States Mint—this time as the director, beginning June 3. Four of his eight predecessors in the position had connections with the Presbyterian Fund: Elias Boudinot (director 1795-1806, elected a corporator 1801); Robert Patterson (director 1806-1824, became a corporator 1795, treasurer 1798-1824); Samuel Moore, M.D., Patterson's son-in-law (director 1824-1835, elected to the annuity corporation, 1828); and Robert M. Patterson (director 1835-1851, joined the corporators 1816, served as treasurer 1824-1828, 1836-1852).

More than friendship and family favoritism were involved in these relationships at the American coin factory. Each director assumed the responsibilities by White House decree. Ross Snowden's book about the Mint contained compliments about each of these men who also made such significant contributions to the annuity corporation. Boudinot, appointed by George Washington, discharged his duties at the Mint "with great fidelity and ability."[8] Robert Patterson, selected by Thomas Jefferson, "filled the office with great reputation."[9] Samuel Moore, named by James Monroe, used his "influence and exertions" to transfer the Mint to a new location.[10] Robert M. Patterson, appointed by Andrew Jackson, prepared "a new law which simplified previous regulations."[11] No wonder, in God's providence, the Presbyterian Fund proved so durable through these years of financial panics and business uncertainty.

Colonel Snowden's years as director of the Mint were flavored with talks and books. In 1856, for example:

"On the 6th of September the services of Baron von Steuben, of Revolutionary fame, were commemorated at Lemon Hill by a picnic, which more than ten thousand people attended. There was also a parade. The career of the German patriot was eulogized by Col. J. Ross Snowden and Dr. Godfrey Vellner, the editor of the German Democrat."[12]

Known later as "a voluminous writer"[13] Snowden wrote a book on ancient and modern coins which appeared in 1860, followed soon thereafter by a volume describing the medals of George Washington.

After eight years of minting and mentioning medals, the institution's director resigned to become prothonotary of the Pennsylvania Supreme Court.[14] Fittingly enough, to commemorate the event, he received a medal with this inscription on the obverse side:

"Presented to James Ross Snowden, Director of the Mint, by his personal friends, as a mark of their regard for him as an officer, and their esteem for him as a citizen."[15]

With the outbreak of the Civil War, 1861, Colonel Snowden advocated making an application to Philadelphia City Council "for an appropriation for the maintenance of the Home Guard."[16]

A book published in 1876 observed that J. Ross Snowden "being an elder in the Presbyterian Church, took an active part in the various courts of that denomination."[17] This included his election as a corporator of the Annuity Fund, June 19, 1863.

This same year, as an ardent Democrat, the lawyer spoke publicly against the war. As a military officer he eschewed pacifism, but he warned his listeners about the financial and legal consequences of the conflict. He worried about the mounting national debt, and expressed concern over suspension of the *habeas corpus* act—declaring Abraham Lincoln possessed neither "ubiquity nor omniscience." The articulate politician even advocated "withdrawal of The Emancipation Proclamation and repeal of the conscription bill."[18]

Colonel Snowden twice offered his volunteer Philadelphia regiment for field service, "but it was not accepted by the government."[19]

With the end of the war and preservation of the Union, Ross Snowden began active participation in the life of the Fund. Named a member of the Finance Committee, he helped prepare the 1871 "Address" to the Presbyterian Church. Although Charles Macalester was president at the time, Snowden did much of the work on this new project. In a sense, he echoed the contribution made by John Kintzing Kane in drafting the Plan of 1852 during the presidency of Alexander Mitchell.

The company office, in those days located at 1334 Chestnut Street, stood only a few blocks from Rittenhouse Square, which later became the home of the Fund. Fanny Kemble, the famous British actress, lived there in 1874 and had this to say about the picturesque area:

"This square is inclosed in an iron railing; it is about as large as Lincoln's Inn Fields, open to the public, and not reserved, as our squares are, for the use of the persons residing in them. There are neither shrubberies nor garden-beds with flowers, but trees, grass, and gravel walks, and it affords a pleasant diagonal short cut across the square."[20]

The first 1874 meeting of the corporation, April 20, initiated Snowden's Fund presidency. At once he proposed a memorial minute to honor his predecessor, Charles Macalester.

The new president then moved swiftly to appoint a special committee to "consider the propriety" of expanding the business to meet the growing needs of the church, and to place the matter before the General Assembly. The committee received instructions to cooperate with "any measures feasible which that reverend body may inaugurate."[21]

This language went beyond conciliation to enthusiasm as it appealed to pre-1837 spirit in the denomination before the doctrinal split and subsequent reconciliation. Perilous times demanded this vigorous approach. Fifty-six life insurance companies failed between 1868-1872. Fourteen others closed their doors in the panic of 1873.[22] The Presbyterian Fund came nowhere near this fate, but it breathed stagnant air. Only 125 persons paid premiums or received benefits!

The new president called the company to a special meeting ten days later to receive the committee's report, approve it, print it, and send it to the General Assembly. The two-page document summarized the purpose and progress of the Fund. It carefully noted its independence from the ecclesiastical body, but indicated a willingness to "act on harmony" with the denominational center if its views were "made known to us."[23]

At the Annual Meeting, October 5, the Board voted the president a $100 annual salary. Since chartered in 1759, that officer had served without remuneration. The Board also asked its leader to prepare a new historical sketch of the company—a task for which he was well qualified. The articulate Snowden published *The Coins of the Bible, and Its Money Terms* (1864); an article on "International Coinage" in the January, 1870, *Lippincott's* magazine; and, three years later, an article on United States Coins for the *National Almanac*.[24]

Treasurer Robert Patterson II reported nine less people in the Fund and only $123 additional assets over the previous year. As a result the men appointed a special committee to review the corporate charter with regard to insuring laymen, and adjourned to meet again at the call of the president.

The group reconvened thirteen days later as Snowden reported the approval he secured from the Synod of Philadelphia and New Jersey. Encouraged by this success and the president's determination, the company moved boldly to: change the charter to permit insurance of laymen; consider renaming the firm "Presbyterian Life Insurance Company"; increase its capital from $20,000 to $500,000; and open an office of its own instead of continuing to meet in space provided by the Presbyterian Board of Publication. The Fund had followed that entity westward on Chestnut Street as it moved from #265 (1853) to #861 (1871) to #1334 (1874). The treasurer's office would remain at the Fidelity Trust and Safe Deposit Company.

What a year it had been for the somnolent enterprise! J. Ross Snowden put the company in motion, and 1875 would bring more of the same.

The Presbyterian Annuity and Life Insurance Company became the new name of the Fund. This and the other proposed changes were confirmed on March 27 by Philadelphia Common Pleas Court #2.

Meeting again May 17 at the call of the president, the corporation made two additional decisions which augured well for the future of the business. Approving appointment of an actuary (also to act as an agent in soliciting prospects), the Board enlarged the Finance Committee's powers to constitute that body an Executive Committee with full powers to act for the company. This began a new arrangement with the Executive group conducting oversight of the officers, and the corporation to meet but once a year.

J. Ross Snowden kept his cohorts busy. Monthly meetings through the summer and into the fall brought J. B. H. Janeway to the position of actuary at a salary of $1,200 per year. Mr. Janeway was also paid $250 for his premium tables, and his work on the new "Address" being prepared for the constituency.

The actuary received authority to employ sub-agents with the clear understanding that their commissions on first-year premiums would not exceed 25 percent. Within four months Janeway enlisted Mr. J. C. Jamison as a traveling agent and the committee endorsed his employment on this basis:

"1. A commission of 30% on all first-year premiums obtained by him personally.
2. A commission of 5% on all first-year premiums obtained by agents of his appointment, over the 25% to be allowed them.
3. His traveling expenses to be paid by this company at the rate of $5 per day when actually on the route."[25]

The "Address" of 1875 merits mention in some detail. In the 116 years since the drafting of the charter, 1759, the Fund published six supplemental communications to the Presbyterian Church. The messages dated 1792, 1824, 1826, 1841, 1852, and 1871 possessed a certain similarity of style. They were dull.

"TO PRESBYTERIAN MINISTERS AND LAYMEN AND FAMILIES INCLUDING ALL OTHER DENOMINATIONS OF SIMILAR POLITY"

furnished the focus for this forty-two-page, 1875 prospectus. An offer to insure laymen appeared right at the start. Snowden, Patterson, and Janeway took no chances that this innovation would be missed.

Colorful language took the place of the pedestrian prose which characterized the earlier addresses. Life assurance was compared with protection against "loss by flames" and "wrecks at sea," with warnings of death's inevitability in contrast to houses "which may never burn" and the ship "which may never be wrecked."[26] Questions and answers followed this ominous distinction. Then came Biblical texts, such as I Timothy 5:8, leading to the dramatic statement: "Five cents a day, at age 30, will provide an ordinary life policy of $1,000," and "eight cents a day at the same age will secure an endowment of $1,133 payable at the age of sixty."[27]

Solemn warnings were included about "survivors accustomed to the intellectual and social refinement of the parsonage" being "poorly prepared, in the event of the husband's or father's death, to endure the rough, cold grasp of penury."[28]

For good measure, London's preaching sensation, Rev. Charles H. Spurgeon, told the reader to practice Christ's command of "taking no thought for the morrow" by paying the policy money once a year in obedience to the spirit and the letter of the Master.

The company then described itself. It stressed the "integrity and wisdom" of the corporation managers, the rigid economy of operations, and the mutual aspect of the plan. Kinds of policies were listed and explained. Individuals were importuned to buy, and churches, colleges, or societies also solicited. Not forgotten were "liberal persons" who might make permanent deposits with the company for future benefit of missionaries or those in any worthy calling who are "devoting their strength to others rather than accumulating for themselves."[29]

Noting the $10,000 insurance limit on a single life, the Address then provided twelve pages of premium tables to conclude with the names of many ministers to whom annuities had been paid or whose survivors had received them. Also listed by name and dollar amount were a number of clergy successfully insured since 1854. The first groups included Samuel Finley, D.D., President of the College of New Jersey; and Robert Smith, Moderator of the General Assembly, 1791. The second list counted Rev. William L. Breckinridge, $1,040.00, and Rev. Nathaniel Burt, $1,759.00

The reader must have been impressed by the geographical diversity of those satisfied clients. The Presbyterian company had reached west to Salt Creek, Nebraska; north to Hampton, New Hampshire; and south to Hebron, Alabama. The Annuity Fund even insured a man who lived in Rio De Janeiro, Rev. Ashbel G. Simonton.

The United States celebrated 100 years as a sovereign nation in 1876, with a giant exposition in Philadelphia. Ulysses S. Grant occupied the White House, and George Armstrong Custer made his last stand at Little Big Horn, Montana. A different but equally serious battle took place in New Jersey, where words instead of bullets were exchanged in heated combat.

The former struggle involved a famous cavalry general and Indian Chief Crazy Horse. The latter featured two Presbyterian ministers in a test case over women preachers. Rev. Elijah Craven attacked Rev. Isaac See for inviting two members of the Women's Christian Temperance Society to speak in his church. The crusty Craven fulminated about "divinely arranged subordination" (of women) as he raged:

"Man's place is on the platform. It is positively base for a woman to speak in the pulpit."[30]

Craven thundered his charges in Presbytery, Synod, and General Assembly, pressing for ecclesiastical condemnation of See. The latter, supported openly by Henry Ward Beecher, and benefitting from the broader endeavors of Susan B. Anthony and other feminist leaders, escaped defrocking. However, the Presbyterian Church successfully resisted the ordination of women ministers of the gospel for another seventy-five years.

As these and other events marked a century of American life, the remarkable annuity and life insurance company reached the 117th year of incorporation and the 159th anniversary of its organization.

February 10 found the Finance-Executive Committee meeting for the first time at the firm's office, 133 South 5th Street. The business occupied the "first floor front," paying $600 annual rent—a figure ingeniously cut in half through a sublease to J. Ross Snowden, Esq., for a law office in the "first floor back."

Convened again, April 3, the committee established a schedule of regular meetings to be held the first Monday of April, July, October, and January. Actuary Janeway reported:

"Since adopting the agency plan the company has secured applications for $151,000 of insurance (less $3,000 for applicants having failed to take their policies). Gross annual premiums for the new business is about $4,000.

The outlook for business, in spite of the hard times, is good."[31]

Stimulated by this success, the men decided to recommend to the Board of Corporators that the officers be authorized to have the company charter changed to allow assuring of "all other persons."[32] Snowden, as president, did not take the lead in this move toward making the firm a general insurance company. It was his associate, William E. Tenbrook (president 1878-1881), who persisted with the idea to insure "all human beings."[33]

The company year ran out with the by-laws revised rather extensively on October 21. Important provisions included ballot election of corporators at any annual meeting; election of seven directors as a board to run the company; selection of a single person to be both president and chairman of the Board; and the requirement that other officers elected not be members of the Board. It was clearly stated that the directors would serve without "emoluments."[34] Another change moved the annual meeting from October to January.

The first 1877 session under the new plan came January 25. After prayer, the minutes, and a report from the actuary, the Board approved a motion that George H. Stuart, Esq., be asked to resign. Elected a corporator in 1853, he had not attended a single meeting in twenty-four years! This family would later take a more active part in the life of the company through the participation of Mr. Stuart's son and grandson.

The directors met for the first time the following day. Immediate decisions were made which reflected the growing professionalism of the officers and the increasing sophistication of the management. Greater responsibilities were recognized and paid for accordingly. The actuary received a raise to $1,800 per annum plus another $250 as assistant to the treasurer. That individual would get $500, and one E. J. Collins was also confirmed as "clerk to the actuary at a salary of $9.61 per week."[35]

Other actions taken that day further expanded the influence and responsibility of the actuary—an officer first authorized only three years previously.

These were times of increasing sales efforts, and sales results. New policies were being issued at the rate of more than thirty-five every two months. They were, in contrast, times of continued investment caution. In early summer, for example, the directors rejected an $8,000 loan request from the First Presbyterian Church, Wilmington, Delaware. Going beyond this specific case, the Board declared: "For the best interest of the policyholders, all applications for loans from churches and eleemosynary institutions be declined." In addition it was also resolved "that loans on bonds and mortgages shall hereafter be confined to improved property in the city of Philadelphia."[36]

As J. Ross Snowden's imaginative administration took the company in new directions, his private law practice must have been shrinking. When the directors decided to explore the merits of doing business in other states, they reduced by one-third the $300 per annum rent charged the president for his office in the back room of company headquarters.

In January 1878, Snowden was elected president for the fifth and last time. He did not attend the corporators' or directors' meetings, but he must have rejoiced in the report of the treasurer given at that time. Policies, assets, and surplus had all grown substantially during his tenure:

Year	Policies	Assets	Surplus
1874	116	$106,630	$28,538
1878	406	146,638	55,732

Within a short time his second "Address" went forth in search of new business. This time it was directed to:

"ALL PERSONS DESIRING SAFE
LIFE INSURANCE AND PROFITABLE ANNUITIES."

Much of the text corresponded to the 1875 publication, but the section describing conditions of insurance began with this bold offer:

"Though formerly restricted to ministers and laymen of the Presbyterian and other denominations of like polity, now any man, woman or child may have insurance effected on his or her life in this corporation . . ."[37]

Snowden did not live to see the result of this gambit. He died, March 31, at Hulmeville, his Bucks County home. A western Pennsylvania historian of the next generation would write of this man:

"There was never a blemish upon his character, nor a suspicion of malfeasance in his long official career."[38]

Policy No. 5381, issued a few months later, affords a measurement of the company and the mores of the community at this time. The eleven-by-seventeen-inch document was issued to Samuel Winchester Adriance, clergyman. Adriance, age twenty-five, of Highland, Ulster County, New York, paid a $16.06 semi-annual premium for $2,000 protection in favor of his wife, Lizzie Phelena Adriance.

The policy required the insured to remain in the United States, Canada, or Europe unless he received prior written approval from the company to travel further. Other than militia duty, Mr. Adriance could not "enter into any military or naval service whatsoever." He was also kept from "work as engineer, fireman, conductor or brakeman upon a railroad." Policy #5381, it was distinctly stated, would be

144

null and void, and of no effect if the assured "shall die by the hands of Justice," or by his own hand "sane or insane."

Adriance outlived his wife, who died November 30, 1930. He requested the beneficiary be changed from his executors, administrators, or assigns to "his son, daughter, and daughter-in-law, if living, share and share alike, their children to have their parents' share as contingent beneficiaries, in the case of the pre-decease of the parents; otherwise to the executors, administrators or assigns of the insured."

For less than three dollars per month a thrifty minister protected his wife through more than fifty years of marriage. Dying at age ninety in 1943, he left this definite pecuniary remembrance for his children.

CHAPTER TEN

Declaring a Dividend
(1880-1887)
Rev. John Welsh Dulles, President

He who would valiant be 'gainst all disaster,

Let him in constancy follow the master.

There's no discouragement shall make him relent

His first avow'd intent to be a pilgrim.

John Bunyan

The 1880's are remembered as one of America's daring decades. These years brought riches, scientific achievement, and zest to the nation now in its second century. A hundred years later the Pennsylvania Academy for the Fine Arts dramatized the era with an exhibit of elegant evening dresses of the time and photographs of palatial homes in the baroque style of architecture, including the Widener mansion of Philadelphia.

Concurrent with these social developments, the already-venerable Presbyterian Annuity and Life Insurance Company chose a new president, Rev. John Welsh Dulles. He was elected May 20, 1880—the first minister to get the job in 101 years!

The first three men to hold the office were clergy: Robert Cross, John Ewing, and James Sproat. Since the latter resigned in 1780, however, the enterprise had been led by four lawyers, three doctors, and four merchants.

The attorneys included George Bryan (1780-1791); John McMullin (1837-1844); John Kintzing Kane (1856-1858); and J. Ross Snowden (1874-1878). The physicians comprised John Redman (1791-1796); Robert Harris (1797-1815); and Alexander Mitchell (1850-1856, 1858-1862). Merchant presidents were Robert Ralston (1815-1836); Matthew L. Bevan (1844-1849); Charles Macalester (1862-1873); and William E. Tenbrook (1878-1880).

The choice of an ordained minister as president, after more than a century of lay leadership for the company, came a few days after the Board of Directors decided to cease offering financial protection "to all human beings,"[1] and to once again restrict insurance to Presbyterian ministers. Dr. Dulles—whose grandson, John Foster Dulles, would achieve world prominence as United States Secretary of State in the administration of Dwight D. Eisenhower—proved effective as a business leader, although his earlier years provided little training or related experience for the responsibility.

Born November 4, 1823, young Dulles, as the son of a prosperous Philadelphia merchant, enjoyed educational privilege from the start. After preparation at the Samuel W. Crawford Academy, he went to Yale, graduating Phi Beta Kappa, 1844. He delivered the commencement oration, "Unity of Purpose." His New Haven years were marked by the close friendship of a fellow student, Allen Macy, who influenced the future president of the Presbyterian Fund to attend Union Seminary. Dulles later named one of his sons for Macy.

1848 found Dulles receiving his theological degree; getting married to Harriet Lathrop Winslow; and taking his bride to Madras, India, October 10, under the American Board of Commissioners for Foreign Missions.

For Mrs. Dulles, born April 19, 1829, Odooville, Ceylon, as the daughter of missionary parents, the 132-day, 14,000-mile voyage to the other side of the world lacked the sparkle it held for the earnest cleric from the Quaker city. John Welsh Dulles kept a daily record of the journey, addressed to his mother. He noted at the beginning it would be April of the following year before those at home would know if the adventurous Christian pair had survived the dangerous passage to arrive safely in the exotic storybook land of Hindustan.

The ship "Bowdich" left Boston with fourteen missionaries embarked. Accommodations aboard the 650-ton, 160-foot vessel were primitive. The Dulles cabin measured "6'6" square, contained two berths, a trunk, washstand and was lighted by a single thick glass bullseye set in the deck overhead."[2] After more than four months of typhoons, dodging whales, a burial at sea, and conversion to Christianity of the ship's captain, the intrepid young couple reached Madras, February 19, 1849.

Soon Rev. Dulles began "making tours about the country

in a palankeen borne on the shoulders of native carriers."[3] In this way the zealous clergyman "acquired a better knowledge of the native peoples and religion of India than is acquired by some missionaries who have longer service in the cities without becoming acquainted with the more primitive life of people in the country."[4]

The Dulles mission to India ended in three years as the preacher became ill and lost his voice. John and Harriet came home with three children, and he obtained an appointment as Secretary of Missions of the American Sunday School Union. His father served that organization as a board member for fifty years. Four years later Rev. Dulles assumed the duties of Secretary and Publication Editor of the Presbyterian General Assembly (New School).

These were worthwhile years professionally, but far from happy ones in a personal sense. In 1861 Mrs. Dulles died, age thirty-two. She had borne six children in eight years. The widow clergyman, to assuage his grief, took a more active part in the life of the Walnut Street Presbyterian Church as Sunday school superintendent.

His involvement with the annuity and insurance company began May 20, 1864, with election as a corporator, the year before his marriage to Mary Nataline Baynard of "Castle Hall," Goldsborough, Maryland, February 2, 1865.[5] Two children were born of this union, but the second Mrs. Dulles died March 25, 1876, leaving the former missionary a widower once more.

Dulles became increasingly active at the insurance Fund. This led to his election as a director, 1877. He and Rev. Thomas L. Janeway were the only two ordained men among the seven persons chosen that year.[6]

By this time the popular minister held the title of Editorial Secretary of the Presbyterian Board of Publication, a position he attained in 1870, with the reunion of the two branches of the church and the consolidation of their publishing houses. This vocational rank would prove helpful to the insurance company when Dulles reached the presidency of the Fund a few years later.

The Philadelphia editor wrote ministers across the denomination who hoped to see their sermons in print. Some responded with alacrity. Others proved desultory, particularly in summertime. One wrote, "I have been so much prostrated by the hot weather that my physician has utterly interdicted toil of any sort."[7]

After a year on the insurance company Board of Directors, Dr. Dulles took an extended vacation for his health. Armed with a letter of introduction from the president of the Pennsylvania Bible Society "to the friends of the Bible cause wherever he may meet with them,"[8] the ailing clergyman sailed for the Mediterranean on November 14, 1878, accompanied by his son, Rev. Joseph Heatley Dulles III, age twenty-five. The men went to Egypt and the Holy Land. Dulles collected stones and shells, and later wrote a book about their trip, *A Ride Through Palestine*.

The Presbyterian Annuity and Insurance Company found May 1880 a month to remember. It was a time of resignations, reorganization, and elections.

A special Board meeting held the first day opened with the reading of a letter from J. B. H. Janeway, relinquishing his positions as secretary and actuary. Poor health prevented his continuation in these roles, which he filled with "zeal and efficiency."[9]

The next order of business that eventful morning came as a memorandum from treasurer Robert Patterson II, an incumbent of twenty-eight years in the position. Patterson took more than 1,500 words to show his colleagues the negative results of insuring all persons. Patterson proved five years of increased business cost the company money. Since 1875 the ratio of assets to liabilities had dropped from 172/100 to 145/100. He found the Fund with "strictly speaking, no capital," and ill-equipped to compete with "the great companies," without a large increase in premium loading charges. Because of various "fearful disadvantages," including the possibility of "annoying litigation caused by an energetic agent writing a contract with a tavern bar-keeper," the treasurer urged the company "to cease the general insurance business and the expensive methods required to secure it."[10]

Impressed with the cogency of these arguments, Dr. Dulles and the other Board members responded with a resolution restricting future business to Presbyterian ministers. The directors also approved additional Patterson proposals to:

1) Combine the offices of treasurer and actuary in Mr. Patterson (at no increase in his salary).
2) Keep the secretary's work separate (at a salary of $75 per annum).
3) Elect Rev. Nathan L. Upham to that post.
4) Select the Fidelity Insurance Trust and Safe Deposit Company as agent to collect premium and other company income.

Nineteen days later, at the regular directors' meeting, William E. Tenbrook resigned as president and a member of the Board. John Welsh Dulles was elected his successor by unanimous vote, and in this manner the former missionary became the fifteenth man to serve as president of the Presbyterian insurance company, now in its 121st year of incorporation. Since his election as a director three years earlier, Dulles had often offered the opening prayer at Board meetings at the request of Mr. Tenbrook. He must have enjoyed the experience, for as president he continued to perform this function instead of assigning it to an associate.

The Fund had published a "Roll of Honor" two years earlier. Several pages of testimonials proclaimed "the safest and cheapest insurance for men, women and children of all denominations." No other insurance company, it matter-of-factly declared, could "show such a noble line of witnesses to its usefulness." Policyholder heroes of the Revolution were featured in one section, insured moderators of the Presbyterian General Assembly in another. College professors, editors of religious journals, and "prominent pastors and laymen who authorized the public use of their names as references for the economy and good management of our time-honored institution" appeared by the score.

Rev. L. M. Miller, First Presbyterian Church, Ogdensburg, N. Y., furnished a typical endorsement:

"I have great confidence in the Presbyterian Annuity Co. . . . Its favorable insurance offers solid foundations upon which to rest expectations for the future."[11]

Despite the impressive list of prestigious clients, and the contagious enthusiasm of such declarations, some clergymen questioned the value of life insurance. Rev. Edward Irving, a minister in the Church of Scotland of a previous generation, actually advised married clerics with children to "put no money in the bank for them, but write prayers in the record of the book of life."[12]

The Fund began in 1881 with a renewed sales effort. From 1759 until 1878, increased financial protection had been offered to an expanding clientele, culminating in the offer of insurance to all persons. The 1880 return to Presbyterian ministers exclusively demanded a fresh approach to this concentrated market.

Accordingly, the year Christianity received the Revised English Bible (representing the first changes in Scriptural language since the King James Version of 1611), the Presbyterian Annuity Company decided to send another bulletin to its denomination. At the January 27 annual meeting of the corporators it was agreed:

"The Board of Directors be requested to take such measures they may deem expedient to bring the claims of this corporation before the General Assembly and other representative bodies of the Presbyterian Church."[13]

Most of the previous communications to its public were given the title "Address." The Dulles presidency undertaking carried the designation "Memorial."

Historical background provided the first part of the notice. Synod meetings of 1717 and later years were recalled which confirmed the origin of the corporation by the denomination. Cordial relations with the General Assembly were tactfully noted. The memorial included a succinct rationale for the unique principle of life insurance:

"No means can be better adapted, to persons in the circumstances of the clergy, to procure from their small savings a provision for their families in the event of their decease or for themselves in old age. It substitutes the certainty of contract for the uncertainty of benevolence or of contributory assessment."[14]

Sound management, low premiums, financial integrity, it declared, had made possible more than a century of service to ministers relieving them of "much distress," while "never failing an obligation."[15] The epistle concluded with a respectful request for "the contenance and the counsel" of the General Assembly as well as "some sort of official recognition."[16]

Considering the consistent independence of the company from ecclesiastical control, the response to this somewhat obsequious proposal should have been predicted. Within two weeks came this terse reply:

"While we thank God for the uniform prosperity which has attended many of the various plans and institutions which have been devised for the maintenance and relief of the poor of the church—yet we are of the opinion that the future usefulness of these institutions must depend upon the continuance of wise and judicious management rather than on the approval of the General Assembly."[17]

1882 brought Hansom cabs to Philadelphia—introduced by the Pennsylvania Railroad. Labor Day was first observed, but the life insurance industry sagged. Of 129 companies operating in 1870, only fifty-five survived at this time.[18]

The Presbyterian company, rebuffed by the Church, continued to operate successfully but without élan. Little was done. Perhaps from discouragement, perhaps from innate modesty, Dr. Dulles nominated Samuel Field for president at the February 3 directors' meeting. This gesture failed, and the distinguished editor was reelected with dispatch. Several subsequent meetings that year adjourned without a quorum, and total company assets declined from $247,303 to $237,947.

Although the directors continued to meet at the company office, 133 South Fifth Street, Dulles, as president and a denominational official, moved the corporators' annual session back to the Assembly Room of the Presbyterian Board of Publication, 1334 Chestnut Street—where the yearly gathering had convened prior to the administration of J. Ross Snowden.

The January 25, 1883, conclave featured for the first time a complete listing of the firm's investments. The gentlemen present learned in detail of temporary loans; four Vine Street mortgages, and a number of other Philadelphia properties; selected municipal bonds; together with numerous railroad bonds, including issues of the Allegheny, Pennsylvania, and Lehigh Valley companies.

Dulles, on a trip to Europe, missed the January 24 corporators' annual meeting in 1884, which began the company's 125th anniversary year. He presided, however, at the three most important assembling of the directors which followed: May 15, September 18, and October 11. These were days of consequences for the annuity and insurance enterprise. They deserve a closer look.

On the first occasion the president received a letter written and read by the treasurer. It began:

"Dear Sir:
Herewith I present to the board of directors my resignation . . . to take effect at the earliest possible date."[19]

Robert Patterson II recounted his thirty-two years in office, and mentioned the eighty-six-year total service as treasurer enjoyed by three generations of his family. "I naturally abandon it with extreme regret," he went on, noting "our business career of a century and a quarter has passed without stain."[20]

The resignation was received but not accepted by the directors. They took no action. This proved fortunate for the company, as Patterson remained on the job despite other obligations which prompted his offer to quit.

The September meeting left the matter unresolved as the Board learned that the president's son, John W. Dulles, Jr., declined an invitation to become assistant treasurer and actuary. The directors put Patterson's resignation aside and approved payment of a substantial cash dividend. "About $15,000" would be divided among all January 1, 1884, policy-holders who had been insured more than one year.

This dividend was not a conventional payment to share owners in the stock-company sense, nor was it a partici-pating distribution of assets provided for in customary mutual company practice. It represented, on the other hand, a new departure for an established corporation which, under God, had earned a profit by consistent wise manage-ment and shrewd investments.

A second Patterson letter came to the Board October 11, This time the veteran official began by pointing out that the "limited nature" of the company precluded payment of a salary "as would authorize any officer to devote his time exclusively to our service."[21] The treasurer proposed to Dulles and the others appointment of Robert P. Field as assistant treasurer and actuary. Field, a mining engineer, University of Pennsylvania graduate, and "of good Presby-terian stock," had his office at nearby 433 Chestnut Street. He was Patterson's nephew, to be sure, but this made no difference. The company had prospered through a number of other family relationships, and experience with this par-ticular line confirmed the advantages of selecting persons on the basis of personal merit regardless of relatives who worked for the company.

Field got the job at $500 per year, but it was made clear he was "chosen by the board and would hold his place at its pleasure."[22] In addition, he had to post a $2,500 personal bond, and agree to collect insurance premiums. This had been done previously for a $210 annual fee by the Fidelity Insurance Trust and Safe Deposit Company. With his assistant handling the details which Patterson found too absorbing, that durable individual retained care of the investments, and continued in office a few additional years. Problem solved and crisis averted.

A month later, as Dulles neared the end of his most eventful year as company president, the nation elected Grover Cleveland to succeed Chester A. Arthur in the White House. A contemporary newspaper account put it this way:

"Vast changes had taken place on the American scene during the decade which preceded the 1884 election. Farmers in the Northwest complained of low crop prices and in the cities a growing labor force organized unions to improve wages. . . . From these groups had emerged the Greenback party, founded on the belief that more paper money would reduce poverty . . . which foreshadowed the importance of currency as a national issue during the next quarter century."[23]

Government and business were far less intertwined in the 1880's than they have become a century later. However, during the Dulles presidency, while Federal authorities were moving to limit the freedom of manufacturing companies, the insurance industry felt the reign of state regulations to an increasing degree. The Presbyterian annuity enterprise, for example, had to meet policy reserve requirements calculated by the actuary of the Pennsylvania Insurance Department.[24]

Actually, the Fund had maintained its pioneering quality since 1759. It provided cash surrender values as early as 1852, although this life insurance feature was not required by law in any state until 1880.[25]

The directors, in addition, could take pride in a record of

financial stability and survival. Growth of the business was another matter. For more than 120 years it had been extremely modest, to say the least. Two other Philadelphia life insurance companies, formed almost 100 years later, far surpassed the Presbyterian annuity firm by 1883:

"Company	Incorporated	Surplus	Assets
American	1850	$ 500,000	$3,204,931
Penn Mutual	1847	1,768,055	8,478,457
Presbyterian	1759	92,000	265,000"[26]

Beginning January 28, 1886, the company office moved to 148 South 4th Street, where it occupied the second-story front section of a building at a rental of $250 per year.

The following month, Robert Patterson resigned once more as treasurer. The directors appointed Mr. Field his successor and agreed to pay him an annual salary of $1,500—three times the sum earned by the valiant Patterson!

President for six years, Dulles tendered his own resignation in March; but the directors took no action on his request until April 7, when he was asked to remain on the job until the next annual meeting. His role as secretary of the Board of Publication, it was felt, would help the company secure additional business. After some negotiation Dr. Dulles withdrew his letter.

When the corporators met again, however, on January 27, 1887, the matter was completely ignored, despite the absence of the president "on account of serious illness."[27] A week later the directors took similar action, and continued Dulles in the position he had held for seven years. Was it sympathy for an ailing friend or refusal to face facts?

Moving to another matter, the Board decided to slightly expand eligibility for company insurance. Since May 7, 1880, only Presbyterian ministers were underwritten, but this practice proved too restrictive. Now wives, widows, and sisters of these men would be included.

A typical policy issued that year provided $1,000 for annual premium of $27.56. This twenty-year ordinary life contract was purchased by a Brooklyn, N.Y., minister, Rev. Thomas Tyack, age thirty-four. Tyack outlived his wife; and, May 23, 1932, made his daughter the beneficiary.

A thirty-five-year endowment contract for the same amount was issued to another cleric at a $21.51 annual premium. Rev. C. S. Nickerson, then twenty-seven, of New York City, also survived his wife, and later changed his beneficiary to his son, Harold L. Nickerson.

John Welsh Dulles ignored the passivity of the board of directors, and died at his Philadelphia home, April 13, after an illness of three months. During his years of corporate guidance the Brooklyn Bridge and the Statue of Liberty were completed. The Interstate Commerce Commission came into being, and Ottman Mergenthaler patented his linotype machine. Within the Fund, nine men joined the corporators between 1881-1887, and total assets of the business rose from $223,000 to $313,104.

Associates on the Board of Publication noted his "innate integrity of purpose founded on truth as apprehended, with all gentleness towards those who held contrary views."[28]

An obituary writer paid Dulles this perceptive compliment:

"He never became 'secularized' as clergymen sometimes do when they give their lives to business and semi-secular occupations."[29]

Years before, when a boy of fourteen, Dr. Dulles received a gift Bible from his father, Joseph Heatley Dulles. The affectionate parent wrote a note on the title page advising the youth to heed the "solemn injunction" of David to his son found in I Chronicles 28:9. The life of this exceptional missionary, editor, and insurance company president confirms his obedience to that teaching:

"Know thou the God of thy father, and serve him with a perfect heart, and with a willing mind."

PART THREE

CHAPTER ELEVEN

Taking the Sting Out of Charity (1909-1930)
Perry S. Allen, D.D., President

They who tread the path of labor,
Follow where my feet have trod;
They who work without complaining
Do the holy will of God.

Henry Van Dyke

Who led the Presbyterian Ministers' Fund longer than any man in its history? Which president wore pince-nez eyeglasses? Who wrote more than 100 million dollars of new life insurance entirely by mail? Which president called one of his daughters an "angel child"? A single name provides the answer to each of these questions: Perry S. Allen.

Dr. Allen held the presidential title twenty-one years beginning in 1909. Since 1894, however, he had been chief executive of the company under the titles of secretary, actuary, and managing director, as other men occupied the position of titular head. Perry S. Allen ran the company these first fifteen years while Rev. Hughes O. Gibbons, Rev. Robert Graham, and Rev. William P. Fulton did little more than preside at meetings of the directors and the corporators. Hughes Gibbons, far from feeling jealous, recognized his associate's remarkable abilities, and proposed the younger man's assumption of responsibility and the authority which went with it.[1]

To clearly understand the state of the business when Perry Allen joined the company in 1893, and fully appreciate his subsequent leadership of the Fund, we should briefly review the years between that event and the administration of John Welsh Dulles which ended six years earlier.

The era began with a name change for the durable enterprise. In 1856 the original twenty-three-word title had become "Presbyterian Annuity Company." Less than two decades later this designation was superseded by "Presbyterian Annuity and Life Insurance Company." Now, March 10, 1888, Philadelphia Common Pleas Court #3 approved a Charter Amendment making it, simply, "Presbyterian Ministers' Fund."

Three reasons prompted the company to take this action. Burton A. Konkle, a corporator writing in the 1920's, notes:

"A return to the original conception of the corporation, an avoidance of some of the odium that attached to insurance companies at that time; and a desire to meet the needs that caused the General Assembly to create the Board of Ministerial Relief."[2]

The corporation first met under this new name, January 28, 1888. The figures revealed that day furnish a statistical benchmark worth noting. After 129 years of cautious operation the Fund could claim:

Assets $360,420.52
Surplus   103,874.09
506 insurance contracts
33 paying annuities
8 paying deferred annuities
Insurance in force $936,064.03.[3]

In 1889, as the nation grew through admission of Montana, North Dakota, South Dakota, and Washington as new states, the Fund added corporators from a wide area, as the Synods of Ohio, Indiana, and Illinois proposed men for this service. Increasingly the company found it important to conduct its affairs within the framework of a developing industry. The Pennsylvania State Insurance Commissioner formally approved the new name of the old firm; and his New Jersey and Ohio counterparts "officially granted permission for PMF to do business in their respective states."[4]

Life insurance, that same year, advanced to a higher level of sophistication with the formation of a professional organization for statisticians of the industry. David Parks Fackler, an actuarial consultant, organized the Actuarial Society of America in New York. It enrolled thirty-eight charter members; and, from the start, insisted upon high standards for those admitted. "Attention was paid not only to professional attainments but also to character and reputation."[5] Sheppard Homans was elected president.

The larger companies might afford a full-time actuary, but the Presbyterian Ministers' Fund continued to combine the function with those of another officer. Robert P. Field served as both actuary and treasurer as had his predecessor, Robert Patterson II. This practice would continue well into the next century.

The National Association of Life Underwriters came into being in 1890, adding a further dimension to cooperative efforts toward better service and protection for the insuring public.

Initial years of the gay nineties brought further refinements to the operation of the Fund. The by-laws now defined greater responsibility for Board committees. President Snowden gave the Finance Committee powers of an Executive group in 1875. Sixteen years later the Auditing Committee became accountable for oversight of the treasurer; the Finance Committee would handle investments; the Executive Committee to supervise sales or "extension."[6]

In all, 854 policies totaling $1,358,456 insurance in force — to say nothing of the eleven Synods and ninety-three Presbyteries represented in the corporation[7] — demanded more formality of management than the pecuniary preachers of Philadelphia had been accustomed to. Hence the changes.

Administrative advancements notwithstanding, the company never forgot the reason for its existence, service to the minister of the gospel — an individual humorously described in this verse of a local rhymester of those days:

"Of manners gentle and of temper even,
He jogs his flocks, with easy pace, to heaven.
In Greek and Latin pious books he keeps,
And, while his clerk sings psalms, he soundly sleeps.
From rustic bridegroom oft he takes the ring,
And hears the milkmaid plaintive ballads sing.
Backgammon cheats whole winter nights away,
And Pilgrims' Progress helps a rainy day."[8]

No wonder the directors rejoiced in the news from Old Pine Street Presbyterian Church dated October 28, 1892.

That congregation purchased a $5,000 life insurance policy for "its pastors in succession as long as they continue to hold their relationship with us." Old Pine hoped its example would stimulate other churches to take similar action, and noted this course would give "the recipient less anxiety about his future."[9] The letter, printed as an advertisement in several newspapers, served to anticipate a more ambitious promotional effort made the following March.

The company commissioned George Tompkins, an independent actuary, to examine the affairs of the Fund, submit a report to describe his findings, and reflect his professional judgment regarding its merit. Tompkins wrote four pages of careful analysis.

He noted the Fund enjoyed a $1.32 ratio of assets to liabilities as compared to the industry average of $1.14. Mutual Life of New York could claim only $1.07. Tompkins also pointed out the Presbyterian company possessed $255.50 in assets for each $1,000 of insurance in force, contrasted to the industry-wide average of $216.

Based on these figures and other calculations, the outside expert could easily declare:

"From these comparisons it appears the condition of the Fund is far above the average condition of all the life insurance companies."[10]

Mr. Tompkins applauded the sound principles and efficient management of the corporation which made it possible for a clergyman to purchase life insurance at the lowest possible cost. His report concluded with the ringing endorsement, "every insurable man of the class to which the advantages of insurance in the Fund are offered should be enrolled among its policyholders."[11]

This actuarial prose received editorial assistance when it reached the clergy. The solid body of text appeared between covers emblazoned with captions in bold-face type:

PRESBYTERIAN MINISTERS' FUND
THE OLDEST THE FOREMOST THE BEST
FOUNDED 176 YEARS AGO
THE MOST PROGRESSIVE
INSURES ALL EVANGELICAL
PROTESTANT MINISTERS

1893 brought the Fund more than this splash of gay-nineties salesmanship. Rev. Perry S. Allen joined the corporators, January 23, and simultaneously found himself elected a director. Three days later he became a member of the Executive Committee, and in this dramatic fashion began his exceptional career with the company. He was thirty-nine years old.

Born the 4th of July, 1854, in Butler County, Pennsylvania, Allen was the son of Richard Boyd Allen and Mary Vanderland Stoops Allen. His father was a farmer and landholder. His grandfather, John Allen, served as an officer in the Revolutionary War. His great-grandfather, Samuel Allen, came to Philadelphia from England, and held a commission as lieutenant at Fort Augusta, Pennsylvania, 1757. This ancestor, as a Presbyterian elder, voted in Synod on the Fund's application for charter.[12]

Young Allen, the youngest of eleven children and a deeply religious person from his earliest years, always wanted to be a minister of the gospel. In adolescence he would come home from church and preach his version of the morning sermon from a tree stump in the backyard.[13]

Allen went to Wooster College in Ohio, selling Bibles farm to farm to pay his tuition. He graduated in 1874, and went on to Western Theological Seminary, Pittsburgh, where he received his degree in 1877. The same year Allen was ordained a minister of the Presbyterian Church.

November 8 the aspiring cleric married Mary T. Kinter of Indiana, Pennsylvania, and took her to the manse of his first pastoral charge, the Presbyterian Church of Edinburg in that state. Rev. and Mrs. Allen stayed a year, then moved to Sharon, where he occupied the pulpit until 1882. The Allens then served five years in Warren—completing a decade of ministry in these three churches within a radius of forty miles, in the northwestern corner of the state.[14]

His apprenticeship completed, Allen felt ready for bigger things. Opportunity came through a call to the church of Saratoga Springs, New York; and the Allens, with their son Harry, came east to that fashionable resort community in 1887. This pastorate would be one of occupational achievement but personal sorrow and difficulty.

During the late 1880's Americans depended heavily upon patent medicines. In the days before the Federal Food and Drug Act, manufacturers were not required to divulge the formulas for these drugs which caught the public fancy.[15]

Unfortunately such nostrums had little value for those seriously ill, including the wife of the energetic pastor from western Pennsylvania. Mary Allen had suffered from tuberculosis for some time. Her condition grew steadily worse. To pay for her medical expenses the young minister needed additional money to augment his modest ministerial salary. He began selling insurance for Equitable Life, and in this manner not only increased his income but also learned that business. This experience and knowledge proved helpful a few years later when he became associated with the Fund.

Mary Allen spent time at Lake Placid in the Adirondack Mountains, but to no avail. She died in 1890, the year the Presbyterian General Assembly came to Saratoga Springs for its 102nd annual meeting. Puritans in Babylon, United States style!

Known as "the king of spas,"[16] Saratoga Springs lay thirty-five miles north of Albany and fourteen miles from the Revolutionary War battlefield. The New York community "drew many visitors who wanted to benefit from the curative effects of its renowned mineral springs."[17] Identified by name with potato chips and a distinctive clothes container, the town found gambling provided its greatest lure. "Famed for its race track, its rich men and beautiful women," notes a modern writer, "Saratoga was the gaudiest of America's nineteenth-century summer resorts."[18]

By the 1890's the vacation center was "wide open and gambling establishments were never closed." The Club House, a particularly notorious establishment, boasted "two faro tables and nine single-end roulette wheels to serve the public in the main gambling room."[19]

Rev. Allen fought gambling, and with the other ministers of the area tried to moderate the influence of the pernicious habit which gripped the community. As a grieving widower struggling to raise his son, however, he often played cards with the boy in the manse—behind closed window curtains, lest a passerby might misunderstand.[20]

Dr. Allen's congregation welcomed the General Assembly on May 15. Twelve days later the clerics and laymen finished their business, and thanked "the pastor, Session, and Trustees of the First Presbyterian Church" for their hospitality; "gratefully recognized the excellent service of the choir"; and "also extended our thanks to the janitor for his services."[21]

The Grand Union Hotel, where many of the delegates stayed, proved as important to Allen as the house of worship during these convention days and nights. Roaming the quarter-mile front porch, frequenting its 306-foot main dining room and conferring with influential leaders amid the black-walnut and French-mirror decor, the host pastor renewed old acquaintances and made new friends. Within two years he received a call to a smaller but more prosperous charge, Green Hill Presbyterian Church, Philadelphia. Allen and his son moved there in 1892. Propinquity did the rest, and soon the popular preacher found himself involved with the ministerial insurance company.

Perry Allen's first contribution to the work of the Fund

came through his vote on an 1893 Executive Committee decision to increase the compensation of existing sales agents, to employ more solicitors, and to hire a new General Agent "to take care of the work in the counties on the eastern border of Pennsylvania and Maryland, and in the State of Delaware."[22] Within a few years Allen would begin to phase out the sales force in a complete reversal of this policy!

The year 1893 found the Fund involved in controversy about the constituency of the company. It was hardly a novel topic. Since 1759, when insurance was offered only to Presbyterian ministers, corporation policy had moved back and forth like the needle on a measuring instrument:

1759 Only Presbyterian clergy insured
1828 All male church membership with eligible clergy
1852 All Presbyterially-governed clergy, but no laymen
1875 Insurance for all human beings
1880 Presbyterian ministers only
1892 All evangelical Protestant ministers.

The corporators approved policy changes through 1875; but after the directors were given power to run the company the following year subsequent decisions of this kind were made by that body. The corporators did not vote on the subject between 1875 and 1894. Certain articles about the company constituency[23] have presented an inaccurate account of this circumstance. While it is true that the corporators did not vote to reduce the scope of coverage until 1894, the directors made the change as early as 1880, and approved other changes in 1892.

After Perry S. Allen's company debut, the Fund spent the rest of that year discussing financial protection for laymen. Should they be offered insurance once more? In the outside world Americans flocked to the Columbian Exposition in Chicago, and financial panic marked these early months of Grover Cleveland's second term as President.

Within the firm the directors debated insuring "lay

members of evangelical Protestant churches." With no decision reached June 22, the issue received attention again on September 26. Still no action was taken. On November 9, despite the opposition of President Hughes O. Gibbons, the directors finally endorsed insurance for laymen as recommended by the Executive Committee on June 14. Gibbons, undaunted, convened a special meeting two weeks later and read his associates a four-page protest of the Board's action—even accusing the membership of extravagance and improper conduct in voting "this proposed radical step."[24] Result: The directors rescinded their November 9 resolution!

Seizing the initiative that day, Perry Allen urged appointment of a special committee to investigate not only this sensitive subject, but also the possibility of company reinsurance proposed by Henry N. Paul, Jr.

The year ran out with two December meetings equally inconclusive. The directors considered four possible plans for the future of the Fund. It was clearly a time of crisis in the history of the company.

January 1894 cleared the air with four meetings within nine days beginning on the 20th. In a series of dramatic strokes the directors struck back at President Gibbons and repudiated his recent charges of mismanagement. The corporators adopted a motion by Robert Patterson II, commending the directors for "energy and good judgment" in the conduct of corporate affairs; and agreed to appoint "a proper person" to fill the post of secretary and expand that position by "any additional duties appropriate to the office."[25]

When Rev. Gibbons was reelected president, Perry S. Allen resigned from the Board on January 25. Four days later, however, he accepted the dual positions of secretary and actuary with the distinct understanding he would "have charge of the office" and that Robert P. Field could continue as treasurer of the Fund "until his successor is appointed."[26]

Insurance would henceforth be issued solely to "ministers Presbyterially governed," and the widower preacher from Saratoga Springs, New York, had the authority to run the Presbyterian Ministers' Fund. Allen believed he served God in this new role as much as through his earlier pulpit ministry.

Perry S. Allen, whose salary in later years would prove controversial, began work as secretary and actuary at a modest $2,500 annual stipend — with $500 extra for expenses and permission to spend up to $1,400 more for office clerk hire. Mr. Field was given three months' notice, and Allen obtained approval to engage a new treasurer at $500 per year. The executive's first report so impressed the directors they ordered part of it printed for circulation in the churches. Never one to miss an opportunity, Allen not only "sent a letter to the ministers of the Presbyterian Church"; he also sent "a serious word to the students of our theological seminaries."[27]

Other changes that dramatic spring included appointment of the company's first medical director, McCluney Radcliffe, M.D. (who lived at 711 N. 16th Street and who served without remuneration) and selection of Rev. James B. Kennedy as treasurer. Both corporators and directors began meeting at the new corporation office, 925 Walnut Street; and if there was any doubt, the assertive leader was officially noted as being "in charge of the office."[28]

Authority invariably requires answers, and the busy boss had to find the right ones for the State of Connecticut Insurance Commissioner, who wrote the Fund that same month requesting information about PMF policy valuations and other matters.[29]

Allen, who would have agreed "no man is born into the world whose work is not born with him,"[30] managed to leave the office for a few summer days to attend his second wedding and take a brief honeymoon. On June 2 he married a young woman from Rochester, New York, Virginia Gertrude Oliver, in a Philadelphia ceremony. It was to be a long and happy union, but the bridegroom was back at work in twelve days.

Two documents of early 1895 characterize the state of the Fund at that time. The 136th *Annual Report*, issued in January, contains information about the corporators as "guardians" of the business, lists them by name and address; does the same for the directors as "management" and includes the dollars and cents resulting from the operations of the previous year—impressive, but essentially a routine insurance company record.

A letter to the directors from Mr. Allen reveals his dramatic style of leadership through these words:

"When I was elected into this Fund I came with a sense of duty. . . .
It will be only a sense of duty that will keep me longer in the office. . . .
If I am to serve you longer it will be necessary for the duties of my office to be more clearly defined . . . and my position in the office as its manager made more emphatic."[31]

Trouble had developed between the manager and the new treasurer, Rev. James B. Kennedy. Allen accused him of creating friction and misunderstanding as well as "talking too freely in the presence of clerks in the office and callers."[32] Kennedy departed and his place was taken by T. N. Rogers, who served only a few months. Allen had greater success with his third treasurer, Jonathan C. Neff. Neff, elected a corporator in 1921, would hold the post fifty years.

Moving into his second leadership year, Allen paid increasing attention to letter writing. The secretary-actuary quickly earned distinction as a master of the epistolary art. From the beginning of his leadership at the Fund he developed a correspondence crusade which comprised three distinct ingredients: letters to ministers distributed in leaflet form; other sales letters reproduced in quantity; and voluminous personal mail communication covering a surprising range of insurance lore. Each category deserves specific illustration.

The leaflets were printed in 3⅜" x 6" size with the heading "A New Series. . . ." No. 1, "to the ministers of the Presbyterian Church," began "Dear Brother," as it challenged each reader with the caption "Some Facts for You to Ponder."[33] Allen occasionally interspersed words of others between his own efforts. Issue No. 3, for example, presented a collection of testimonials with the title *What Eminent Men Say about the Presbyterian Ministers' Fund.* The front page contained this squib from *"The Spectator,* which is the leading insurance journal in the country:"

"In the first place it outranks in point of age every life insurance company of the United States, being over eighty years older than the Mutual of New York; secondly, it is the only company restricting its field to a preferred class of insurers, and, thirdly, in ratio of assets to liabilities it surpasses most companies, thus ranking among the strongest. The sole object of the managers is to serve the ministry of the Presbyterian Church, by giving them lower premiums, by easy terms for the payment of such premiums, and by giving them every possible advantage insurancewise."[34]

After this introduction came a cluster of brief recommendations from policyholders. Rev. Joseph H. Dubbs, a Franklin and Marshall college professor, said this about PMF:

"I have for several years held a policy in it and am thoroughly satisfied with the investment."[35]

Rev. Robert P. Kerr, D.D., Pastor of the First Presbyterian Church, Richmond, Virginia, declared:

"I consider the Presbyterian Ministers' Fund, in which I carry $5,000 insurance, one of the very best in America, and absolutely safe."[36]

Rev. W. H. Roberts, D.D., L.L.D., Secretary of the Alliance of Reformed Churches, and Stated Clerk of the General Assembly, exclaimed:

"The Presbyterian Ministers' Fund is an admirable institution, long-established and efficiently managed. Familiar with its history, its methods, and its objects, I commend it cordially to all ministers of the Presbyterian and Reformed Churches."[37]

Before long the articulate Allen composed another effective appeal of his own built around the words "An Imperative Duty." In response to the posed question, "Why Am I Not Under the Protection of the Fund?" ten answers were proferred with vivid expressions such as "neglect of the obligation is selfish and sinful," and "if you should overwork and involve your brain, and suicide should follow, it would not affect the value of your policy in the Fund one iota."

This forthright approach produced results. Allen sold $175,000 insurance by mail his first year; and reached the level of 221 policies worth $315,787 in 1895 — about half the company total business for that period. His third year produced sales of 336 policies valued at $543,950, yielding premium income of $19,510. Not bad for a neophyte!

His success did not go unnoticed in the industry. A New York company vice president advised:

"We have at this time a very good thing to offer the right man and have to ask whether or not you are in a position to consider a proposition."[38]

The energizer of the Fund asked for details but apparently found them unacceptable and kept them to himself, for no mention is made in company records of even a possible departure of the audacious secretary, actuary, and managing director.

In addition to these printed messages reproduced by the tens of thousands, the full-time occupant of the company office wrote personal letters to many existing policyholders and sales representatives in the field. Allen drove a hard bargain, when it came to protection for foreign missionaries, as excerpts from two notes to the Orient confirm.

Rev. T. C. Winn, Kanazawa, Japan, sold policies to several fellow ministers in that country, but the actuary in

Philadelphia showed little enthusiasm for the new business. Pointing out that most companies added to their regular premium in the case of foreign missionaries, Allen refused to pay the agent for his endeavors. Winn was told:

"The Fund cannot possibly afford to carry such risks and pay at the same time for getting them. The company ought to be paid a premium for placing its protection on such lives . . . if you insist upon your commission on these applications we must decline to carry the risks."[39]

Rev. E. L. Mattox, Hangchow, China, received a similar dispatch. Mattox interested another missionary, Joshua Crowe Garritt, in the Fund and sent the home office two applications for life insurance from that person. Mattox requested permission to keep the first premium payments on the Garritt policies for his "time, trouble and expense of medical examinations."

Allen declared this would be impossible, and that the Fund preferred not to write missionaries "if it had to pay these large commissions for the business." Cost conscious to the end, Mr. Allen extolled the virtues of volunteer service to his fellow Christian on the other side of the world:

"If the missionaries who are already in the Fund and realize its benefits and who are in the way of sharing those benefits that will be increased by the growth of the Fund, cannot render the service that is necessary to interest their brethren in their own company and from a desire to benefit their friends who are laboring with them in the Lord . . . we shall have to let foreign missionaries to go to other companies where they will have to pay very much larger premiums and an extra premium cost besides."[40]

Nearer to home and later that year the secretary corresponded with a Pittsburgh policyholder, Rev. J. Shaw Nicholls. A series of December 1896 letters between the two men centered upon the dubious activities of a former Fund salesman whom Nicholls averred "is trying to do us an injury."[41] Perry Allen appreciated this information about the disgruntled ex-employee. Allen called him "that most malicious creature,"[42] and confided to his informant that the problem represented "the kind of nasty work that life insurance men have to meet all the time." Allen later referred to the man in question as a "nasty, pesty creature who deserves utter extermination."[43]

As the decade neared its end the company counted substantial gains in every aspect of the business. After four years of the new management these figures were made public:

Total insurance written	$3,459,224
Gain in insurance in force	1,959,803
New premium income	82,763
100% gain in premium income over 1894	
Gain in assets	314,363
Gain in surplus	82,138
Gain in ratio of assets to liabilities from 123% to 128%[44]	

No wonder the preacher from Saratoga Springs increased his influence and consolidated his position at the Fund as Rev. Robert Graham succeeded Hughes O. Gibbons as president and a number of new corporators joined the Board. One of these, George H. Stuart, Jr., would come to be one of Allen's closest friends.

It would be a mistake to suppose, however, that the secretary, actuary, and managing director enjoyed absolute power. His relationship with the Board of Directors at this time is illustrated by the attitudes expressed at the appointment of George W. Sparks, M.D., as the second medical director of the Fund in 1897.

Sparks, already serving in a like capacity for Manhattan Life Insurance Company, Massachusetts Mutual, and Berkshire Life, had a reputation for shrewd selection of risks, and was obviously worth his $600 per year beginning salary. The secretary recommended Sparks provide a list of life insurance applicants rejected by another company, but the executive committee waived this requirement "in view of the fact we are dealing with ministers of the gospel and can trust their honesty."[45]

Perry Allen's candid comments and colorful vocabulary helped define his personality as an insurance executive, but with his brusqueness of manner went a warmness of heart and truly compassionate nature. His sales letters, for example, carried a blend of insurance knowledge and pastoral concern. He wrote a man in Hagerstown, Maryland:

"If I could but see the sheltering arms of this grand old Fund spread over you and your little brood . . . I should feel that I had done a great service to you and your household."[46]

Rev. A. J. Waugh, Phelps, New York received this advice when he confessed his further purchase of protection depended upon greater enthusiasm from Mrs. Waugh:

"I wish I could drop into your study and have a little talk with that dear wife of yours. She does not know how soon she may be a widow and dependent upon the proceeds of your insurance. Death comes like a thief in the night."[47]

New business aside, the Presbyterian minister who ran the Fund so effectively found time to counsel and console his commercial flock on a surprising variety of topics both trivial and profound.

Regarding the plight of a certain overweight pastor, the corporation manager declared to a mutual friend: "There are two extremes a minister ought to avoid if he can in order to be successful: he should neither be too skeletonized nor too fat."[48]

To a Chicago preacher who surrendered a life insurance policy because it hindered his absolute life of trust in God, PSA replied:

"There is a Scriptural foundation for life insurance, and there is no other form of duty known to man that so completely carries out the Scriptural injunction: 'Bear ye one another's burdens and so fulfill the law of Christ.' "[49]

A Michigan minister, who charged PMF with deceptive sales letters, received this personal reply based on the belief that the cleric knew more about theology than he did life insurance:

"If you were in the active life insurance business you would find an entirely different kind of life from that you lead as a pastor; and you would soon learn to possess your soul in calmness and patience with the cannons booming all around you and aimed at you from every direction."[50]

The Spanish-American War brought special problems to PMF. In the spring of 1898, Leslie R. Groves, "Post Chaplain, USA" Vancouver Barracks, Washington, noted his life insurance policy did not permit travel outside the United States, Canada, or Europe without written permission from the company. Anticipating his regiment might receive orders to Cuba, Chaplain Groves requested such permission. Allen wrote:

"My Dear Brother: I shall bring the matter before the attention of our Executive Committee as soon as possible. In the meantime you can give yourself no concern as I have no doubt about the permission to go to Cuba if you should be ordered there in the discharge of your duty."[51]

Perry Allen loved his work. Seldom has a company gained an employee with greater esprit. As merchant and minister he made his endeavors a labor of love. The man also loved his family and spent his leisure time with them, a circumstance made easy by proximity of home and office. The Allens lived in a rented house on Chester Avenue, where their daughter, Agnes, was born June 22, 1897.

Presbyterian Ministers' Fund enjoyed an easy transition to the twentieth century, moving into the new era on the momentum of a series of late 1890's achievements which came with almost monotonous regularity: 1898, insurance in force reached five million dollars; 1899, assets passed one million dollars.

The turn of the century found operating expenses, which had been greatly reduced, reaching the 1894 level for the first time — with three times the business on the books! Rev. William P. Fulton became president; Francis and Sterrett were retained as the firm's first independent auditor; and J. Hewson Bradford, M.D., was elected medical director. The Annual Report, for the first time, contained a forthright list of "Death Claims Paid" instead of the oblique "Necrological Statement" used the previous four years.

Another advance came with the Fund's first use of the typewriter. Actions of the Board of Directors, March 14, were partially recorded with this device. What a relief after the vagaries of human penmanship displayed in early Minute Books by secretaries from Francis Allen through Nathan L. Upham. One incumbent, Joseph H. Jones (1852-1869) achieved the distinction of noting events in an almost indecipherable scrawl.

The early 1900's brought Presbyterians comfort through changes in the Westminster Confession of Faith; changes, which for the first time since the 1640's, placed greater emphasis upon God's love for mankind. Publication of the American Standard Version gave Protestants generally a new Bible. Rhodes Scholarships and Nobel Prizes became important annual events of international significance. Germans Wilhelm Roentgen and Emil von Behring received the first of the latter awards for their respective discovery of X-rays and development of diphtheria antitoxin.

Queen Victoria's death united the affairs of the world with the activities of the Philadelphia insurance company as that organization saw fit to mark the passing of the famous British monarch. The corporators, January 28, 1901, sent condolences to her son, His Majesty Edward VII, basing their action upon the fact that the Fund's corporate life "emanated from the Crown"; and observing that the late Queen's "long and glorious reign covered a period coexistent with that of our own highest development and usefulness"[52]

The corporators achieved greater visibility in other ways as well. At the 1902 meeting six members were dropped for persistent failure to attend the annual conclaves or even send excuses for their absence. From this time forward members would be reimbursed for travel expenses to and from the Philadelphia gatherings, and nominal affiliation with the Fund would no longer suffice. Appreciation for the unique corporators' role came that year with the first annual dinner in their honor—given at the Hotel Lorraine by the Board of Directors, who appropriated $400 for the occasion.

Perry S. Allen, receiving the Doctor of Divinity degree from the University of Omaha, 1902, made good use of his time and these years of increasing influence in the company. He prodded the directors to approval of radical changes in the PMF insurance contract including the installment settlement options, changing of the beneficiary privileges, and separation of the application from the policy itself.[53] The company limit for coverage on a single life rose to $7,500.

He experienced continuing trouble with a number of the diminishing sales force. C. W. Hibbs, who had been with the Fund for some time prior to Allen's arrival, provoked a hostile reaction from a number of policyholders in New Jersey. On one occasion Allen wrote Mr. Hibbs: "I will not allow the insolent manner that you have under taken to run the business of this Fund another day or hour."[54] Hibbs apparently regained the good graces of his superior, but Allen found later occasions to lament the poor sales record of his controversial field representative. On a day in July the secretary wrote:

"I don't want to disturb your peace of mind, nor do I wish to discourage you about your work. . . . This letter is written for the only purpose of stirring you up to do a very much better business than your year thus far has been."[55]

Allen's annual salary had doubled, from $2,500 to $5,000, since 1894. He also received a 10 percent commission on premiums received for all policies he sold. In 1903 the directors recognized his devotion to duty with a $1,000 bonus and strong recommendation he take a vacation that summer. Although he had taken no time off in a decade, the industrious Allen stayed on the job completely satisfied and totally oblivious to the negative connotations of all work and no play.

On July 20, 1905, the New York legislature appointed a special committee to investigate the insurance industry. State Senator William W. Armstrong was named chairman, with Charles Evans Hughes, Chief Counsel. The committee convened September 6 and worked until December 30 at New York City Hall. The investigation came as part of the social clamor of the time for muckraking and exposure of all business evils. The press fanned the flames. Life insurance had been guilty of certain excesses by a few companies who gave the industry a bad name. The Armstrong investigation brought strengthened state governmental regulations. Investment rules were tightened, greater nonforfeiture values established, and standard policy forms came into use.[56]

PMF, completely free from the management mistakes and expense excesses of the "Big Three" companies which sparked the Armstrong investigation (Equitable, Mutual, and New York Life), nevertheless found it convenient to adopt new investment policies and improve the management capacity of the directors. Company records reveal a sequence of by-law revision actions, 1906-1908, designed for these purposes.

Despite the San Francisco earthquake and the Panic of 1907, PMF prospered as did its aggressive leader. The Allen family and the Fund both expanded. A second daughter, Mary Virginia, arrived November 10, 1906, and the following spring insurance protection was extended from "ministers Presbyterially governed" to "all Protestant Evangelical Ministers." Allen's friend, George H. Stuart, Jr., assumed chairmanship of the Executive Committee; and, once again, the company office moved to a new location—914 Commonwealth Building.[57]

Presbyterian Ministers' Fund more than kept pace with the growth of life insurance in the United States during the first nine years of the twentieth century. Nationwide, Americans doubled their personal protection in this period while the Fund grew from insurance in force of $6,015,000 to $13,236,000.[58] Yet life insurance is more than mathematics, as a force for good in human affairs.

Perry S. Allen kept this concept ever foremost in his early years of successful selling as secretary, actuary, and managing director. On one occasion he said:

"It is a painful thing to contemplate leaving this world without adequate provision for wife and children. Poverty leads not only to misery but to crime, and a good policy of insurance is the best protection against these sad and awful possibilities."[59]

And in a 1907 tract to policyholders he wrote philosophically:

"When the fraternal spirit is receiving emphasis throughout all Christendom, the ministers identified with this Fund could well afford to contribute to this pre-eminently Christian spirit by sharing the advantages of the Fund with their brethren of other denominations."[60]

Allen felt so strongly about the matter, he experimented with "A year's insurance without cost." A bulletin offered PMF coverage for twelve months before payment of the first premium. This unusual proposition was withdrawn after a short trial period when industry competition, in the form of rebates, stopped as a result of the Armstrong investigation.

When named president of the company in 1909, Perry Allen was fifty-five, close to the average age of all men elected to that office. His predecessors had assumed the post as old as seventy (Robert Cross) and as young as thirty-five (John Ewing).

The new president reinforced this theme of social benefit from life insurance with his first public pronouncement at a January 26 dinner held at the Bellevue-Stratford Hotel, Philadelphia to commemorate the 150th anniversary of the Fund. Allen, likened in creative capacity to Michelangelo, when introduced by his predecessor, Rev. William P. Fulton, described his company's product as a blend of Scriptural teaching with the laws of life:

"That charity might lose its sting, and the widow and fatherless children come into their own and continue to live without hunger and without wanting for clothes and shelter."[61]

Allen reminded his audience that PMF pioneered the nonforfeiture principle (1792); introduced cash surrender values (1852); and never contested a single policy claim in 150 years of business. He also compared the first 135 years of operations with the period of his leadership since 1893. He pointed out the fivefold increase in number of policyholders, the sixfold increase in insurance in force, and the sevenfold increase in assets during this short period—a time when "its benefits to policyholders were about threefold those covering the entire previous history of the Fund."[62]

A typical PMF contract that year was sold to Rev. Edward Arthur Bowden, age forty-one, who began paying an $87.40 annual premium for a 2,000-dollar Twenty Year Saving Fund Endowment. Allen personally signed the policy after carefully crossing out the printed word "Treasurer" at the bottom of the page and noting "President" below his flamboyant scrawl. When thirty-five years later, Bowden's wife died, the durable clergyman changed the beneficiary to his daughter.

Three years raced by. The General Assembly had this to say about the surge of wealth resulting from national business growth of all kinds, including life insurance:

"The church declares that the getting of wealth must be in obedience to the Christian ideals, and that all wealth, from whatever source acquired, must be held or administered as a trust from God for the good of fellowmen."[63]

Reflecting continued maturation of the industry, the American Institute of Actuaries was formed in Chicago in 1909, as a supplement to the Actuarial Society of America organized in New York, 1889.

The Fund moved to a different level of governance with the first authorized director's fees. Starting January 1910, each member would receive five dollars for every Board meeting attended. Following a consistent program of expansion of the business to cover ministers of other denominations, PMF nevertheless set certain limits. For example, it "recognized with hearty approval" the work of the Salvation Army, but sternly ruled "its officers not qualified for insurance with the company."[64]

Dr. Allen represented the company at the funeral of Dr. Gibbons at Old Pine Street Church, where he had served as pastor twenty-eight years. The same year he had his portrait painted by Frank Linton because he could not bear the thought of dying suddenly before his four-year-old daughter, Mary Virginia, could remember him. Allen negotiated terms which provided he would pay the painter nothing unless the portrait was entirely satisfactory. Linton surpassed his expectations as Allen wrote a friend, "he painted my personality into my face. It is a portrait that lives and breathes and speaks and for one thousand years it will tell the story of my exact likeness to all who follow me."[65] This painting is now a part of the permanent collection of the Presbyterian Historical Society, Philadelphia.

Fire destroyed the New York headquarters of Equitable Life (built 1870 at a cost of $4,000,000), January 9, 1912. PMF, without a home of its own after 153 years, still occupied rented quarters, and would continue to do so for more than another decade. Short on real estate but long on liquid assets and Christian spirit, the company that same month recognized its president for eighteen years of distinguished service by adopting a special resolution of the Board of Directors.

The feisty executive appreciated these compliments, but each year as the corporation scored new gains by every insurance measurement, he grew more apprehensive about the security of his loved ones. Although since January 1912, he earned an annual salary of $15,000, and also enjoyed company-paid insurance in the amount of $10,000, Dr. Allen sought assurance of additional help. He asked that the directors and corporators:

"Charge themselves with the sacred responsibility of some interest in the welfare of my family, and especially so in the event of the death of the mother of my children, in which event, they would otherwise be thrown entirely upon a cold friendless world."[66]

These early World War I years were times of PMF annual income exceeding one million dollars, and total assets reaching six-and-a-half million. Yet the practices of the past died slowly. For example, the Executive Committee of the Board of Directors met in solemn conclave April 8, 1915, with the complete agenda for that occasion involving approval of the following items from John Wanamaker's store:

4 Clothes poles	$18.00
1 Step ladder	1.50
Arm chair and 3 tables	49.73
	$69.23

and these goods from Hardwick and Magee Company:

14 rugs, 12¾ yds. linoleum	$358.67.[67]

This same year Edgar Lee Masters published *Spoon River Anthology*, and Carl Sandburg startled the literary world with his *Chicago Poems*.

By 1920 America had suffered its first polio attack, its worst influenza epidemic, and emerged from its most serious foreign war. The Philadelphia ministerial insurance company suffered high mortuary loss from the flu; and, true to its tradition of helping the nation in time of armed conflict, had invested heavily in Liberty and Victory bonds. PMF committed a total of $2,567,000 for this purpose.[68]

Consistently higher company earnings made possible extra dividends for policyholders on two occasions between 1915-1920 with an accumulated total paid since 1904 of more than $1,327,000. These dividends were reversionary, a term the president explained in this way:

"A reversionary dividend is in terms of insurance, adding the amount of same to the face value of the policy, and payable as per terms of the original policy. Our dividends will hereafter be declared in this form, but this will in no wise interfere with the immediate use of such dividends in amount of their cash surrender value which may be used at once to reduce premiums, or payable in cash."[69]

1918 had been a year of three important anniversaries for the Fund: the 202nd of its organization as a beneficent agency, the 160th of its incorporation, and the 25th of its current management. Dr. Allen had increased company assets from $517,542 to $9,087,033. Benefits paid policyholders for the quarter century came to more than $6,000,000 compared with only $400,000 paid in the entire previous 135-year history of the corporation. The president's personal sales of several million dollars annually saved the Fund agents' commissions far in excess of the chief executive's salary. These savings made possible reduced premiums for lower cost insurance than that offered by any other company. No wonder the directors recognized Allen's "ability, fidelity and consecrated services" with a raise in salary to $25,000. PMF also continued to pay the premium on his personal life insurance policy with Massachusetts Mutual.[70]

How had the former preacher achieved these impressive results? By what method had he quickened the leisurely company pace of more than a century to lead the business to these previously unthinkable levels of profitability? The first president to serve full time and for pay, Allen made the most of these circumstances. He built his management style on personal endeavor, exemplified the Puritan work ethic, and became a "company man" in the best sense of that word. He lived PMF.

The industrious clergyman belonged to no clubs, avoided the theater, and pursued no hobbies. As we have seen, he rarely took a vacation. Allen took his work home in the sense that he made family dinner-table conversation about impoverished ministers who had trouble paying the premiums on their insurance. Conversely, the dynamic executive brought his family to the office. Frequently paying a visit to his desk Sunday afternoons, Dr. Allen often took along his younger daughter. Mary Virginia loved to "play the typewriters" as her father attended to business.

The president had two close friends: Robert Dick Wilson, a Princeton Seminary professor and authority on dead languages; and George H. Stuart, Jr., an officer of the Girard Trust Company. Both men were corporators of the Fund. Wilson, elected in 1899, served thirty years. Stuart joined the corporation in 1895, and became a director two years later. He resigned in 1911, but was reelected in 1916, and played an important part in the life of the company as an active member of the executive committee. Perhaps with these two relationships in mind, Perry Allen wrote this definition of friendship:

"The longer I live the more I value friendship. True friendship: the friendship that is as true as the planets are to their orbits or as breath is to life, the friendship that lifts up the hands that hang down and rest the weary feet; the friendship that is not fickle or selfish, but steadfast and self-sacrificing, that 'sticketh closer than a brother'!

The friendship that will walk with you on the broad pathway of prosperity under the blue skies and by the flowers and fountains, or that will sail with you over the summer seas for rest and pleasure; and yet will not desert you when the clouds gather and grow dark and the storms burst and beat upon you and the night overtakes you; the friendship that rejoices in your joys and that comes yet closer and more tender and precious in your sorrows; that will mingle its laughter with your life and also its tears.

To cultivate such friendship in ourselves for others will make us more worthy of such friendship in return."

The "Roaring Twenties" got underway with Warren G. Harding in the White House as the nation tried to get back to "normalcy." The times were anything but normal for the energetic president of the Fund. The indefatigable Perry S. Allen became seriously ill in February of 1921.

The directors had empowered T. Elliot Patterson to act in Dr. Allen's absence. As the president's condition worsened, Patterson (named a corporator, 1904 and a director, 1908) was elected vice-president.[71] Despite the efforts of his doctors, Allen lapsed into a coma. The end seemed near. PMF employees and friends held a prayer meeting in Holy Trinity Church on Rittenhouse Square for the ailing executive. Prayers and the determination of his wife brought eventual recovery after doctors gave up. Mrs. Allen, according to a newspaper account, "took the case in her own hands. She began feeding him freshly squeezed beef juice from a medicine dropper, just a drop or two at a time, placed at the root of his tongue."[72]

When April came Allen felt able to write his associates on the Board to express appreciation for the prayer support. He also declared in utter candor:

"You will not be surprised when I say that the office has never given me the slightest anxiety."

Allen reminded his colleagues that he organized operations in such a way as to obviate the need for an understudy to function in his absence. He referred to his system of correspondence for getting new business. He paid tribute to the abilities of Mrs. M. S. Johnson, Secretary of the Corporation, and Mrs. M. L. Ehrenzeller. He concluded with, "I have had absolute relief of all worry on account of business."[73]

The Fund gained valuable public notice from the dedication of a commemorative tablet in the First Presbyterian Church, Washington Square, Philadelphia, January 24, 1922. The event marked the Philadelphia Synod's 1717 action in creating the "Fund for Pious Uses." Dr. Allen read the lauditory inscription and his daughter, Mary Virginia, unveiled the slab whose message concluded with:

IN THE PROVIDENCE OF GOD
THIS FUND HAS BEEN UNTOLD BENEFIT AND
BLESSING TO THOUSANDS OF MINISTERS
AND THEIR FAMILIES.[74]

"Nothing succeeds like success,"[75] Alexander Dumas had written in 1854, and the events of the next few years substantiated this maxim as PMF's leader earned a series of accolades from both within and without company circles.

In early 1924 the corporators adopted George H. Stuart, Jr.'s, resolution which concluded a compendium of credits with this panegyric:

"Born in the inspiration of love for the welfare of the weak and dependent, this child has grown into its manhood of strength and has been for many years reared under the guiding hand and intelligent purpose of Doctor Allen. His name has been truly woven into its warp and its woof and in the years to come may the purpose of this Fund and his personality stand linked together to furnish the motive which the one may inspire and the skill which he shall contribute to the consummation of its highest destiny."[76]

Not to be outdone, the directors raised Dr. Allen's salary to $30,000 two days later, and continued to pay the premium on his personal life insurance policy.

The Insurance Department of Pennsylvania went beyond the customary stilted language of officialdom in its endorsement of the company at this time. Perry Allen, called "apostle of the Fund's ideals," received praise for "putting the firm on the map" by doing more than "any other individual at any time connected with the Fund during its long two hundred years of history."[77]

The United States Review published another piece on the "Old Fund Without Parallel" which enthused about its president with this salutation:

"As the lives of great men by devotion and labor are indelibly imprinted on the history of corporations, so the life of Rev. Perry S. Allen has become forever woven into the structure and fabric of that grand old institution. Other men have filled their places in its history, but he has been the great builder of the Fund."[78]

A lesser man might have had his head turned by such adulation. With praise from every quarter, Dr. Allen could easily have forgotten the Biblical injunction for humility and become conceited. From all accounts, however, he did not. Allen considered his Fund responsibility as much a ministry as his earlier pulpit years. Amid continuing business achievements and the plaudits they produced the consistent executive kept hard at work, looking to the future and composing correspondence to his ordained flock. He compared ministers without life insurance to the foolish virgins of the Gospel parable.[79] He asked others, "Are you insurable?" and warned, "In less than a week it may be impossible for you to get it . . . you may be dead!"[80]

Miss Vivian Fenstamacher, who began work at the Fund in 1922, and who remained with the company until her retirement forty-five years later, remembered this president as a "fatherly type, considerate, kind and so full of humor!"[81]

Actually Perry Allen had no time for vainglory. In addition to normal business demands the mid-decade years brought the company to the realization of a long-held dream — a home office building of its own. After conducting its affairs since 1759 in thirteen temporary locations, PMF dedicated its new headquarters, 1805-07 Walnut Street, Philadelphia, on January 25, 1925. The 166th Annual Meeting of the corporators, held there at that time, provided a splendid opportunity for appropriate recognition of the

Fund. The directors made the most of it. As the president observed:

"For a corporation doing millions of dollars of business and responsible for many millions of dollars held in trust for the benefit of the clergy the world over, it became impossible, and well nigh unthinkable for its management to drift from one office building to another in search of more adequate quarters of administration."[82]

As we have seen, the corporation first met at "Mr. Bell's in Market Street." For many years the annual sessions convened at different Presbyterian churches in Philadelphia. These gatherings were succeeded by meetings at the Presbyterian Board of Publication as that enterprise moved steadily west on Chestnut Street. The directors rented modest office space at several locations in the 1880's, and later came the leases at the Stephen Girard Building and the Commonwealth Building, where business was conducted and meetings of both corporators and directors scheduled since 1907. Then, fifteen years later, with twenty-nine clerks and six salaried officers employed, to say nothing of an annual rental cost of $9,036, something had to be done!

The directors appointed a new committee to handle the matter on September 14, 1922. Three months later property was purchased at 1805-07 Walnut Street for $201,618.53. Craig N. Ligget, building committee chairman, soon reported the engagement of Paul A. Davis III as architect. Before long a contract was signed with builder Frank G. Stewart, who got the job with a bid of $203,914. Construction went ahead at a brisk pace with virtual completion achieved by the end of 1924.

Three men spoke at the memorable dedication ceremonies. Mr. Ligget presented the building to the corporators with the prediction that rental receipts from that part of the structure not occupied by PMF would entirely carry the overhead charges within ten years. George H. Stuart, Jr., brought this message, noting:

"the immeasurable blessings which flow from life insurance, stimulating principles of economy in life and providing for the wants of dependent families."[83]

Dr. Allen, who termed his friend's remarks "tender and effective,"[84] presented a vivid historical sketch of the Fund built around seven cardinal points. He concluded with recognition for the entire building committee, and asked God to "continue to bless and prosper this Ministers' Fund and extend and increase its usefulness."[85]

With his beloved Fund established in larger quarters, Dr. Allen moved his family to smaller accommodations that same year. The Allens' daughter, Mary Virginia, was introduced to society at a party given in the Bellevue-Stratford Hotel, and her parents left their house at 2124 Spruce Street for an apartment at 135 South 18th.

The booming, optimistic years between the Great War and the economic collapse of the 1930's brought not only a big jump in life insurance sales, but increasing professional stature to the industry as well. Two important things happened October 1927 at the Peabody Hotel, Memphis, Tennessee. The National Association of Life Underwriters, at that meeting, created the American College of Life Underwriters to improve the education of the life insurance agent. At the same time, they also established the Million Dollar Round Table to recognize outstanding achievement in the industry. A man named Paul Clark played a big part in these endeavors, and in later years he became president and board chairman of John Hancock Mutual Life.[86]

In 1927 Perry Allen, now seventy-three, relinquished the title of actuary which he had held since 1893 when appointed secretary of the company, and which he retained in 1909 after being elected to the presidency. John Leslie Milne, named assistant two years before, now moved up to the title role to become the fifth man to formally hold this position in the history of the corporation.

Dr. Allen, heretofore positively addicted to work and suspicious of vacations, adopted a more relaxed attitude toward time off. For years, Mrs. Allen wished a change of pace and scene, but to no avail. Her husband would not travel. Finally, in desperation, one summer she took their two daughters on a trip to Europe. The dogged man of the house remained behind, but agreed to some sea air at Atlantic City, New Jersey. He took a room at the Marlborough Blenheim Hotel, commuting to the office each business day by train, and writing his family long letters every evening.

In the late 1920's, he consented to spending July and August in Bar Harbor, Maine, but got the directors to approve his employment of a secretary to handle correspondence during his sojourns at that New England resort. It takes little imagination to visualize the restless president, ever an inveterate writer, composing his next major company treatise while free from daily office routine.

This production appeared in 1928, and ran twenty-three printed pages. Allen called it an "Historical Sketch." Commenting upon the early years of the Fund, Allen noted "the great majority of the ministers, whom it was designed to benefit, were never identified with it."[87] He then went on to say:

"The chief cause of failure of the corporation to realize its benefits in fullest measure to all the ministers was in the fact that, while great and good men were giving much thought to the cause, there was not one man to devote his entire time and energies to it.

No cause, however commendable, can hope for success without personal energy back of it.

Resolutions and addresses and articles of agreement, and ecclesiastical deliverances may be helpful, but they will not do the work."[88]

At the end of the decade PMF celebrated its 170th anniversary with Perry S. Allen at the pinnacle of his financial ministry. His first daughter, Agnes, had completed her studies at the Pennsylvania Academy of Fine Arts, and was getting started in her career as a portrait painter. In later years she would achieve prominence in the field as her pictures became part of the permanent collections of the University of Pennsylvania, the Insurance Company of North America, American Oncologic Hospital, and the Philadelphia Atheneum. Her outstanding likeness of Eugene Ormandy hangs in the Academy of Music.

1928 proved to be one of the Fund's most impressive years in a succession of annual record breakers:

New business written .... $ 6,710,379
Insurance in force 55,357,224
Income 3,491,498
Assets....................................... 18,487,911
Paid to policyholders .... 2,212,417[89]

The directors voted Dr. Allen a raise in salary to $40,000 per year, and continued to pay the premium on his $10,000 life insurance policy with Massachusetts Mutual. A British writer exclaimed, in a 1929 biographical sketch of the American company president:

"Ridiculed by many journals which predicted his failure to secure business by correspondence, these journals today speak loud in his praise for being able to write over six million dollars of business annually from his desk."[90]

With gross assets up thirty-sixfold in as many years (1894-1930) from $517,000 to $20,000,000; with insurance in force increased during this time from $2½ million to $57 million; and with annual income multiplied twenty-eight times from $92,000 to over $2½ million, is it any wonder the company and its leader provoked constant comment in trade publications? "There is nothing like it in the world," a reporter enthused in 1930. He described Allen's efforts as "the hand of a master who guided it to greater destiny."[91]

Particularly satisfying to Allen, the directors, and the board of corporators, were the consistently low ratios of expense to income (5.27—5.40 percent) and of expense to assets (1 percent). Regardless of dazzling figures and startling economies of operations, however, the essence of the Presbyterian Ministers' Fund comes to focus in a letter written that year by an officer of the Equitable Life Assurance Society of the United States:

"My father had been insured in the Presbyterian Ministers' Fund of Philadelphia, and that after his death that insurance was paid as an annuity to my mother. It was that annuity that enabled her to send me to college, and if I had not received that college education I would not have been fitted for the work assigned to me when I entered the Equitable office. This was the first service rendered to me by life insurance. It has served me in many ways since then. In my case it has proved to be the most beneficial and the safest of my investments."[92]

The first week of November 1930 brought the earthly life of Perry S. Allen to a dramatic end. Knocked down by a taxi at 18th and Walnut Streets, as he returned to the office after luncheon with Mrs. Allen at their apartment only a block away, the seventy-six-year-old executive insisted on being taken home instead of to a hospital. He lingered a few days and died Saturday the 8th. A local newspaper attributed his demise to "an acute attack of grippe."[93] It failed to mention the accident or an incident which took place the following day. The cab driver came to the Allen apartment, 135 South 18th Street, with a statement exonerating that individual of all blame. He asked the failing minister to sign the release to save his job with the taxi company. Allen signed and died the next day.[94]

Not long before his death Allen wrote these verses which the Philadelphia Presbytery quoted in its memorial minutes to the life and work of the fallen leader. It epitomized his faith and confidence:

"God Will Be with Me

There are mysteries in life to be solved,
There are crises in life to be passed,
When the ways of the world are involved

With no haven for anchor at last;
When the skies seem to frown and appall,
But God will be with me through all.

It has always been thus in my life,
And supported by memories dear,
I have nothing to dread in the strife,
And there is nought to discourage nor fear,
As by faith I triumphant recall
That God will be with me through all.

Whatsoever the crises may be,
And whatever its gain or its loss,
If it should be God's will to call me,
I shall answer my name at the cross,
And before his great white throne I shall fall,
For God will be with me through all."

CHAPTER TWELVE

Earthen Vessels
(1936-1963)
Alexander Mackie, D.D., President

A mighty fortress is our God,
A bulwark never failing;
Our helper He, amid the flood
Of mortal ills prevailing.

Martin Luther

Interplay of personality and clash of character has saved many business biographies from what one contemporary writer calls "a ponderous air."[1] PMF, as a Christian pecuniary mission nonpareil, transcends the dry stuff of ordinary life insurance history. It moves beyond actuarial accounting and investment intricacy through the collective commitment of its corporators and directors on the one hand, balanced with the individuality of its presidents on the other. The tensions of these relationships came into sharp focus in the 1930's when the Fund experienced greater management stress than at any period in its history.

Ravages of the great depression brought times which Thomas Paine would have said "tried men's souls,"[2] with bread lines, soup kitchens, and unemployed men selling apples on the street. The years also brought crisis to the venerable company which a trade publication reported "glaringly displayed in the columns of the daily newspapers."[3]

One era ended with the death of Perry S. Allen, and the next began before the interment of his remains. Planning for the election of his successor started on the steps of the Second Presbyterian Church, 21st and Walnut Streets, Philadelphia, as the bereaved left the funeral service for the deceased president. Two men quit the building and entered into conversation. One was the minister of the Ridley Park Presbyterian Church, and later president of Bloomfield College and Seminary, Rev. Frederick Schweitzer.

"That's a job for you," he said to the other mourner. They walked down Walnut Street to Broad, went into the Manufacturer's Club, and talked about the idea over coffee.[4]

His friend, Rev. Alexander Mackie, pastor of another suburban Presbyterian church, Sharon Hill's Tully Memorial, would eventually become president of the Fund. Ahead, however, lay more than five years of intrigue and conflict before the goal would be reached. To fully understand those tempestuous days we need to know more about the central figure of the evolving insurance trauma.

Mackie, born on September 26, 1885, in the Frankford section of Philadelphia, grew up in comfortable circumstances as the son of Alexander J. H. Mackie and Alice Bolton Copper Mackie. There were three other children. The father, a successful businessman often called "doctor" and an active Mason, served as ruling elder of the Hermon Presbyterian Church. The paternal forebears were Scottish. They included the famous Biblical commentator, Matthew Henry, and John K. Howie of Lougoin, author of *Scot's Worthies*.[5] Dr. Mackie's ancestors on the distaff side came to Bucks County, Pennsylvania before the arrival of William Penn. Many of them were Quakers.[6] The young man graduated in 1903 from Philadelphia's Central High School, where he took courses in both Latin and Greek. He entered Princeton University that summer, and four years later earned his Bachelor of Arts degree with honors in philosophy from that institution. The next, last, and most dramatic phase of Alexander Mackie's formal education came with his three years at Princeton Theological Seminary, which began in this manner:

"How well I remember that first hour in a Princeton Seminary classroom. It was in Stuart Hall, the room on the first floor to your right as you enter. There were windows in this room. As far as I could find out, they had never been opened since good Mr. Stuart had donated the building in the 1860's. I should have known as I entered the door and sniffed the musty, before air-conditioning atmosphere, that I was in for three years of mustiness."[7]

Students' complaints about their teachers are not new. A famous British poet described his Rugby School instructors as "a set of Philistine, soulless, dull, ugly, unintelligent bat-eyed idiots."[8] The forthright Pennsylvania minister-to-be expressed similar sentiments about the faculty he found in graduate school, declaring the professors "dwelt in fog and mist unapproachable." He called one with whiskers, who wore a high silk hat and frock coat to class, "Pompous Johnie."[9]

After a year at seminary Mackie was charged with twenty-eight unexcused academic absences, and told his behavior in elocution classes "had not been becoming or helpful." This verbal tit-for-tat between the theological tyro and his mentors reached a climax in the 1909 student rebellion, which eventually led to the resignation of President Francis Landley Patton.

Mackie organized a meeting of students, February 18. The dissidents sent two letters to the Board of Directors and another to the faculty. This brazen audacity brought a demand for their apology and a 1,500-word rebuke from the indignant Dr. Patton. Mackie and his cohorts refused to apologize. They continued to deplore what they considered to be archaic teaching methods.

The enfant terrible of the venerable Presbyterian institution graduated in May 1910. Although he was president of his class, the faculty refused to recommend him to any church. He was the last man to receive a call to service in the pastorate, and was offered the lowest salary tendered to any senior that year ($900 with no manse).[10]

Like Isaiah of old, the fledgling preacher had gained little faith in religious leaders. He carried this opinion for the rest of his life, and soon after assuming his first charge found occasion to state "there could be found chislers and double-crossers in our Presbyterian ministry."[11]

After a few months working in a gospel tent at 24th and Reed Streets, Philadelphia, Mackie was ordained on November 14 at Sherwood Presbyterian Church, 58th and Hoffman Avenue. He described this house of worship as "a large weather-beaten chicken coop." He stayed a year, during which time he conducted a trolleycar courtship of Miss Ethel Dean Walton in Frankford. His fiancee received her education at the Philadelphia Collegiate Institute and Miss Hart's School. They were married November 14, 1911.

The same month, they began a new ministry together at the Sharon Hill Presbyterian Church, Borough Hall and Chester Pike: salary $1,200 and no manse. The Mackies paid $28 for an apartment nearby.

The church owned land for a future building, but services at this time were held on the second floor of the Borough Hall over the fire department. During Mackie's installation the alarm bell sounded and many of the men rushed out in response to its strident clamor. From this undignified beginning the church soon knew better days. Within a year membership jumped from eighty persons to 130. The name was changed to Tully Memorial; and, at a special ceremony on April 20, 1912, the faithful band and their purposeful leader broke ground for a new church building.

Erecting the sanctuary proved to be easier than paying for it, but the entire congregation became involved in meeting the challenge. Each Sunday school class had its own project for raising money. One sold candy eggs. The ladies ran rummage sales. The pastor noted in his journal:

"I remember that I saved all my Lincoln pennies for the church. Mrs. Mackie saved tin foil. Unfortunately I let it be known that I liked Devil's Food cake. . . . I think I must have bought and eaten several hundred dollars worth of Devil's Food cake to help build the church."[12]

Within a few years the debt had been paid in full: $50,000.

Membership grew each year and by 1918 reached a total of 381. Tully Memorial survived the influenza epidemic and the First World War. It was the young Presbyterian cleric who rang the Borough Hall fire bell with joy and vigor to celebrate the armistice, November 11.

Alexander Mackie enlarged his world in the 1920's. Early in the decade he published a book on the subject of speaking in tongues. Never one to flinch from confrontation, the author declared the phenomenon "a fraud" and not of

God.[13] Eight years later, when Mackie became a Princeton Seminary trustee, the J. Gresham Machem-Clarence Macartney faction of the denomination in the Fundamentalist controversy of the time, described the book as "one of the most radical and destructive books ever written by a graduate [of the school]."[14] Mackie served only a year on the Board.

Taking a more active part in the religious life of the community, he served as chairman of the Chester Presbytery Mission Committee. In 1924 PMF made him a corporator, and the following year he received the Doctor of Divinity degree from Parsons College, Fairfield, Iowa.

At Tully Memorial, A. M. took the most audacious step of his twenty-five years in that pastorate. He started a church country club! Using the Swartley farm on Ashland Avenue and other parcels of land purchased by the enterprising minister comprising some eighty-five acres, the church built a swimming pool, baseball diamond, tennis courts, and even a nine-hole golf course. Originally conceived as a war memorial for the men of the congregation who had died in that conflict, the country club proved "a blessing and source of happiness." It let Mackie show "Christianity was something more than words and talking about words that had lost their meaning."[15]

Things went well until the 1929 stock market crash, which began the great depression. The country club, the church itself, and its aggressive pastor faced financial stringency. Mackie, while never paid more than a $5,000 salary, had inherited some money and business acumen from his maternal grandfather Cooper.[16] He owned considerable real estate in the 1920's as well as a substantial stock position in the Darby Bank and Trust Company of which he was a director. As conditions worsened, many families had trouble paying their rent to the landlord minister, and the bank eventually closed its doors.

Within two weeks of Perry Allen's death, the Board of

Directors elected one of its members, John Henry Radey Acker, acting president of the Fund. The Philadelphia lawyer found it a thankless job from the start. That very day, Director George H. Stuart, Jr., died; Dr. Allen's widow declared it God's will that the company pay her $200,000 for 40 letters written by her deceased husband;[17] J. Gray Bolton, another director, resigned from the Board; and a group of insured ministers formed a "Policy Holder's Protective Association" to force changes in the Fund management. Frederick Schweitzer was the secretary-treasurer of this self-styled organization, and J. B. C. Mackie, Alexander's brother, served on the Executive Committee. In addition to the officers, certain corporators joined in the campaign. Herbert A. Gibbons, for example, wrote eleven of his fellow members of that group "to work for Alex." He monitored their progress as he traveled to Paris, Port Said, and Manila.[18]

Faced with a crescendo of criticism, Acker asked the corporators to postpone election of directors at the January 27, 1931, Annual Meeting; and to appoint a committee to answer nine questions concerning future operations of the company. This committee was directed to present its report within six weeks.[19]

Actually, 1930 had been a relatively good year for the Fund. Despite the depression, company assets reached $20 million for the first time. Best's Life Insurance Reports stated: "It is managed with phenomenal economy. . . . Its policies show the lowest net cost of any company. . . . Our rating of this company is A [excellent]."[20] The dissidents, however, were not to be denied. Dr. Allen's long tenure brought a desire for a new direction; depression hardships aggravated the situation; and the determined little band had its way.

March 24 brought a seventy-page report from the committee and a director's election beyond belief. Four candidates were defeated, including John A. MacCallum and

Alexander Mackie. The issue turned on the principle of cumulative voting (whereby each elector may vote as many times as there are candidates, giving his votes to one candidate). This system was legal in Pennsylvania, but had not been used previously within the Fund.

April 6, Mackie, MacCallum, and Robert C. Ligget brought suit against Acker and the four victorious-but-disputed directors, charging these gentlemen:

"unlawfully intruded into, usurped, and exercised the offices, franchises, rights, duties, and powers and prerogatives of directors of the said Presbyterian Ministers' Fund."[21]

April 9 the Board elected Henry Acker president of the Fund. Offered a salary of $25,000, he accepted $20 thousand. Acting or actual president, Mr. Acker found himself sorely tried. His accession was hailed in the press as bringing to the company "practical experience, valuable legal training, and close and intimate familiarity" with its affairs.[22] He was mentioned as a person who "at once commands one's confidence."[23] The Protective Association, however, felt otherwise. The corporators soon received a caustic critique of the committee report, the Board meeting, and the salaries of company officers.

May 31 the insurgents solicited support among the delegates at the Pittsburgh General Assembly. They gave those individuals a tract attacking the officers' compensation and "demanding a complete mutualization of the Fund."[24]

Acker and Schweitzer kept the corporators informed through lengthy letters which reflected their respective points of view.

On September 21 the Court Referee issued his report on the Mackie suit. Proxy votes were voided, cumulative voting approved, Rev. John MacCallum elected a director, and the choice between William P. Fulton and John Grant Newman referred to the corporators. Mackie and his cohorts were victorious in many respects, but he would have to wait for his own election to the Board.

On November 10 the Common Pleas Court affirmed the referee's findings of fact and conclusions of law, but Acker and the others appealed to the Pennsylvania Supreme Court.

Policy Holder Protective Association officials wanted to meet the corporators, but settled for a rendezvous with the directors on December 22. Robert B. Whyte, Frederick Schweitzer, and William T. M. Beale pressed for "Fund administration on the basis of various boards of the church" as well as "complete mutualization of the management, permitting policy holders to vote for the Board of Directors."[25]

The year thus ended on an unresolved note. The corporators' committee confirmed that officers' salaries at the Fund were higher than those paid by other companies of similar size.[26] On the other hand, no critic could deny the Fund "its absolute solvency, the character and diversity of its investments, the adequacy of its reserves, its rates lower than those of any standard life insurance company in the country."[27] Acker blamed the controversy on:

"A hostile movement which sprang up immediately upon Dr. Allen's death on the part of a few men who sought to gain control of the management of the Fund and to install a particular man as president."[28]

The first six months of 1932 were a time of continued agitation within the Fund. The corporators refused to elect John MacCallum and Alexander Mackie directors (although the men received sufficient cumulative votes at the January 26 Annual Meeting) until the state Supreme Court acted upon the Fund appeal then before it.

Henry Acker, reelected president two days later, experienced two kinds of reading between that time and the May 15 Board meeting. *United States Review*[29] and *The Weekly Underwriter*[30] printed laudatory statements about the Fund and its leadership. *The Christian Century*[31] and *The Church-*

man[32] published defamatory articles which the chief executive did his best to refute.

In March the Supreme Court of Pennsylvania upheld the legality of cumulative voting in Fund elections.[33] MacCallum and Mackie joined the Board in triumph! The latter soon enjoyed election to the Executive Committee, but the former found himself exposed as having misled the directors about his part in Robert Whyte's article in *The Churchman*. His integrity impugned, MacCallum threatened to resign and "fight from outside."[34] He and Mackie attempted to have all reference to MacCallum's role in *The Churchman* affair expunged from the minutes, but they were outvoted and the record stood.

This publicity, reported in the press and nurtured by the Policy Holder's Association, brought letters from many parts of the country. Some were helpful, most were sincere. A few sounded vindictive. Henry Acker's mail in these contentious days contained these typical comments and questions:

"Have expenses increased or decreased since 1929?" asked a New York clergyman.[35] Two letters from Iowa reflected opposite opinions. From Dubuque came, "I have unbounded confidence in the Presbyterian Ministers' Fund."[36] From Waterloo the message was, "No wonder there are complaints and criticisms, the way the Fund is managed."[37] A minister in Cape May, New Jersey, urged the Fund to discover the author or instigator of the recent articles in denominational papers and "ask him to resign."[38] This particular policyholder also expressed his distaste for cumulative voting used by those who "evince more interest in personal schemes than in advancing the interests of the Fund."[39]

1933 brought new leadership to both the United States of America and the Presbyterian Ministers' Fund. The people elected Franklin D. Roosevelt President of the country. The directors elected Matthew J. Hyndman president of the company. Rev. Hyndman, sixty-five, succeeded Henry Acker, who died suddenly while vacationing at Pinehurst, North Carolina, on February 23.

A memorial booklet mentioned his twenty-five years of service to the Fund, beginning as a corporator, January 28, 1908. It also stressed the "difficulties of a perplexing and astonishing nature,"[40] which beset the deceased president during his two years in office, as it confirmed the impressive business record scored during this time. This tribute echoes the unanimous resolution of the corporators passed the previous month, which stated in part:

"WHEREAS, during the year of unprecedented economic and financial depression the Fund has not only maintained its traditional soundness but has actually increased its usefulness by writing more new insurance in the year 1932 than in the previous years. . . .

WHEREAS, the assets of the company reached the impressive sum of $21,877,000, a sum substantially greater than at any time since its incorporation in 1759. . . .

NOW THEREFORE, We commend the Officers of the company and the Board of Directors for their accomplishment during these difficult days."[41]

Hyndman took office May 18 at a salary of $10,000. Mackie placed his name in nomination, but he privately described the new president as: "A thoroughly upright, honorable, orthodox Presbyterian clergyman who walked trails that were already blazed."[42]

Dr. Hyndman's election was reported as one bringing "stability to the Fund," as he was "widely known and trusted."[43]

Between Acker's demise and Hyndman's succession the directors elected J. C. Neff (treasurer since 1895) first vice-president, and William S. Furst attorney for the Fund. Mackie confided to a friend that he supported these actions as "very wise."[44] He also confessed a fondness for mystery stories — particularly those appearing in *True Detective* magazine.[45]

1933 found the nation "teetering on the edge of chaos."[46] In Philadelphia, for example, "400,000 people, many stooped and bedraggled, wandered through the city streets vainly searching for work."[47] It was a never-to-be-forgotten year with "the government closing the banks, the flight from the Gold Standard, the adoption of the N.R.A., and the restrictions placed upon life insurance companies to moderate the payments made by them for loans and cash surrender."[48]

Yet the Fund pressed ahead with new insurance offerings to its ministerial family. "Let us reason together!" one began.[49] "Important Announcement to the Ministers of America" another proclaimed.[50] These sales efforts emphasized the Fund's low expense ratio (less than 5 percent of income) and its lowest-in-the-nation net cost of insurance.[51] No wonder its strength increased as it provided immediate estates for ministers deceased, the very thought of which, the company promised, freed the insured

"to do his best work, his fears set at rest that he need not save every single penny against the possibility ever before him of premature death with dependents who would then be in need of the actual necessities of life."[52]

PMF faced 1934 with both a reduction and an increase. Salaries went down and the number of directors went up. Alexander Mackie played an active part in each decision.

January 25 the Board reelected President Matthew Hyndman at his existing $10 thousand salary, but other officers took cuts of 10 to 15 percent. Mackie advocated 20 percent. He also urged that Perry Allen's widow be dropped as "second Assistant Secretary" — a pension designation she had enjoyed for three years. He was overruled and Virginia Allen would continue to receive a $3,600 stipend until her death some years later. Mackie (and Robert C. Ligget) specifically requested their dissent be recorded.[53]

The Board of Directors grew from eleven to eighteen. Of

the group serving with Dr. Allen, November, 1930, only six men remained in office. In less than three and a half years a resignation and four deaths left Rev. William P. Fulton, Rev. Matthew J. Hyndman, Rev. Edward Yates Hill, Walter K. Hardt, J. C. Neff, and Morris Williams still active in the government of the company. To these survivors had been added Rev. J. A. MacCallum, Rev. Alexander Mackie, Rev. John Grant Newman, Rev. George W. Richards, and George H. Stuart III.

The corporators, on Dr. Mackie's motion, first approved a change in the firm's Constitution authorizing the new number of directors. The existing Board was then augmented by six additional ministers and one layman: Rev. Robert Scott Inglis, Rev. Charles M. Jacobs, Rev. James A. Kelso, Rev. Harris E. Kirk, Rev. F. W. Loetscher, Rev. Daniel A. Poling, and Robert C. Ligget, Esq.[54]

The larger number would facilitate committee work and be more appropriate to a company which claimed assets of $22,720,108.23. The action also effectively diminished the influence of the holdovers from the Allen and Acker administrations. Mackie noted, "We struck our first body blow at the old guard."[55]

These strategic maneuvers came during continued efforts to expand company benefits to a larger number of clergymen and their families. Dr. Hyndman posed two questions and provided the answers in a tract entitled "A Thoughtful Minister's Soliloquy," sent to 60,000 prospects. Hyndman made seven arguments why a preacher should insure his life, and added ten reasons why it should be done in the Fund. Rev. George L. Glunt of Pittsburgh was engaged as a sales representative for Western Pennsylvania.

The efforts brought tangible results. Premium and total income for the year increased over 1933, as did disbursements to policyholders and their survivors. To match the January salary reductions the Executive Committee, on which Mackie served, proposed a 10 percent dividend cut for 1935, but the Board decided against taking this step.[56]

Presbyterian Ministers' Fund, 175 years old, continued to demonstrate a remarkable financial vitality. The emphasis made and results produced stood in clear contrast to the theoretical pronouncements of certain other Christians of these depression days. The Federal Council of Churches had adopted a "Social Creed" which denigrated the profit motive and subordinated it to the "principle of social well-being."[57] Congregationalists at Oberlin, Ohio, passed a resolution denouncing the competitive profit-seeking economy as "increasingly self-destructive."[58]

Five depression years failed to deflect the persistent growth of the extraordinary insurance enterprise. The bankruptcy of many companies, numerous bank failures, and the countless personal catastrophes brought about by job loss and currency deflation, compounding a sense of hopelessness, may have slowed the Fund's progress; but they could not halt it. These factors were somehow surmounted. Income grew each year, despite the calamitous financial climate. Sinclair Lewis won the first Nobel Prize for American literature at this time. The Presbyterian Ministers' Fund deserved another prize for its sustained performance from the end of 1929 to the beginning of 1935, when assets increased almost $5,550,000.[59]

Prayer, careful scrutiny of costs (some home office salaries fell to fifteen dollars per week), and a change of sales tactics contributed to the record. Rev. Hugh McCrone began work as a Fund representative for Eastern Pennsylvania, and others were appointed. Alexander Mackie favored the idea, but knew disappointment in some cases. He referred to one agent as "a broken-down Presbyterian preacher who attached himself to us like a barnacle."[60]

Sensing the potential of this sales program, the directors approved a special drive for the final three months of 1935. They selected Dr. Mackie to represent them "in close and constant cooperation with the president" for the continual oversight of the project.[61] On September 12 the Board voted Mackie an office, asked him to take the state insurance examination, and told him to hire a stenographer (at not more than twenty dollars per week). He would be paid $400 each month.

On December 12 Dr. Hyndman submitted his resignation as president, to take effect the following month, and in this manner another era came to a close in the life of the company.

OLDEST LIFE COMPANY
ELECTS NEW PRESIDENT
Dr. Alexander Mackie, Noted
Clergyman, Accepts Post in
Presbyterian Ministers' Fund

proclaimed an important insurance weekly in early 1936.[62] Wednesday, January 29, the pastor from Sharon Hill achieved his goal at a turbulent Board meeting, which caused the resignation of one irate director, George H. Stuart III. "Acceptance" is a misnomer. Mackie admitted, "I had been working for over four years to get the job, and my friends had been working."[63] Besides, his Tully Memorial Church $3,600 salary had not been paid for more than a year (and twenty-five years later his pension dues were still unpaid).[64]

In a year in which the Million Dollar Round Table claimed less than 150 members when it convened at the Jefferson Hotel, St. Louis, and Margaret Mitchell published her famous novel *Gone with the Wind*, Alexander Mackie had these thoughts about his condition:

"I was now the president of a life insurance company . . . and I didn't know anything about life insurance except that it was a good thing. I made up my mind to proceed slowly. It was also very clear to me in spite of our criticisms of the last years of the Allen management that somebody somewhere in the Fund knew something about how a life insurance company ought to be run. . . . I made up my mind I would find out what Dr. Allen did under like circumstances, and do it."[65]

The new president took office as the Board voted to move the Fund from Philadelphia if that step became necessary to escape a threatened city property tax.

His initial sales letter to the Fund family bore the innocuous title "Just Another Report," but carried the unmistakable flavor of what would come to be recognized as the Mackie style: erudite but not dull, forthright but obviously sincere, poetic in a manner in which the average person could appreciate. That first letter spoke of "romance," and "Home Sweet Home," and "the unflinching bravery of the poor parson." It ended with mention of Immanuel's Land and the "Delectable mountains."[66]

Proceeding slowly or not, AM, by December, got the directors to approve the acquisition of the Boston-based Ministers' Mutual Life Insurance Company.[67] The agreement was signed by the 28th of the month. This seemingly forward-looking step brought discord to the Fund, produced clashes between the directors, and would be soon reversed as the relationship grew increasingly unsatisfactory.

The arrangement began with Dr. Mackie becoming president of the New England company, and its chief executive, Daniel E. Marsh, taking the vice-presidency. PMF elected Rev. Marsh simultaneously a corporator-director. John MacCallum, designated "Secretary-Manager" at $3,000 per year, was to spend one day each week in Boston. The fiery Philadelphian soon reduced this schedule, eventually to once a month. Mackie hoped MacCallum would resign the post, and toward this end helped his colleague secure the editorship of the *Presbyterian Tribune*, an independent church weekly published in New York. MacCallum continued to hold both positions.[68]

The quickened pace of the Fund in the late 1930's took other forms as well. Salesman Carleton C. Loeble organized, under the president's direction, a "New Business Department." This brought a series of promotional pieces describing new policies as they were introduced. July 1937 featured a leaflet entitled "Are You Satisfied?" Another emphasized the "Retirement Income Endowment Policy." A minister's "Budget Book" and a folder about life insurance and Social Security came next in this agressive program which produced results of several kinds. Sales increased, but so did the hostility of Mackie's erstwhile friends, who helped him gain office — John MacCallum and Robert Ligget. Ligget fumed at the president's flirtation with Ohio Conference Methodists. He spoke against Fund business methods in states other than Pennsylvania and called them "illegal."[69]

Mackie proposed restoring the salary cuts made under Hyndman. MacCallum opposed the idea and the president appointed a special committee to the study of the matter. Mackie prepared a handsome Fund souvenir brochure in limited edition for the Commissioners to the 150th General Assembly meeting in Philadelphia, May, 1938. Much to his indignation the committee held a secret conclave without him at that event. The committee retained the firm of Ernst and Ernst,

"For the purpose of obtaining an independent and experienced viewpoint on salaries and general organization and personnel activities pertinent to any consideration of employment and remuneration."[70]

Further points of controversy arose over Dr. Mackie's proposals to make the medical director, J. Melvin Smith, M.D., full time to better protect the Fund from insuring poor health risks, and his wish to maintain company dividends in those years. MacCallum opposed him on the first issue, and Actuary John L. Milne fought against the latter.

Amid the turmoil of these years came an occasional victory for the feisty president. PMF and three other insurance companies (Penn Mutual, Provident Mutual, and Fidelity Mutual) defeated the Philadelphia plan to tax as "personal property" the securities held by these concerns. The Fund abandoned its threat to move and would stay in the Quaker City.

Mackie, described as "tall, sandy-haired, and crinkley-eyed," by a reporter from a national magazine, made the most of the occasion. He explained the success of his company over the years by noting the longevity of clergymen in these words: "They rarely commit suicide, and darn few preachers are murdered by their wives."[71]

Differences of opinion deepened. The Massachusetts Mutual arrangement soured. Bickering continued over methods of doing business in other states. The directors took two steps to check the president. They installed a chairman to preside at Board meetings. They paid Vice-president Walter K. Hardt a $5,000 salary and greatly expanded his duties. This action particularly rankled Dr. Mackie, who believed his own business judgment superior to that of many laymen. He once began a talk about the Fund with this declaration:

"The object of this paper is to prove that your preacher . . . is a very smart man and that if you would entrust him with a little more money he would show you how to manage it."[72]

The president ended 1939 by bringing a special report to the December directors' meeting. He crammed thirty-nine pages with legal opinions which supported his handling of a number of difficult matters that year in which he had been opposed by MacCallum and Ligget: the Rev. Manuel H. Snow case, and the Fred Pierce Corson affair. In the former he protected the Fund from an unwarranted claim which would have set a dangerous company precedent for future policy conversions. In the latter he agreed with the Methodist bishop who had been given short shrift by officials of the firm.[73]

Mackie had had enough. After four difficult years he "reached a state of desperation," and felt "the time had come for a showdown."[74] Laying aside his "modesty and reluctance," the president "blew his own horn" at the 1940 corporators' conclave.[75]

In a stinging rebuke to those who charged him with management inefficiencies, Dr. Mackie reported gains in every company measurement: insurance in force; net admitted assets; surplus; premium income; and total income.

He described changes in salesmanship, and boasted of keeping the office open Saturday mornings to better serve small-town preachers coming to Philadelphia about their insurance. He reminded his audience of the New Business Department and the Purchasing Department; mentioned the first budget in company history, and described methods used to bring lower costs. He railed against the "vicious habit" of directors earning Fund salaries, calling it "bad business, bad practice, and distinctly bad ethics."[76] He reported "over-riding on my own authority, opinions and mandates from the attorney of the Fund which ran contrary to common sense and common insurance practice."[77] He ended one section of this *tour de force* with an eloquent challenge:

"I have dared to say 'NO' to directors—and to a director when he threatened 'to blast the Fund to bits,' and to resort to newspaper publicity and to cumulative voting if I persisted in my plan to close the Ministers Mutual and to conserve its assets for its policyholders. And if I am elected again to the Board of Directors, and if I am elected again to the presidency of the Fund, I shall continue to say 'NO.' "

This challenge brought adjournment of the meeting. Chairman Lewis Seymour Mudge appointed a Committee of Inquiry, with Rev. Harry Lathrop Reed, Chairman.[78] The Adjourned Corporators' Meeting convened May 5. As the men assembled, Mr. Ligget distributed his own report as Counsel in which he scored Dr. Mackie:

"The last two years of his four-year rule, as you can imagine, have been nothing but turmoil, destructive of officers and employees."[79]

Dr. Reed's candid report noted MacCallum and Ligget's attack on the president for "extravagance, illegal methods of operation, and a sort of nepotism," and Mackie's counter thrust toward his former friends on the basis of "incapacity, vindictiveness, and personal truculence."[80] The document also contained three specific recommendations.

The by-laws should be changed to prohibit salaries for directors (excepting the president and present treasurer); the directors should be "staggered" (elected in three classes of six men each); and each year the president should appoint a Nominating Committee to select candidates for the Board of Corporators and the Board of Directors. Four men then serving on the Board should not be reelected as directors: Walter K. Hardt, Robert Ligget, John MacCallum, and Alexander Mackie. Cumulative voting should no longer be practiced within the Fund.[81]

The president remained calm through this period of anxiety. He even made the motion to receive the Report and consider each proposal. Behind his outward aplomb, however, AM had "cleaned out" his desk "preparatory to moving."[82]

The directors met promptly, dropped Mackie, but retained MacCallum and Ligget, who nominated each other! Ligget attempted to make Dr. Hyndman president, but was rebuffed. With assistance from William A. Schnader, Esquire, Dr. Mackie found himself reelected to head the company, but not as a voting member of the Board. The crisis outwardly abated for a time, and 1940 passed quickly without further open conflict.

J. Melvin Smith, M.D., presented a detailed report from the Medical Department. Smith revealed 41 percent of current death claims came from cardiovascular disease. Tuberculosis had been completely removed from the illness list, although thirty years earlier it had posed a major threat to life.

Mackie, perhaps unduly conscious of previous office informality, and irked by the conduct of several colleagues, listed new regulations which required all employees (including officers of the Fund) "to be at their desks ready for work at 9 o'clock." Each had to sign in and out. "Officers obliged to be late or absent will telephone their secretaries who will inform the President in writing."[83]

Robert Ligget then mounted his final assault on the former pastor from Sharon Hill at the next meeting of the corporators.[84] His statement claimed:

"Dr. Mackie has been guilty of conduct unbecoming the President of an honorable institution such as the Presbyterian Ministers' Fund.

Dr. Mackie has tried to terrorize and crush his subordinate officers.

Dr. Mackie has violated the insurance laws in many of our states: New Jersey and Ohio, for example.

Dr. Mackie is incompetent to run the Presbyterian Ministers' Fund as he has made a failure of his own financial affairs."[85]

The lawyer warned impending by-law changes (to appoint a separate secretary of the Board in addition to that officer of the corporation, and require the vice-president to be a member of the Board) would "produce an absolute one-man control of the operation of the Fund."[86]

Rhetoric rebounded to its perpetrator's detriment as the directors dropped Mr. Ligget from the Board.[87] Later his lease of an office on the fourth floor of Fund headquarters was not renewed, and he left without further ado. Ligget continued as an active corporator until 1976. He and Dr. Mackie at least partially resolved their differences.

In the reorganization effected at this time, Walter K. Hardt's vice-presidential rank was terminated but he remained on the job. The chairman and president "were obliged to take the carpet off the floor and move his desk" before the former official actually departed![88]

Other changes followed. Rev. Frederick W. Loetscher became Board secretary, replacing Mrs. Maude Johnson. Jonathan C. Neff retired after an exceptional career as treasurer. The president's sister-in-law, Helen Mackie, now a widow, came to work in the Old Business Department. She would stay twenty years. Rev. Matthew Hyndman and Robert S. Inglis retired as directors.

Dr. Mackie's salary rose to $12 thousand, and for the first time since achieving the leadership of the Fund he felt worthy of the words which appeared on the front page of the 1936 Annual Report, issued at the end of his first year in office: "I am among you as he that serveth."

1941, which began with acrid international discord, ended peacefully within the company — as the Japanese attack on Pearl Harbor, December 7, stunned the world and brought war to America.

The ensuing years of deadly conflict found the Fund playing its traditionally active part in support of the nation at a time of military crisis. From the French and Indian War, when Rev. Charles Beatty served at Fort Allen, Pennsylvania, throughout the Second World War, when Director Daniel A. Poling's son gave his life in the sinking of the *S.S. Dorchester;* PMF loaned money to the government and served policyholders without additional premium.

Twelve patriotic advertising blotters issued in the early 1940's proclaimed this proud message. The company remembered the Alamo and asked clergymen to remember the extraordinary insurance enterprise at 1805 Walnut Street, Philadelphia. Many ministers heeded this advice and made possible fruitful years when premium income rose from $2,647,000 to $3,191,419; the number of policies increased from 25,516 to 28,241; dividends paid grew from $504,592 to $586,000; and total company assets showed a gain of $8,242,000 to a new high of $40,578,000. By war's end more than 730 armed forces chaplains had been protected by insurance worth $4,086,725, with death claims paid of only $57,210.[89]

These results reflected more than momentum. Two 1943 new policies proved very attractive to eligible preachers. Both the "Whole Life Special Five" and the "Double Protection" contracts called for low initial premiums and offered generous special benefits.

The second of these proved a wise investment for the survivors of one minister, age forty-one, who bought $1,250 coverage with a first year premium of $18.59. Paying only $37.18 for five other years, he died and the company paid his widow $2,500.

The Board at this time experienced changes in its customs and membership. July and August meetings were discontinued. Beginning June 8, 1944, the directors had luncheon together before taking up their business agenda. More than half of the men died or retired within a four-year period in the early forties, to be replaced by an equal number of new ministers and business executives. Departing as directors were Rev. Edward Yates Hill, Rev. Matthew J. Hyndman, Rev. Robert S. Inglis, Rev. Frederick H. Knubel, Rev. John A. MacCallum, Rev. Lewis S. Mudge, and Rev. Charles F. Wishart, in addition to William M. Lewis and Jonathan C. Neff.

The new members included three clergy and six laymen. Rev. John R. Cunningham, Rev. Norman Vincent Peale, and Rev. Robert B. Whyte represented the former. Whyte was an old friend of Dr. Mackie from the days of the Policy Holder's Protective Association. Within twelve years he would be elected chairman. The laymen comprised Theodore A. Distler, President of Franklin and Marshall College; D. Irvin Fulton; Russell H. MacBride, a mortgage broker; Henry D. M. Sherrerd; J. H. R. Timanus, Secretary of the Philadelphia Contributionship; and Charles S. Walton, Jr., Philadelphia industrialist.

Mackie wrote, "I now had as strong a group of men directing the affairs of the Fund as were associated with Francis Alison in our first days."[90]

Fund prosperity in the early 40's came from the customary blend of investment income, increased sales, and careful monitoring of costs. Employees of the home office had every right to feel they contributed to this state of affairs in their response to constant prodding from the president.[91] On one occasion they were admonished to conserve paper by using every line on both sides of each shorthand notebook page.[92] At another time they were forbidden to visit from desk to desk.[93] The 1945 yuletide message from the boss advised "the practice of allowing time off for Christmas shopping has been discontinued in all departments."[94]

Mackie also made a number of changes in the administrative offices. Mrs. M. L. Ehrenzeller succeeded Mr. Neff as treasurer. Horace T. Allen took the place of Maude S. Johnson, who had held the secretaryship since 1921. Actuary John Leslie Milne resigned and his position was filled by Bernard S. Haines. After ten years in office the president at last felt comfortable with the directors and the officers.

Secure in office but ever unsatisfied in the spirit of duty, Alexander Mackie continued to feel the restlessness of concern which marked his life. Before the end of the decade he said:

"Many are the humble widows; the poor and distressed widows of poor and distressed ministers of the gospel who are with us today to listen to our Report, to admonish us if, as stewards, we have been found unfaithful."[95]

A few years later he reminded his colleagues, "In the world of good deeds we have only made a beginning."[96]

The conscientious executive never ceased his efforts to make the Fund go beyond annual growth statistics, no matter how impressive, and manifest "the worthiest impulses of men."[97]

He wound up the Ministers' Mutual Life by surrendering the charter of that company and having PMF assume its total business. He sought more policyholders through a mixture of new programs and different ways of presenting traditional coverage. Children's insurance up to five thousand dollars appeared at this time. The clergyman's "Road Map to Easy Street," as well as a series of sales talks built around the Ten Commandments, made ordinary and endowment protection hard to resist. Lloyd C. Douglas endorsed the Fund in a pamphlet called "Make Full Proof the Ministry." Douglas, who published his famous novel, *The Big Fisherman*, in 1948, was nominated for corporator but never served.

Some risks were not welcome. After four death claims within a few months from aviation accidents, PMF began asking applicants about their flying with amateur pilots.[98] In such cases future claims paid would be limited to return of premiums.

Persons actually insured could count on swift answers to their queries. Rev. Hugh B. McCrone, who served in both the policy-writing department and as librarian, took pride in promptness. He wrote reply letters in ink on a yellow pad. They were then typed by a stenographer and mailed at once. A typical response began this way:

"Your application came to my desk a few moments ago, with the approval of our medical director. Your premium accompanied your application, so that I am happy to have you numbered among the family of the Presbyterian Ministers' Fund."[99]

On October 14, 1948, he furnished facts about a new policy taken out by a young minister in Narberth, Pennsylvania, Rev. Robert J. Lamont.

McCrone also arranged dinners for seminary students given by the company. Seniors from Drew came to such an event December 7 at the Hotel William Pitt, Chatham, New Jersey. They enjoyed:

Fruit Cup with Sherbert
Roast Loin of Beef
Potatoes and Two Vegetables

Salad and Rolls
Celery and Olives
Chocolate Ice Cream Sandwich
Coffee

It cost the Fund only $2.25 per person, tip included!

Three men elected corporators in 1947 merit specific mention: Rev. Arthur M. Adams, Rev. Raymond I. Lindquist, and Rev. Frederick Schweitzer. Adams, the president's first cousin once removed, became a director the same year, and later chairman of the Board. Lindquist soon joined Adams as director and (more than thirty years later) would follow him as chairman. Schweitzer, of Policy Holder's Protective Association repute, would also be elected director and eventually secretary of the Board. All three would serve many years with distinction.

After nineteen decades of business transacted entirely from Philadelphia, PMF opened its initial branch office in Boston. The Fund then added sales centers in St. Louis and Atlanta. By the end of 1949 this outreach accounted for 28.9% of total sales or $2,118,387.[100]

As the century mid-point approached, the company noted two mergers of organizations related to its operation. The historic First and Second Presbyterian churches, Philadelphia, came together as a new First Church, 21st and Walnut Streets, adjacent to Fund headquarters. A newspaper reporter observed that the corporation "was established, 1717, through the efforts of the ministers of these churches."[101] The Actuarial Society of America (1889) joined the American Institute of Actuaries (1909) to form The Society of Actuaries. The new entity kept as its motto the one adopted by the older parent organization in 1892: "The work of science is to substitute facts for appearances and demonstrations for impressions."[102]

PMF won an important victory at this time through a ruling by the Pennsylvania Deputy Attorney General, who concurred with Fund counsel, William A. Schnader, Esq., regarding the true status of the company. State Insurance Examiners claimed the Fund was a mutual company, and tried to force it to reduce its surplus and pay larger dividends to the policyholders. Schnader wrote Ralph B. Umsted a reasoned but forceful argument that PMF was neither a stock nor a mutual concern, but, *sui generis*, unique one of a kind, and therefore exempt from state laws applicable to mutual companies.[103]

The company moved into the second half of the twentieth century with insurance in force passing the $100,000,000 mark for the first time. Assets now exceeded $50,000,000. Two additional branch offices opened in 1950: Chicago and Dallas. And a university president, Dr. Francis P. Gaines of Washington and Lee, provided thoughtful insight for the mystique of life insurance in a talk given at the American Life Convention, Chicago:

"It seems to me to be the final invitation to character as developed in the economic world . . . by incentive.

Life insurance builds in men the character by which they can sacrifice the desire of the moment for some great advantage of the future years; and therefore, it goes beyond character and by building character, builds the only kind of security that has any meaning."[104]

1951 brought Rev. S. Carson Wasson to the Fund Board of Corporators. Branch offices were opened in Columbus, Ohio, and Pasadena, California, as the company enjoyed continued progress in both investment income and mortality experience. The first figure rose to 3.58 percent (from a 1945 low of only 3.02 percent). The second fell to 32.62 of actual from 38.92 percent the year before. These statistics reinforced Dr. Mackie's operational credo. He believed the company could be run successfully with the right combination of these factors.

The mortality advantage of clergymen (about six years better than the actuarial table) finds illustration in the case of a policyholder who outlived two beneficiaries and made arrangement for benefits to be paid a third person at this time. Rev. Will D. Landis, age twenty-three in 1896, bought a $1,000 twenty-year Savings Endowment policy payable to his wife Pearl. She died in 1935. A second wife, Grace, died in 1948. In 1950 Mr. Landis, now seventy-seven, named his son, William, to receive the benefits at his death.

Alexander Mackie did more than make executive decisions. Throughout his administration he never lost a love for office minutiae, nor did he relax his vigilance regarding adverse comment from outsiders. A memorandum from the president illustrates his difficulty in delegating details while a series of letters to assorted Philadelphians reveals his response to error on the part of persons misinformed or critical.

June 13, 1951, he ordained:

"Each desk receiving mail shall have an 'In' and 'Out' box. These boxes are to be distinctly marked 'In' and 'Out,' and the 'In' box to be to the right and the 'Out' box to the left of the person sitting at the desk."[105]

Mackie advised the editor of *Philadelphia Magazine* he "missed a bet" in omitting PMF from an article "In Banking and Insurance" which appeared in that periodical.[106]

Rev. W. Sherman Skinner, Presbyterian Church Board of Pensions President, was told his organization should "discontinue the mistake claim" it evolved from The Fund for Pious Uses. Mother's Day church bulletin covers carried this inaccurate data and AM objected![107]

The Philadelphia Inquirer published an editorial, "Highbinders Horrified," which described two PMF directors with words which the doughty president declared reflected upon "the competence or the integrity" of his company. Mackie protested the newspaper's calling Daniel A. Poling "a beautiful facade" and William A. Schnader a person who "would look well in a halo."[108] Poling was running for mayor of the city at this time.

Not all public notice of the Fund was negative, to be sure. Ten Philadelphia firms, in continuous operation for at least 175 years, were honored July 4 that year as part of the city's anniversary celebration of the signing of the Declaration of Independence. Included in the prestige list were the Franklin Printing Company, and *The Saturday Evening Post* (both 1778) as well as the Presbyterian Ministers' Fund (1717).[109]

In sharper focus came the activities connected with the enlargement of company headquarters. The first, held October 11, 1951, included an actual cornerstone laying ceremony as well as a convocation in the First Presbyterian Church, Walnut Street at 21st. The second occasion followed, January 27, 1953, with the Dedication Service at the time of the annual meeting of the corporators.[110]

Characteristically, Alexander Mackie took no part in these formalities. As a member of the "Committee on Arrangements" he planned two memorable events, supervised every detail, involved celebrities as participants, but remained in the background.

Twelve men, including Pennsylvania Governor John S. Fine; Philadelphia Mayor Bernard Samuel; Methodist Bishop Fred Pierce Corson; University of Pennsylvania Executive Vice-president William H. Du Barry, and University of Delaware President John A. Perkins wielded the trowel, offered the prayers, or occupied the podium as the Fund president assumed an outwardly passive role to start the project. He followed a similar procedure at its conclusion when Rev. Daniel L. Marsh, Board chairman; Howell Lewis Shay, architect; and Rev. Robert B. Whyte occupied the platform while AM kept a low profile.[111] Both days concluded with a dinner at the Union League.

The cornerstone observation carried a Masonic flavor "in recognition of Chief Justice William Allen, the first grandmaster of the Pennsylvania Grand Lodge of Freemasons, and the Fund's first treasurer."[112]

The handsome structure, substantially enlarged from its original size to accommodate the larger staff of a growing business (and named for Francis Alison) was "dedicated to the memory of the first officers and directors of the Fund."[113]

Through the years of the decade Mackie maintained momentum with a distinctive blend of board strengthening, branch office expansion, imaginative sales ideas, employment-practice nit-picking, colorful public utterance, and occasional dramatic episodes.

Rev. Frederick Schweitzer joined the directors (1952) as did Millard E. Gladfelter, and Rev. S. Carson Wasson (1957). The eighth branch office opened in Pittsburgh, increasing the contribution of these centers to total sales. They furnished $7,731,113 or 60 percent of the 1952 total.[114] Branch office conferences were held each year in the Alison Building; but, in addition, the president found it necessary to send special communiques to the field:

"Fees for medical examinations have been mounting at a startling rate.

You are requested hereafter to state in conversation or in a letter on the subject: 'Our regular fee for a medical examination is $3.00.' DO NOT state: 'If your doctor charges more we will be glad to pay it.' Because we will not be glad to do so."[115]

Prior to 1955, when Rev. Lester Paul reached the rank of vice-president in charge of sales, Dr. Mackie functioned personally in this capacity. One application for life insurance reached 100,000 preachers in newspaper format. It exposed the disadvantages of term insurance through a clever editorial entitled "Dog Days." Four policies were presented at another time by a brochure called "Emergency Aid" whose cover pictured the president and five directors in an open car ready to assist the minister as he traveled the road of life.

Presidential views on baseball reached the clerical staff one early autumn afternoon in this form:

"We understand that the World Series is to be played during the week of September 27. And we realize that this matter is of supreme international importance.

We also consider the conduct of our business to be of very considerable importance. And we are also of the opinion that working hours are short.

We do not think that radios should be in use on the second, third, fourth, or fifth floors during working hours."[116]

Not long before, the articulate executive had made national news with a blast at the General Assembly plan to change the Lord's Prayer at the 164th meeting of that body in New York City:

"Why all this silly tampering with the Lord's Prayer?

As a Republican I consider it a serious invasion of private rights to tell me how to pray."[117]

Corporators and directors responded to this brand of leadership with resolutions of praise and continued increases in salary ($22,500 by 1953). They also commissioned a noted Washington, D.C., artist to paint Dr. Mackie's portrait.

Alfred Jonniaux, favorably compared by the *Boston Herald* with Copley and John Singer Sargent, did the work that summer for a fee of $4,000. The picture was featured in a New York art show, November 6-21, with other Jonniaux portraits, including those of Clare Boothe Luce and Alfred P. Sloan, Jr.[118]

The corporators presented Mackie's portrait to the Fund, January 26, 1954, in a special solarium ceremony which included dedication of a memorial tablet to one of the original twelve founders of the company, Dr. Samuel Finley.

The president achieved visibility in other ways as the Fund's 200th anniversary drew near. His community leadership brought not only publicity but prestige to the ancient company. As trustee chairman of the Friends of Old Pine Street Church he led a committee to raise $200,000 for restoration of that early American shrine.[119] He took an active part in the programs of the Pennsylvania Historical Association.[120] The College of the Ozarks, where he served as trustee, gave him an honorary Doctor of Letters, 1956.[121]

A consistent writer, the insurance executive kept the presses rolling. "Life Insurance Answers Cynics of Modern Era," he stated in an article which appeared in a leading trade journal.[122] The company credo found expression in this message one January afternoon:

"The corporators and directors of the Presbyterian Ministers' Fund are not proprietors or owners. They have no personal vested rights. They are trustees. If there is any lesson which it is my heartfelt wish and prayer and purpose to transmit to those who come after us in the administration of this Fund, it is that it is a Ministers' Fund. It exists solely for the service of the minister."[123]

His book, *Facile Princeps*, appeared in 1956. The fluent president used this Latin-phrase title not only to describe the first one hundred years of the company, but to accentuate its essential thrust—"easily the first."[124] Through tales about the men who guided the pioneer firm from its earliest days, Mackie reinforced his thesis that success in life insurance comes from a combination of common sense, learning, and character.

Dedicated to his deceased brother, Rev. Joseph B. C. Mackie, and his friend, William A. Schnader, Esq.,—two "gentlemen unafraid"—*Facile Princeps* closed with these words:

"There was something more that accounted for the survival and the ultimate progress of the Corporation—that something was the character of the men who managed it. Some of them were very pompous, and some of them very tiresome, and some of them reasonably stupid. But the men who managed the first life insurance company in America were men who believed that the Ten Commandments had a place in modern business. And they were men who knew how to make only one answer to the ancient question, 'Am I my brother's keeper?' "[125]

Two centuries of successful business life received appropriate recognition in 1959. The observation began with a commemorative service at Old Pine Street Church, Philadelphia. The corporators on January 27 received impressive statistics concerning the state of the Fund, and they responded with a special resolution to honor the president, then marking his twenty-third year in office.

Insurance in force passed the $200,000,000 level; assets came to almost $73,000,000; and surplus totaled $6,337,534. Careful risk selection reduced the ratio of actual to expected mortality to a record low of only 27.11%.

The corporators declared, in part:

"We, your associates, gratefully acknowledge your superb leadership.

Yours is a composite excellence. You are a dedicated man whose life is an unselfish ministry to your brother ministers and to their families.

You excel as a dreamer of dreams that are made to come true.

You have an unfailing sense of humor which is an infiltrating lubricant.

You share yourself."[126]

The Bicentennial Annual Meeting also featured particular mention of three men for their exceptional contribution to the life of the company: Robert Patterson II, Hughes O. Gibbons, and Perry S. Allen. Extensive by-law changes were voted which served to improve managerial functions as well as redefine the firm's essential mission at that time:

"The Fund will issue policies of life insurance and annuities only to ministers and theological students of any Protestant denomination . . .

The wives and minor children of such ministers . . .

And the officers and employees of the Fund."[127]

J. B. Millard Tyson, Esq., was elected a corporator on this occasion, and the Rev. S. Carson Wasson gave the after-dinner address at the Union League that evening. Wasson, elected a corporator (1951) and a director (1957) would soon earn a further promotion as the anniversary year progressed.

A birthday bonus paid to employees recognized the longevity of service of many who confirmed the "Perseverance of the Saints."[128] The largest premium went to Mrs. Kathryn Ettenger, a devout Baptist worker and widow of a Baptist minister, whose achievement emphasized that the Fund was "ecumenical to the Nth degree."[129]

The Newcomen Society in North America recognized PMF with a dinner on April 16, in honor of Dr. Mackie, who delivered a seventeen-page speech at the event.

That same month, Mackie, thinking about his mandatory retirement in 1963, proposed that the directors appoint a committee of eight to study the advisability of electing an executive vice-president, and to nominate a suitable person for that position. The committee selected S. Carson Wasson. He assumed the post on February 1, 1960, and thereby introduced a new dimension to the management of the Fund. Mackie, relieved of certain details, found time in his remaining presidential years to extend his passion for community outreach. For example, he took the lead in organizing the Conwell School of Theology which succeeded Temple University's school of religion.[130] Daniel A. Poling, Fred P. Corson, Millard Gladfelter, and William A. Schnader served on the Conwell board with Dr. Mackie.

The early 1960's were days of the first American in space; of Rev. Robert J. Lamont's election as a corporator; and of Mrs. Mackie's death at age seventy-five. The Fund continued its steady growth with insurance in force climbing to $276,207,024 by the end of 1962. Assets at that time reached $86,036,486. The president occasionally reminded male employees to take their hats off in the elevator or chided the switchboard operators for reading the newspaper during business hours. In a more serious vein he labored for higher standards, new ideas, and a sense of humility for those guiding the company.

His final report to the corporators carried the title "Farewell and Hail." He reminded the Fund family it had a rendezvous with duty and destiny; destiny being "what we make it."[131]

A $100,000 scholarship fund for education of children of PMF employees was established at his retirement. It was presented by Theodore C. Distler, Executive Director of the Association of American Colleges, at a dinner in the Union League of Philadelphia that evening.

Methodist Bishop Corson reflected the sentiments of many when he expressed his gratitude for the manner in which Dr. Mackie conducted the business of the company:

"Not only have you made it a sound insurance company but always you have had the thought of the preachers and their families uppermost in your mind and given them a personal service which the commercial insurance companies do not render."[132]

Years later a memorial tablet to Alexander Mackie was dedicated in the main hall of the Alison building. That tablet described the extraordinary president as the servant of the servants of God.

SERVUS SERVORUM DEI

PART FOUR

A Modern
Life Insurance
Company

CHAPTER THIRTEEN

Following Different Paths
(1963-1973)
S. Carson Wasson, D.D., President

Jerusalem the golden, with milk and honey blest!
Beneath thy contemplation sink heart and voice oppressed
I know not, oh, I know not, what joys await us there;
What radiancy of glory, what light beyond compare.

Bernard of Cluny

"There's nothing wrong with life insurance but the people who administer and sell it,"[1] cried a 1963 critic of the industry as the Presbyterian Ministers' Fund selected a new president to head the old company. The attack was not directed at PMF's incoming leader nor any other specific individual. It reflected a broader attitude of hostility toward the risk protection business which found varied expression in different eras. For example, in 1845 some felt life insurance "wicked."[2] On another occasion Elizur Wright heard "life insurance is the greatest humbug in Christendom."[3]

The early 1960's version declared that "those who dare to point the finger of criticism at life insurance are not answered with reasoned argument but are as bitterly assailed as if they had attacked motherhood or the flag."[4]

The Fund's new chief executive officer did not assail the dissident author nor anyone else. Instead, as a "greenhorn vice-president" he modestly "climbed into the saddle"[5] vacated by his predecessor Alexander Mackie. That individual officially retired, January 22, to be succeeded by S. Carson Wasson, who became the twenty-third man elected to the presidency of the company since its incorporation in 1759.

A more striking contrast between two personalities can scarcely be imagined. Two Presbyterian preachers with utterly different management styles thus served back to back as leaders of the original American life insurance enterprise. Mackie talked; Wasson listened. The former declared; the latter questioned. AM exuded warmth; SCW seemed reserved.

Each man's presidential record verified Winston Churchill's observation that most big decisions are made by amateurs. Benjamin Franklin, son of a soapmaker without even a secondary school education, became both a statesman and a scientist. S. Carson Wasson, a clergyman (as were ten of his predecessors) not only went into business, but successfully headed a concern with assets of $86 million and annual sales in excess of $24 million. Mackie and Wasson, through opposite methods, brought individual meaning to Jonathan Swift's definition of style: "proper words in proper places."[6]

Each man's contribution strengthened the company, but each remained subordinate to the Fund itself. A modern life insurance writer described this relationship between a corporation and those who serve it:

"To be sure, the people are the company. But they come and go, enter here and leave there, by retirement or otherwise. The company goes on. And towering above the storms and trials, the news and weather below, there stands this abiding, majestic being, nearly ineffable yet very real, a being of power, sovereignty, and compassion"[7]

1963 may be described as a pivot in PMF history around which turned contrasting presidential postures. Alexander Mackie took the company as far as it could go under what we see today as "old-fashioned" management. S. Carson Wasson made possible a move toward modern corporate life for the Presbyterian institution. The first exercised a colorful, benevolent despotism. His successor adopted a bland team approach. Dr. Mackie kept officers and employees poor. Dr. Wasson improved salaries and increased pensions. One man clung to outdated techniques. The other agreed to experiment with unfamiliar methods.

Before telling the story of the Fund's "Wasson decade" we need to know more about the person God guided to the president's chair in the 204th year of its remarkable history.

Samuel C. Wasson, son of a Presbyterian minister, was born December 9, 1908, in Churchville, Maryland. He had one brother. Within six years his father died, and the child was raised by his widowed mother who moved to the Govans section of Baltimore. A teenager in the roaring 20's, young Wasson graduated from Baltimore High School, 1926, and Johns Hopkins University, 1930.

After two unsatisfying years with Goodyear Tire Company, he entered Princeton Theological Seminary. At Commencement, on May 15, 1935, Wasson won the Hugh Davies Homiletics Prize as the best preacher in his class. That summer he went to St. Paul's Presbyterian Church, Philadelphia, as minister to youth and assistant to the pastor, Dr. Burleigh Cruikshank.

Within twenty-one months Rev. Wasson moved to Jeanette, Pennsylvania, to become the pastor of the First Presbyterian Church in that city. Installed April 8, 1937, the new preacher startled the 1,000-person congregation by wearing academic garb in the pulpit. His former boss, Dr. Cruikshank, came from Philadelphia to preach the sermon on this occasion.

Wasson's engagement to Miss M. Elizabeth Ellis, a graduate of Mount Holyoke College, was announced ten days later by her Philadelphia parents. The couple were married September 17 at St. Paul's Presbyterian Church, where they met during his short ministry there. At the Springhaven Country Club wedding reception a telegram arrived from the Jeanette congregation, signed by the Clerk of Sessions:

"To uphold the Presbyterian reputation of being cold a refrigerator has been installed in the manse as a gift from the congregation."

The Wassons stayed less than three years in Western Pennsylvania, but helped the church observe its fiftieth anniversary on September 29, 1939. During this period the clergyman's views were published in both the local newspaper and a national magazine. In the former he defended reciprocal international trade.[8] In the latter he wrote, "The church is the one agency that looks at the present scene with unblinking eye."[9]

On May 21, 1940, Wasson assumed his next charge when

installed as minister of the Wayne Presbyterian Church in suburban Philadelphia. Burleigh Cruikshank, still at St. Paul's, took part in the service. This time he delivered the charge to the new pastor.

World war came the following year. Wasson took special leave and toured Army camps in the South. In seven years at Wayne, 450 new members were added to the flock, and the church celebrated its seventy-fifth anniversary in June 1945. The maturing clergyman continued to reach beyond his immediate congregation through published writings[10] and local community service.[11] The Presbyterian General Assembly elected him a trustee, and *The Presbyterian* made him literary editor. He also achieved the chairmanship of the General Council's national magazine for pastors, *Monday Morning*.

In 1947 the Rye, New York, Presbyterian Church, organized 152 years earlier, considered a list of 100 ministers before calling S. Carson Wasson to its prestigious pulpit. It installed him as pastor, October 14, and the charge was given by Dr. Alexander Mackie, who traveled from his PMF office in Philadelphia to do the job.

Wasson wrote his friend and mentor that "the congregation was unanimously enthusiastic about the charge to the minister."[12] He thanked Mackie for coming; and he added, by postscript, "Now all I need is a D.D."[13]

Rev. and Mrs. Wasson became parents for the third time soon after their arrival in Rye. Samuel C., Jr., who had been born January 14, 1939; and Diana, born June 19, 1943; were joined by a brother, Ellis, who completed the family, December 31, 1947.

That same month the 1,100-member church was rededicated, following renovations which cost $200,000. The future insurance company president was clearly off to an impressive start in what would be his final pastorate.

Rye, N.Y., proved to be a strategic post for the man from Maryland. His ministry included congregational duties such as conducting a memorial service for the William Freng family of three, killed in a plane accident over Lake Michigan, which took fifty-eight lives in the worst disaster of United States commercial aviation. The historic church also gave Wasson the opportunity for writing and participation in denominational programs and international events. He enjoyed these activities and became an ecclesiastical organization man.

Presbyterian Life published his "Alive to God."[14] Freedoms Foundation at Valley Forge gave him a gold medal for his July 3, 1949, sermon.[15] Wasson went to Amsterdam, August 1948, as a delegate to the founding assembly of the World Council of Churches.

The mid-century decade brought election as a PMF corporator (1951) and director (1957); made him a trustee of Princeton Theological Seminary; and brought him election to the board of the National Presbyterian Foundation. He picked up not one but two D.D.'s as both Temple University, Philadelphia, and the College of the Ozarks, Clarksville, Arkansas, awarded him this honorary degree within five days in May, 1955.

Great satisfaction came from his work as a member of the Permanent Commission on Interchurch Relations. Dr. Wasson helped effect the merger between the United Presbyterian Church of North America and the Presbyterian Church to form the United Presbyterian Church in the U.S.A.

The New York Times printed a 1959 story headed

RYE MINISTER TO QUIT

in which readers discovered Rev. Wasson would resign in February to accept the executive vice-presidency of the Presbyterian Ministers' Fund.[16] A souvenir book of Wasson's suburban New York City preaching appeared soon after his departure for Philadelphia. *Eleven O'Clock Sunday Morning* contained twenty-seven sermons ranging from "Ye and Sympathy" and "Is the Bible True?" to "A Rising Standard of Living" and "Divine Compensation."[17]

The Wassons moved to the Philadelphia suburb of Rosemont, and bought a house on Orchard Way as the fledgling insurance company officer took up his work at 1809 Walnut Street in center city. SCW's diary contained this comment: "In a large house everyone can satisfy his own interest without interfering with someone else." Bricks placed in their toilet tanks saved water.

The successful pastor from an affluent congregation had little business experience. Corporate Secretary Horace T. Allen familiarized Dr. Wasson with company operations, and the neophyte augmented this on-the-job education with academic work at the University of Pennsylvania, where he took a course in accounting.

The executive apprentice, a good listener, learned quickly. He took advantage of every opportunity to gain experience and information. He manned the PMF exhibit booth at the 174th General Assembly held in Denver in May 1962. He also joined the newly-organized Conwell School of Theology's Board of Trustees. Nevertheless, the three years before Alexander Mackie's retirement were difficult for the future president. Office strain and stress caused eye problems and required frequent visits to an ophthalmologist.

Wasson's presidency began January 22, 1963. It was time for a change. PMF had assets of more than $86 million and annual sales in excess of $24 million. However, net gain from operations showed a cumulative six-figure loss for the five-year period ending December 31, 1962. The Fund had sustained a $129,304 deficit since 1957.

A first order of business came with lower rates for insurance protection. They were based upon the 1958 Commissioners Standard Ordinary Mortality Table with a 2½ percent interest assumption. Values continued to be on the

Net Level Premium basis with no loading factor built into the premium base.

All PMF employees were told about the Alexander Mackie Scholarship Fund with income from $100,000 to provide educational aid for their children. Applications were due "not later than May 29."[18]

Fund offices were informed of mechanical details effecting premium collection and policy services. Wisconsin and Minnesota were assigned to the Chicago office, North and South Dakota to Kansas City.[19]

Dr. Wasson also proposed the first in a series of by-law changes which would characterize his tenure. The Finance Committee received broader powers in an initial move. The following year a revised Article IX provided for the company to designate "other officers."[20]

The Million Dollar Round Table counted 3,240 members by this time, and held its 1963 meeting in Bermuda.

The freshman president wrote his first sales letter, which offered information about life insurance as the ideal way for a minister to ease the burden of his children's education. Addressed to "Dear Sir and Brother," the letter offered "practical, low cost figures and plans" for this purpose.[21]

Sales may be the bloodstream of a life insurance company, but unfortunately part of the vital flow runs in the opposite direction. Lapses and surrenders never cease. This first year of the Fund's new leadership brought letters on the subject from faroff places as well as nearby locations. Typical overseas communications included a letter from West Pakistan in which a minister terminated his coverage for two daughters recently married. A policyholder with the Gospel Literature Service, Bombay, India, turned in his protection "as necessity forces me to."[22] Rev. Choo Pyung Kim wrote from Korea, "Foreign currency problems prevent continuance of policy #129856."[23]

The company introduced a variety of special plans that October to stimulate new business: Ten Year and Twenty

Year Term, Family Income Term Rider, Reducing Term, Reducing Term to Sixty-five, and Family Renewable Term.[24] These new policies reflected the president's conviction that PMF contracts should be kept simple and free from the "gimmicks and gadgets" which "riddle the industry and confuse the buyer."[25]

The directors ended 1963 with a decision that the Presbyterian Ministers' Fund purchase the adjoining Penn Athletic Club building on the northwest corner of 18th and Walnut Streets for a price of $300,000. This action helped "round out" the corporate presence in the area and offered opportunities for future growth. Passing years, however, would not prove the move a particularly good investment, as successive commercial tenants vainly struggled to make a profit in the aging former mansion.

After a year's experience as president, Carson Wasson began 1964 with a resolution to honor William A. Schnader, Esq., who retired from the Board of Directors:

"His unerring and good judgment saved us from many a mistake. . . . His unfailing devotion to that which is true, that which is honest and that which is of good report, kept us ever with our faces toward the things that endure and are best."[26]

Schnader's place on the Board was taken by Donald L. Helfferich, President of Ursinus College. Schnader's place as Finance Committee Chairman (a position he held twenty-four years) was taken by J. B. Millard Tyson, Esq., a member of the departing leader's law firm.

The Presbyterian Ministers' Fund Finance Committee, greatly strengthened by J. Ross Snowden in 1875, had played a consistently important part in the life of the company. Alexander Mackie, who dominated almost everyone with whom he came in contact, bowed to Mr. Schnader's judgment when it came to investments. The committee functioned without the assistance of professional advisors and achieved a remarkable record. And 31.9¢ of each PMF

1963 income dollar came from this source. The average for all U.S. life insurance companies was only 22¢.

Despite this splendid showing, the aged Philadelphia corporation followed narrow investment policies. Only small loans were approved, and borrowers had to accept rigid terms for these loans. Dr. Wasson, with the cooperation of Mr. Tyson, encouraged the Finance Committee to take a broader view. New opportunities were explored, and PMF gradually made larger loans, at better rates, under more flexible conditions. It became a pioneer in the field of private placements, finding in these non-public issues higher returns for both bonds (loans up to twenty years) and equipment trust certificates (loans not over ten years).

"No one will lose a job,"[27] the directors assured employees at year's end as the Board voted to partially automate company operations by an order for an electronic marvel of the time, the IBM "360" computer. This action would have been unthinkable five years earlier. In fact, the former president refused to consider such a step. Rapid technological development overtook the Presbyterian organization within this short time; and, with a receptive chief executive in the president's office, the deed was done.

Two anniversaries were marked by Fund employees that winter. SCW finished five years on the payroll (three as executive vice-president), and Mrs. Fern Klapeshaw received recognition for completing forty-four years of work without missing a single day because of illness. She began February 22, 1921, in the PMF Commonwealth Building office, and thereby served under five presidents.[28]

Dr. Wasson did more than note occupational birthdays in the company personnel paper. He urged the Board to provide greater benefits for officers and staff. Later in 1965 the Fund began a Group Term Life Insurance plan which guaranteed each full-time employee coverage equal to one year's salary.[29]

It would be a mistake to suppose, however, the president

did not expect diligent subordinates. He noted late arrivals and early departures on the part of some workers with these words:

"I expect an *immediate* and *marked improvement* in the observance of the rules laid down in the Employees' Manual. If the improvement is not sufficient or does not show indications that it will be lasting, more drastic ways will be found to attain full cooperation."[30]

Concurrent with these internal changes came greater activity in the field. When Wasson succeeded Dr. Mackie, the Fund was licensed to do business in seventeen states. Soon Colorado and Minnesota were added; and, in 1965, Kansas and Iowa joined the list of operational areas. Before long Rev. Wesley W. Martin, Assistant Secretary in charge of the Atlanta office, was brought to Philadelphia and made Sales Vice-president.

Business was stimulated by the lifting of insurance limits:

1) from $50,000 to $75,000
2) Term from $25,000 to $50,000
3) Juvenile from $5,000 to $10,000.

Chaplains serving in Vietnam were eligible for $10,000 coverage, but could not purchase the Whole Life Special Five policy, obtain Family Income benefits, nor any other Term contracts.[31]

In the year Norman Mailer published his novel, *An American Dream*, PMF did its best to help clergymen realize their dream of better family protection. The company asked a postal-card question: "Does your insurance match your current responsibilities?" It urged ministers to review their policies as they would revise their wills to allow for changing circumstances. Three particular annuity plans were emphasized at this time: Joint Life and Last Survivor, Installment Refund, and Immediate Life.

The durability of the Fund received public notice at this time through a trade publication which carried a front-page story:

"24 Life Insurance Companies
In Business Over a Century."[32]

This article noted the existence of 1,600 mutual and stock United States life companies, pointed with pride that two dozen had survived more than 100 years, and concluded with mention of PMF as "the oldest" which "began business January 11, 1759."

Sales jumped 20 percent, 1966, from $35,322,565 to $42,470,025. Doing business in more states proved a factor, as did coordination by Vice-president Wesley Martin. A new policy also helped. Developed with assistance from consulting actuaries, Huggins and Company, the "Decreasing Whole Life Policy Paid Up At Age 70" sold well under its abbreviated name, "Family Security Policy." To help things along, the company spent $40,000 for a public relations and advertising program prepared by Gerald F. Selinger Associates, Philadelphia.

Important Board changes came with the Annual Meeting. D. Irvin Fulton and Rev. Robert W. Whyte retired as directors. Their places were taken by Hon. Brooks Hays, former U.S. Congressman from Arkansas, and Rev. Robert J. Lamont, senior minister of the famed First Presbyterian Church, Pittsburgh. Dr. Whyte's role as chairman was assumed by Rev. John R. Cunningham.

The methodical Dr. Wasson kept a daily diary as president. His 1966 volume began, "Being a continuance of some of the acts and none of the thoughts of S. Carson Wasson." The diary reveals few specific references to named company officers, directors, or corporators. It does furnish, on the other hand, a personal portrait of the company leader not discernible from official reports or corporate minutes.

A typical day began early. SCW took the 7:17 train from Bryn Mawr. He reached his office by 7:45, closed the door, and devoted an hour to reading *The New York Times* and doing its crossword puzzle. He was ready for business at 8:45 a.m.

The president seldom visited with the officers or other employees. Perhaps he remembered Dr. Mackie's strictures against the practice. Unless attending a Board meeting or lunching with a Fund committee at the Union League, the diarist usually ate the noon meal alone at the nearby Colonnade Cafeteria. He took the 4:24 train home.

Betsy Wasson set a good dinner table. Her husband regularly listed the menu with appreciative exclamations including, "Oh, Golly," "Oh, Boy," or "Glory Be." The Wassons often enjoyed roasted chestnuts before the meal.

Bird-watching with binoculars and furniture-making in a basement workshop were two hobbies the president pursued on a regular basis. He also did a great deal of housepainting. The record of most days ended with mention of "reading, listening to music, and early to bed."

Weekends at home found Dr. Wasson going to the local newsstand for the papers instead of having them delivered to the house. Weekends away as well as vacations were usually spent at a New Jersey cottage by the sea named "Summer Salts."

To supplement the group life coverage voted employees the previous year, the Board approved a 1966 pension plan for salaried workers. The considerate president rejoiced in the liberal benefits which required eight pages to describe.[33] The new plan represented great improvement over the existing arrangement adopted two decades before.

The president's 1967 diary included numerous references to the directors, as well it might. This fifth year of Wasson's tenure brought trouble a plenty:

"January 24—The Board met and I had to divulge a $750,000 loss in operations for 1966.

The Board members are magnificent to a man. They said they believed in me 100%. What a relief!"

By 3:30 that day, SCW, "exhausted by nervous debilitation of energy," rested in his ante-room after telephoning Betsy he "still had a job."

"February 6—Bernie Haines found they had found an error in an adding machine tape and that instead of a loss for 1966 we had a gain. Hallelujah! Praise the Lord!

February 8—There was a mistake in the annual statement. 1966 should have shown a $784,000 gain instead of a $750,000 loss. Outrageous!"

As a result of the fiasco the Board changed the annual meeting from January to March. This gave the actuarial department more time to prepare the year-end financial statement.

These were "doleful"[34] days when the recently-installed computer caused additional problems, and some thousand premium checks disappeared in the mail. In a "melancholy" mood,[35] Wasson announced the retirement of two Fund officers who had served "faithfully and well":[36] Corporate Secretary Horace T. Allen, and Medical Director Vincent Shipley, M.D. Allen also kept the books for the Conwell School of Theology.

The Fund elected C. Bradley Eisley as secretary, and William J. Erdman, M.D., medical director.

A further 1967 retirement, that of Frederick Schweitzer as a director, provided the opportunity to institute a gracious custom which reinforced the diary notes of those days:

"February 9—The directors are competent and kindly men.

May 11—The directors really enjoy each other. They are of many theological persuasions, and many different positions of church order, polity and liturgy; but they love each other because they love the Fund, and because above all they love Christ.

With that as a basis we can do our work together in protecting the clergyman and his family through life insurance. A glorious work.

June 8—The directors are a fine bunch."

Rev. Schweitzer took with him the handsome ladderback chair he had used as a member of the Board. His name and dates of service were inscribed on a brass plate affixed to the back.

PMF extended operations into five other states at this

time: New York, Oklahoma, South Carolina, Virginia, and Wisconsin. Admission to the first of these made necessary a third by-law revision of this administration. A rewritten Article One took the Fund beyond Protestants to a clientele described as those "who are actively engaged, on a career basis, in religious activities under the authority of a recognized religious body."[37] Priests and rabbis thus became prospects for the Presbyterian Ministers' Fund.

Occasional mistakes were made. One sales representative got into trouble with the law. Another committed suicide. A more serious corporate problem than these personnel misadventures was the Board's November 9 action "to erect a mutual fund."[38] Dr. Wasson included this step as one of several "cheerful themes" described to the corporators the following January. The "Harvest Fund" seemed like a good idea at the start. It would offer ministers an opportunity to supplement their fixed-dollar protection with inflation-fighting growth stocks. For a variety of reasons the Harvest Fund never realized its potential; and within a few years it would be sold to a Delaware investment company, Sigma Capital Shares, Inc.

Company crises and calamities notwithstanding, 1967 ended with significant gains for the Fund in sales, policies, assets, investment income percentage, mortality experience, and surplus. The five-year statistical comparison of SCW's incumbency looked like this:

	1962	1967
Assets	$ 86,036,486	$109,338,064
Policies	68,932	85,731
Insurance in force	$276,207,024	$420,258,671
Sales	$ 24,358,085	$ 53,146,583
Surplus	$ 6,271,545	$ 8,918,121

Insurance company prosperity has never been guaranteed. As we have noted, only a small number of firms entering the industry achieve consistent success. Momentum cannot be ignored completely, but progress and profit come from good management based upon aggressive sales, wise investments, and careful selection of risks. The Presbyterian Ministers' Fund, regardless of the person serving as president, paid consistent attention to all three with growing benefit to its policyholders and their dependents who enjoyed increasing dividends and family security at modest cost.

New business depends increasingly upon more than a representative's knowledge and salesmanship. Clergy prospects buy policies which meet current needs by providing flexible financial planning.

The Fund introduced new coverage opportunities once again toward the end of 1968 with a spread of four new policies with net level premium:

a) A term insurance rider with premiums payable on a 5-year basis.
b) A reducing term insurance rider providing term insurance for periods of 10, 15, or 20 years.
c) A reducing term insurance policy for mortgage protection providing term protection for periods of 20 or 25 years.
d) Family rider per unit providing term insurance on wife to husband's age 65.[39]

Simultaneously the Board voted an extra-budgetary $17,500 for purchase of an Addressograph-Multigraph machine with allied equipment "for publicity and printing of the business of the Fund."[40]

The same month PMF issued revised eligibility rules to better define the broader constituency required by revised company by-laws. Secretary C. Bradley Eisley noted:

"It is only by limiting our risks to those in religious occupations that we are able to keep down our mortality and to maintain our historic low ratio of actual to expected mortality."[41]

Ordained ministers of twenty-six denominations, from Adventists to United Church of Christ, made the list. Also approved were clergy of the Ethical Culture Society, Four Square Gospel Church, Greek Orthodox Church, and Latter Day Saints. Salvation Army officers, yes. Christian Scientist practitioners, no.

These decisions changed PMF's slogan from "An Interdenominational Life Insurance Company for all Protestant Ministers" to "A Non-denominational Life Insurance Company for the Clergy." These staid descriptions were a far cry from Prudential's "The Rock of Gibralter" or Mutual Trust Life's "As Faithful as Old Faithful," but business increased and insurance in force passed $500,000,000.[42] Medically-rated coverage was offered for the first time in the Fund's history through a re-insurance arrangement with the Insurance Company of North America.[43]

The chairmanship of the Board of Directors changed once again in 1968, with the retirement of John Rood Cunningham and the election of Millard Elwood Gladfelter. Dr. Gladfelter, the Lutheran Chancellor of Philadelphia's Temple University, and a member of the Board since 1957, thus began a decade of exceptional leadership in this important position.

As the 1960's drew to a close the president found satisfaction in progress made toward better salaries for PMF people. In addition to more liberal pensions and life insurance protection, at least a start had been made in the direction of lifting compensation to levels paid by competitors. In seven years, officers had received increases ranging from 10 to 70 percent. Pernicious inflation demanded other measures which led to 5 percent cost-of-living raises for all clerical workers in both 1968 and 1969.

As the new decade began both corporators and directors gave the president "a rising vote of thanks for his excellent work."[44] Wasson's accomplishments within the company were matched by community recognition of his volunteer interests. He served on the boards of numerous Christian organizations including the Philadelphia Presbytery and the General Assembly of the Presbyterian Church, USA. He continued Alexander Mackie's work with the Friends of Old

Pine, the Presbyterian Historical Society, the Canterbury Cleric, and the Conwell School of Theology. He particularly enjoyed the monthly meetings of the United Presbyterian Church Foundation at 475 Riverside Drive, New York City.

SCW, now in his sixty-second year and looking forward to retirement in 1973, took this time to urge the Board of Directors' appointment of a committee to select his successor: Chairman Millard E. Gladfelter; Theodore A. Distler; J. B. Millard Tyson; and Arthur M. Adams. Within a year the choice would be made, but kept secret within the Board until a later date.

Other 1970 changes among the officers took effect without delay. January 1, Franklin M. Henzel went from Comptroller to operations vice-president. Nicholas M. Saitto, former assistant secretary, became investments vice-president. Treasurer (Mrs.) Martha G. Eppihimer retired on April 30, after fourteen years in that office and twenty-eight years of PMF employment. Her resignation was received "with reluctance," for she had demonstrated both "energy and accuracy."[45]

Mrs. Eppihimer was preceded in the position by Mrs. M. L. Ehrenzeller, elected treasurer 1945. Jean K. Knapp took the place of the departed chief financial officer to be the third member of her sex to hold this rank in Fund history. PMF, long before the current feminist revolution, had been a pioneer in naming women officials. Miss A. M. Clifford held the corporate secretaryship, 1909-1921, to be followed by Miss M. S. Johnson, who retained the office for twenty-five years. Jean K. Knapp, therefore, became the sixth female to achieve executive status with the perceptive company. Before long she would receive further promotion.

Mrs. Knapp came to PMF with Alexander Mackie, for whom she had done stenographic work as Miss Jean Kevis, high school student, during the final years of his Tully Memorial pastorate. When Mackie went to the Fund as president, she became his secretary at 1807 Walnut Street.

The ill-fated Harvest Fund, entered into as part of the euphoria about mutual funds experienced in the late 1960's, received legal status through registration with the Securities and Exchange Commission. Shares were first offered for sale in Pennsylvania and Delaware.

July 1970 the Wassons traveled to Japan for the International Insurance Conference. Burglars broke into their Rosemont home while they were overseas.

That September the directors voted to purchase a miniature replica of the Liberty Bell to call future meetings to order and to "proclaim liberty throughout the land."[46]

America's oldest life insurance company held its 212th annual meeting the following spring. News released at that time appeared in the local press under this headline:

OLDEST INSURER THRIVING
DESPITE TAXES, POLICY LOANS[47]

Readers learned of increases in sales to $66,000,000; insurance in force to $550,810,000; and assets to $123,160,000. J. B. Millard Tyson declared, "Clergymen aren't generally considered financially sophisticated, but they showed they were pretty smart."[48]

PMF success came from its individual management of the basic industry credo described in a contemporary book about another company. Life insurance, it pointed out, is based upon the fact of:

"an average duration of life and a calculable cost for insurance. The level annual premium had been devised for the distribution of the cost of the risk."[49]

The presidential succession committee completed its work and presented the directors with an employment contract which would "begin no later than October 1, 1973." The next chief executive's name did not appear in the minutes.[50]

With Fund leadership continuity assured, the Board approved a further by-law revision to create a new committee on "Budget and Salary."[51] Certain special committees were also formed on a temporary basis with directors grouped for emphasis upon Building Study, Branch Offices, Personnel and Public Relations. The latter seemed important as PMF began its own advertising department under the guidance of Rev. Charles D. Robison, who came to the company from the Narberth, Pennsylvania, Presbyterian Church where he served as assistant minister.

Philadelphia can claim both America's first life insurance company and the birth of modern advertising. It was John Wanamaker who had placed the first full-page newspaper ad (in the *Philadelphia Record*, December 1878).[52] For this reason the Fund's decision to handle its own promotional program seemed particularly fitting.

Robison, who married the president's daughter, introduced a thirty-three-page advertising plan early in Dr. Wasson's final year of leadership. Its chief goal: support for sales which needed to increase at a brisker pace. The directors approved a panoply of projects ranging from PMF bookplates, seminary posters, and new brochures, to magazine advertising in such publications as *American Baptist*, *Christianity Today*, and *The Living Church*.

One of the first advertisements featured a photograph of children on a beach raising their hands to a flock of seagulls overhead. It carried the caption, "NOW THAT YOUR CHILDREN ARE STARTING TO REACH OUT." Another early ad portrayed a nun holding her PMF policy with the question, "Why did Sister Mary Margaret buy life insurance from Presbyterians?" A companion piece posed the same question for "Rabbi Steinberg."

SCW had long dreamed of erecting a new high-rise office building on the northwest corner of 18th and Walnut Streets to replace the former Penn Athletic Club building, several adjacent stores, and existing Fund facilities. The skyscraper would give PMF a new home and provide substantial income from rental space to other firms. One of the directors' special committees studied the matter intensely. A combination of factors, however, kept the idea from becoming a reality. Of major concern was the number of other office structures already planned or actually under construction by this time. June 8, 1972, the Fund leased the former club edifice ten years to Binswanger-Herman Company for extensive interior improvements and rental to commercial tenants.

Wasson, with retirement scheduled the following year, made an extra effort in several directions. He authorized Vice-president and Actuary Bernard S. Haines to employ a student assistant to strengthen that important part of the company. Richard C. Dutton started work July 1st. The president brought about further improvement in employee benefits. This time pensions were liberalized. He also paid attention to sales but without a developed marketing strategy.

The Million Dollar Round Table met that year at the Queen Elizabeth Hotel, Montreal. The industry's prestige sales organization now numbered 8,361 members in contrast to only 3,340 the decade before. Fund sales for the period showed consistent increase, but the rate of growth curved downward. Between 1962-1967 they more than doubled from $24,358,085 to $53,146,583. Between 1967-1972 they climbed only 32% to $70,991,201. During the last year they barely exceeded the previous annual period.

The number of sales representatives increased to sixty-two and eight regional managers were in the field in the United States and Canada. A new policy appeared known as "$25 Thousand Minimum Life Paid-Up at 95." Most ministers carried low amounts of coverage. This larger protection sum sold for a premium which reflected reduced company costs for higher dollar values.

The final item of business for the Board of Directors that year came December 14 through its revelation that Rev.

Robert J. Lamont would become PMF's next president beginning October 1, 1973.[53]

This arrangement meant Dr. Wasson made a final report to the corporators six months before relinquishing his post. At the 214th Annual Meeting the president talked about "the danger of corporate senility" for PMF as he recounted his effort "to fight the good fight, to hold aloft the torch, and to keep the Fund on the move."[54]

In preparation for things to come a special Board committee of Rev. Arthur M. Adams, John A. Baird, Jr., and Robert Lamont reviewed the by-laws and job descriptions of all officers.

Directors' fees were paid by check for the first time beginning with the June meeting.

The company offered a WATS (wide area telephone service) line which policyholders could use for toll-free calls to the home office.

S. Carson Wasson welcomed his successor with the admission that he was "content to see the changing of the guard."[55]

CHAPTER FOURTEEN

Business with Biblical Values (1973-1980)
Robert J. Lamont, D.D., President

Let us with a gladsome mind

Praise the Lord, for He is kind;

For His mercies aye endure,

Ever faithful, ever sure.

John Milton

"As far as Americans are concerned, life insurance is well-nigh universal," an industry publication recently declared. "Along with the automobile and the telephone, life insurance is part of the way of life of the American family."[1] Simultaneously a Phoenix Mutual Life official revealed the dramatic expansion of the 1950's when he reported:

"In a four year period no fewer than 836 new insurers began business—almost double the total number of companies existing in the United States at the close of World War II."[2]

As the Federal government confirms that of each one hundred men starting their productive lives (age 25) thirty-six die within forty years, and fifty-four others are not self-supporting at sixty-five; is it any wonder "insurance" conveys "assurance" and stability to the average citizen?

Yet Presbyterian Ministers' Fund faced great challenges when Robert J. Lamont took the president's chair in October 1973. Costs were too high; sales were weak; and inflation outpaced earnings. The company could no longer be run on Alexander Mackie's formula of mortality advantage and investment income. AM offered a combination of low premiums; high cash values in the early years; and low dividends. This no longer sufficed. Something had to be done.

Lamont did not consult a well-publicized clairvoyant who offered card and tea leaf readings to help her clients with all their problems. Instead he found a tattered Bible in the president's desk. Inside the front cover he discovered this note:

"No man can be president of this corporation without this Bible. It was used by Perry Allen, Matthew J. Hyndman, and the undersigned. Search the Scriptures.

Alexander Mackie
January 28, 1963"

RJL had the volume rebound with the corporate seal on the cover for use in future corporators' meetings. He also searched the Scriptures and found Ezekiel 36:11 particularly pertinent: "God will do unto us better than at our beginnings."

From his experience as a corporator and director, the president knew the Fund enjoyed a low mortality experience. Careful risk selection, clergy longevity, and seminary students buying insurance at lower ages than previous generations assured it. He also knew a PMF representative might have to travel one hundred miles between sales calls. In the words of Bernard S. Haines, vice-president and actuary at the time: "Dr. Lamont began to learn what made PMF tick. He researched the company from A to Z. His first three years were learning years."[3]

RJL did more than study investments, operations, and sales. From the start, he looked beyond management to leadership. He began the quest for a company dream. It would involve corporate planning on a scale never before attempted at the Fund. It would be based upon a Biblical value system which had crystalized in his mind while he was still a pastor in Pittsburgh. Management basics from books loaned him by corporate executive friends reminded the president-elect of lessons learned in Sunday school. Contemporary office credos seemed similar to the ancient teachings about talents, laborers, and stewardship.

Fifty-four years old when installed as company president, Dr. Lamont approximated the average election age of his thirteen predecessors featured in this book. A Philadelphian, born April 12, 1919, Robert Lamont graduated from Olney High School and Maryville (Tennessee) College before entering Princeton Theological Seminary. While a student there, Philadelphia Presbytery ordained him, June 23, 1943; and he assumed the first of his three pastorates, First Presbyterian Church, Darby, Pennsylvania. Four years later he moved to the manse of the nearby Narberth Presbyterian Church, where he remained until 1953. During this time he was elected to the General Council of the General Assembly.

These experiences led to a call from the famous First Presbyterian Church, Pittsburgh. His ministry there took the annual budget to more than a million dollars and the endowment to four times that figure. Through extensive radio and television preaching the minister discovered constituencies beyond the immediate parish. His popular Tuesday luncheons, attended by more than 1,000 men, helped develop an outreach to the Pittsburgh business community. Lamont became chairman of the city's Labor-Management Council. At the suggestion of Westinghouse Electric Company President Donald Burnham the minister took a six-month Executive Training Course offered by that firm. The intrepid pastor achieved recognition from the Junior Chamber of Commerce, which named him 1969 "Man of the Year in Religion."[4]

These experiences, and all the others of a thirty-year ministry, were shared by his wife, Edna Weisner Lamont. High school sweethearts, they were married December 26, 1942. The groom reached the church on time, but barely — having come from the hospital where he had undergone an emergency appendectomy a few days before. The Lamonts had four children, one of whom died in infancy.

Mrs. Lamont did not rejoice when her husband was first approached to take the PMF presidency. He felt the challenge of business success; and, through his service as a corporator (since 1962) and a director (from 1967) recognized the Fund as a specialized ministry. His wife, however, was troubled at "leaving the church." Lamont did not accept the initial offer, but the committee practiced patience and renewed the invitation eight months later.

During the interval Edna Lamont, a person of uncommon spiritual perception and extensive Scriptural knowledge, had a change of heart and mind. She found comfort in a Bible verse which seemed to describe their situation and authenticate acceptance of the surprising career opportunity which had come their way.[5]

This time Dr. Lamont accepted the job with the proviso he would ask professionals to measure his executive ability and determine if he would enjoy the work. On his own initiative he had Arthur Hays Associates test both capacities and received definite assurance on each count. Thus prepared, the Lamonts moved back to Philadelphia and bought a house in suburban Bryn Mawr.

Michael Novak, a perceptive modern writer, notes:

"The principle of history is liberty. The liberty of human beings, individually, to imagine a vision, to conceive plans and to execute actions, creates the possibility of history."[6]

Robert Lamont's vision and plans for the Fund centered upon making the company ideal to buy from and ideal to work for achieved by moving beyond the routine of daily business decisions to a new level of planned executive guidance. The new president determined to go beyond Horatio Alger qualities of goodness, courage, and luck to create leadership involving genuine expertise. He knew the life insurance industry depended too much upon financial momentum and too little on long-range planning. He also realized PMF had to overcome its traditional complacency about size and its lack of market aggressiveness.

RJL led the group singing at Dr. Wasson's testimonial dinner, October 24, 1973, but as the Fund family saluted the former president with "For He's a Jolly Good Fellow," the new chief executive officer was thinking about the challenges of the future and how best to meet them. Blessed with the self-esteem needed by any successful leader, Dr. Lamont recognized from the beginning of his tenure the need for outside help. He did not hesitate to seek specialized knowledge from management and marketing consultants.

The extraordinary results achieved in the past eight years are best explained by a review of the Fund's current approach to operations, investments, and sales as developed by the new president.

A dictionary equates "operations" with mode of action. The life insurance industry uses the word to designate those home office functions which provide policyholder service. At PMF these responsibilities are shared by Actuary Richard Dutton and Vice-presidents C. Bradley Eisley, William J. Erdman II, M.D., and Franklin Henzel. In 1974 the number of Fund office employees reached 137. Within years twice the dollar volume of new protection was handled by ninety-six.

Two hundred years took the corporation from a single eighteenth century policy to the impressive array of protection contracts offered in the 1970's. Francis Alison purchased a single annuity for his widow, but his modern counterparts may choose from a variety of coverage including ordinary life, endowment, annuity, and term. Alison's "Indenture" took only thirty printed lines to confirm the agreement. Contemporary PMF policies reach ten pages of fine print.

Policy service at 1809 Walnut Street, Philadelphia, has come a long way in fifty years. From the green eyeshade manual posting days before the Second World War, through the gradual introduction of calculators between 1950-1965, to the computers of the last decade, more and better work is done by fewer people at lower costs.

Successful company operations depend heavily upon actuarial skill and medical knowledge. Policies are built around accurate mortality mathematics which relate directly to life expectancy experience. The 1970's have increased the Fund's actuarial strength and medical sophistication. Enlightened management has made the most of these advances with the result that, by 1979, 20 percent of all PMF contracts were issued to substandard medical risks.

The Fund, however, has wisely avoided the "rampant substandard underwriting which afflicts the industry today."[7] The Lamont administration has made it possible to insure some who previously would have been ineligible for PMF protection, while maintaining its traditional conservative posture. A. B. Best Company, analysts of the industry since 1899, reports "Careful selection and underwriting of business has produced a very favorable mortality experience."[8]

Despite office mechanization, people provide the basic factor in successful home office activity. Giving these PMF men and women a vital sense of personhood has brought Dr. Lamont one of his greatest satisfactions, and fulfilled an essential objective of his management credo.

Unlike Carson Wasson, who worked three years at the Fund learning the business as Dr. Mackie's understudy, Robert Lamont assumed the presidency with different ideas. He would lead the company by setting the proper climate, getting people to work together, and making decisions within a Biblical value system to produce corporate financial success. His leadership style reflects the attitude of contemporary business writer Marvin Bower, who observes:

"Managing is the activity of determining the objectives of an organization and then guiding the people and other resources of the organization in the successful achievement of these objectives."[9]

The president created the desired environment through a series of acts which grew out of the final Corporate Development Task Force report, January 5, 1975. Building upon an Affirmative Action Policy to assure equal opportunity to all qualified persons "on the basis of merit alone," the company made the physical facilities "beautiful and functional";[10] started raising the salaries of the better-organized work force; and urged employees to continue their education.

Richard J. Cifelli became the Fund's first internal auditor. Walter J. Clyde was named controller and would soon be a vice-president. Jean Knapp moved up from assistant to the president to corporate secretary. Others moved out. The home office work force fell 32 percent through retirement, general attrition, and some terminations. The president reported these were handled with "understanding, concern and generous settlements."[11]

Unlike the dreadful 1920's experience of the British Admiralty, where ships in commission dropped 67 percent while officials and clerks increased 78 percent,[12] the Presbyterian Ministers' Fund in the 1970's achieved greater production with fewer employees. PMF conducted a work measurement and management program to evaluate jobs, work flow, and individual productivity. It was called Project Pride. Each worker felt a sense of pride in being part of a company which recognized every individual as a unique creation of God, and provided opportunity for the employee to exercise his or her full potential.

Dr. Lamont and his associates have built a commercial Christian community based upon personal responsibility, the taking of risks, and the acceptance of authority. ID cards permit the bearer to pass building security guards. They also symbolize a precious fellowship.

Every U.S. corporation can claim a board of directors, but only one enjoys a premier governing body called corporators. PMF's distinctive arrangement began in 1759 and continues to this day.

Until 1876, when President J. Ross Snowden created the Board of Directors, the corporators ran the company. For the past 104 years these "Members of the Fund"[13] have played a lesser role. Today the corporators meet annually, elect the directors from among their number, and have the power to amend the by-laws.

The initial group numbered twelve, five ministers and

seven laymen. All were leading churchmen, whether active in the pulpit or the pew. This approximate mix has been maintained for 221 years with about half the Board ordained and the remainder from commerce, law, and other professions. From the original dozen members, the group grew to thirty-four by 1890. In 1895 it reached fifty-seven, and since 1905 has been maintained at a maximum of sixty persons. The corporators had become casual about their affiliation at the start of this century. Actual attendance or a proxy vote were first required in 1902. This imposed duty caused a number of resignations, but the company benefitted and participation improved at once.

From "Acker" to "Young," 469 persons have served as corporators. Six were named Allen; five, Patterson; ten, Smith. Bishops and judges, captains and colonels, doctors and lawyers have worked together with gospel ministers to guide the company. Between 1789 and 1935 twenty-one corporators functioned as moderator of the Presbyterian General Assembly. Ten have filled the office of Stated Clerk. The first women elected were: Lois Stair, 1974; Colleen T. Evans, 1976; and Jean K. Knapp, 1977.

The present corporators represent some twelve denominations, but half of the group are Presbyterian. Corporators come from fourteen states and the District of Columbia. The majority are Pennsylvanians. Senior citizens predominate among the members. A study of forty-five of the most active revealed one over ninety, six in their eighties, and the majority between sixty and seventy-nine. Only two were under fifty. Corporators are elected for an indefinite term and may actually serve for life unless absent without excuse for two successive annual meetings.

Without exception, the members prize their relationship to the Fund. "It's a pleasure to serve," says Hurst R. Anderson. "PMF is a great company and I am glad to be insured with it and be a part of it," explains Rev. Russell Bishop. "An honor," adds Rev. Donald K. Campbell.

These sentiments explain the low turnover among the sixty corporators now on the active list. At the present time a roster of ninety-eight men and women eligible for nomination awaits future consideration of the Board as openings occur.

Present corporators who are not also directors include Eugene Carson Blake, former General Secretary of the World Council of Churches; George P. Jenkins, Chairman of Metropolitan Life; James I. McCord, President of Princeton Theological Seminary; and Hamilton M. Redman, former Vice-president of the Berkshire Life Insurance Company.

Corporators, a current survey confirms, think of life insurance as family protection rather than retirement security by a margin of eight to one. They believe a minister should carry coverage equal to three years' salary, and that the ravages of inflation make this protection more important than ever before.

The same opinion poll reveals a definite concensus regarding the strengths of the Fund: low costs, conservative investments, trustworthy agents, and a family atmosphere throughout the organization. The corporators give Dr. Lamont high marks for his outstanding performance and the remarkable results achieved during the first seven years of his presidency.

Whether from California, Florida, New York, or other parts of the country, these faithful men and women acknowledge their position as watchdogs, take seriously the responsibility to elect capable directors, and rejoice in the role of advocate for the company which has been so successful with the slogan, "He that soweth bountifully shall reap bountifully."

Collection of premium incomes comes first for any insurance company, but advantageous investment of this money is vital for consistent success. The Fund's investment record traditionally has surpassed industry averages, and the past decade brought an even better performance. Three measurements prove it. 1979 PMF investments produced 41.5 percent of each income dollar in contrast to a figure of only 26.2 percent for all U.S. life companies. The same year Fund investments yielded 7.80 percent as compared to 7.78 percent for the industry. Finally, a national reporting service told its clients PMF did better than the nation's twenty-five largest life companies in the matter of investment earnings surpassing each $100 required to maintain policy reserves, $292.40 vs $242.19.

"Today few business men are consulted for opinions. In their stead we have the apercus of rock stars, media mandarins, professional pundits, and bureaucratic boffins,"

claims a contemporary social critic.[14] Robert J. Lamont feels otherwise; and, as did his two immediate predecessors, depends upon the experience and judgment of the company's Finance Committee. Credit for the Fund's investment record goes to this group of lawyers and corporate executives from the Board of Directors. The men meet weekly with RJL and Vice-president Nicholas M. Saitto. Without professional investment counsel they have outdone the experts through a shrewd blend of prudence and imagination which provides impressive income from this source.

Corporator John Templeton, one of America's most noted financial authorities, serves as a consultant to the Finance Committee. Book value of all mortgages, bonds, and stocks stood at more than $159 million December 31, 1979. Thirty-one million dollars in policy loans accounted for the other major segment of corporate assets, and these commitments deserve special mention.

As M. Albert Linton observed a generation earlier:

"A life insurance loan is quite different from an ordinary loan. The policy contains a guarantee that the company will make loans at a named rate of interest according to a schedule contained in the policy extending into the future for a generation or more."[15]

This guarantee caused trouble throughout the industry in April 1980, when rampant inflation created sensational money market opportunities for policyholders. Many borrowed against their protection at 6 percent and placed the proceeds in other investments paying three times this amount. Equitable Life (with 25 percent of its assets in policy loans) and other leading companies were forced to liquidate securities to pay these obligations.[16]

PMF (with only 17 percent of its assets so invested) fared better; but enough of its insured caught the speculation fever to justify the Board approving an 8 percent loan rate to begin early in 1981. Low interest policy loans are particularly helpful to clergy; and, in this sense, reflect the Fund's historic position of service to God's servants. They can cause company problems, however, and also jeopardize protection of loved ones. Many policies with big loans lapse.

The Presbyterian Ministers' Fund corporate headquarters building contains a room with fifty-two brass plates on the walls. The building is named for Francis Alison. The room is named for Perry Allen. The metal plaques contain names and service dates of the most recent former directors. The Board meets here each month, except for July and August, to "do all things not inconsistent with the Fund's Charter or these BY-LAWS which in its judgment are necessary and proper for accomplishing the purposes of the Fund."[17]

The power and influence of the Fund Board has varied during the past one hundred years. It fell to a low level during the Mackie period when that determined individual kept conversation away from serious matters and focused upon funny stories. Chairman Millard Gladfelter brought perception and panache to the Board through the 1960's; and the present posture represents a stimulating, participative arrangement thoughtfully fostered by Dr. Lamont who, like his predecessors, reached the president's office through election by his colleagues.

275

Lamont's board room portrait includes three clues to his management style: the Bible, for evangelical emphasis; his layman's collar, for business orientation; and a clearly-visible wrist watch to signify a sense of time. RJL's first seven years in office confirm his possession of the qualities considered most important in a company head. One of these, "Interdependence," describes his role with the directors:

"Stands on his own, but invites information, criticism, and cooperation from others. Can yield temporarily to the lead of a more competent, specialized person without feeling loss of leadership role."[18]

Board members receive copious reports at the monthly meetings. Management furnishes more than twenty pages of statistical data: an operations summary, balance sheet, investment income analysis (as well as capital gains and losses), actual and budgeted general expenses, sales performance by age, denomination, and region, as well as a five-year historical comparison. Company officers attend the Executive Committee get-together which comes first. Deaths within five years of the date of policy are noted in some detail. A recent compendium included two auto accident fatalities and one murder!

The directors serve on five committees where most of the Board work is done. In addition to the already-mentioned Executive and Finance groups, the members give their attention to auditing, budget, and salary, and the Alexander Mackie Scholarship Fund.

Each director is elected for three years, and may be chosen for additional terms until his seventy-fifth birthday. The 1970's was a time of multiple retirements as eight men reached this age. The departing included: Methodist Bishop Fred Pierce Corson; Paul J. Cupp, Chairman of the Board, Retired, American Stores Company; Dr. Theodore A. Distler, former Franklin and Marshall College President; Dr. Millard E. Gladfelter, Chancellor, Temple University; Dr.

Donald L. Helfferich, Chancellor, Ursinus College; The Hon. Brooks Hays, previously U.S. Congressman from Arkansas; Baltimore industrialist, Arthur N. Morris; and Dr. Norman Vincent Peale.

Two directors died during the decade: S. Carson Wasson, 1976; and Arthur M. Adams, 1979. Former President Wasson and Board Chairman Adams (Dean, Princeton Theological Seminary) served nineteen and twenty-five years respectively. Wasson, in the period following his presidential term, devoted much time and great effort to helping the Friends of Old Pine and carrying on the work there begun by Alexander Mackie. Adams, an experienced and knowledgeable Board member, who performed capably in many previous responsibilities, had less than two years as chairman. Both men fell to cancer, and the former's demise carried a poignant overtone by which the inveterate tobacco user ended a board room custom of several generations. In 1922 Perry S. Allen asked the men to reimburse their associate, William S. Furst, for the cigars he furnished for smoking at directors' meetings. In 1976 Robert J. Lamont decorated the board room table with signs which said

PLEASE
NO SMOKING

One of America's most gifted pulpit men and Minister-at-Large of the Hollywood, California, First Presbyterian Church, Rev. Raymond I. Lindquist, heads the Board today, having been elected chairman in 1980. Lindquist became a corporator in 1947, and a director the following year. Rev. Francis B. Sayre, Jr., former Dean, the Washington Cathedral, and currently a director of the Woodrow Wilson Foundation, continues to hold the secretaryship of the Board—an office to which he brings both diligence and distinction. J. B. Millard Tyson, a director and Finance Committee Chairman, also serves as corporate vice-president, legal counsel.

After five years as president, Dr. Lamont told the corporation he believed the Board of Directors to be "among the finest in corporate life in America," and expressed appreciation for its "incredible combination of business know-how and financial acumen, blended with understanding, compassion, and sensitivity to people and their needs."[19]

Visions of department store bargain sale crowds waiting outside from dawn until opening time and then storming the merchandise counters in a frenzy of buying do not come to mind when life insurance is mentioned. Although this product can be one of life's greatest bargains, most people agree it's a good thing, but defer a decision to purchase. Buying a refrigerator or television set brings immediate pleasure, while purchasing future financial protection is similar to making a will and something to be done later.

Curtis L. North, a colorful agent of Aetna Life in the early days of that company, improved his sales of life insurance by also offering sewing machines and Bibles on the side.[20] Today such a varied product line would be unthinkable. To make matters worse, even a PMF typical policy application now contains dozens of family and health questions which demand accurate answers. A prospective buyer must give details if afflicted by maladies from diabetes to diverticulitis, he must reveal any alcoholism or drug addiction, and report his or her scuba diving and motorcycle racing activity!

The 1970's aggravated traditional life insurance selling trials in three new areas: vicious inflation, consumerism, and social malaise took their toll. A trade journal offered twelve specific suggestions to help keep the agent from being "literally squeezed out of the business."[21] Bankers Life Company built an advertising program on the consumerism theme by frankly confronting the issue in a national magazine,[22] and the Federal Trade Commission issued a *Life Insurance Cost Disclosure* report which appalled some readers.[23] A social scientist defined the third obstacle as:

"A distrust of action, a denigration of success—such appear to constitute the chief strands of social thought of the day. None of this allows much leeway for the use of intelligence, courage, and resolution on the part of individuals."[24]

PMF, with a restricted clientele, conservative management, and low costs, suffered less than the industry as a whole or even some of the giants. At the same time the Presbyterian Fund could not completely escape these blows, and realized it must heed the ominous warnings of an even grimmer economic future. President Lamont responded to this challenge with a 1974 Corporate Development Plan of intensive company-wide self-study which he correctly forecast would "position PMF for continuing leadership in the decade ahead of us."[25]

Sales received rigorous scrutiny as part of a broader concept-marketing. A consultant, C. R. Stigelman, was retained to conduct a marketing audit of the Fund. It included actuarial foundations, policy design, advertising, and pricing as well as actual salesmanship. The Task Force which initiated operations improvements had corresponding impact on sales.

Within a year PMF introduced a quartet of new policies which found favor with the religious professional. Renewable Term went with the Flexible Annuity Plan to provide a combination of low-cost, high-value family protection with a tax-sheltered retirement opportunity for the minister. The flexible premium feature of the deferred annuity proved popular from its introduction in 1977. The Student Protector policy guaranteed seminarians $25,000 of convertible term coverage for the equivalent of only 10¢ a day.

The marketing of these products by Communications Vice-president Alfred A. O'Shields, and a better-compensated sales force took the Fund, during Robert Lamont's first eight years as president, to record levels of achievement in a remarkably short time. It required 233 years (1717-1950) to reach $100,000,000 total insurance in force; ten years (1951-1960) to double this figure; ten additional years (1961-1970) to reach $500,000,000; and only eight more (1971-1978) to hit $1 billion.

This tremendous surge in business took total assets from $144,775,684 to $233,547,830 between 1973 and 1980. It also brought annual net gains from operations in excess of a million dollars, beginning in 1976; two million dollars, 1977; and three million dollars, 1979 and 1980. Nothing like it occurred in more than 220 years since incorporation of the Fund!

Is it any wonder Wittreich Associates, Philadelphia psychological consultants, found leadership to be "RJL's dominant life theme"? Three colleges and two theological seminaries elected him a trustee. Six colleges conferred honorary degrees; and he joined the boards of the American Bible Society and the University of Pennsylvania-Presbyterian Medical Center. His prescient reorganization paid off with lower costs, higher earnings, and increased dividends for policyholders. By the end of the 1970's PMF ranked forty-ninth among all U.S. mutual life companies.[26]

Warren Wittreich also noted Lamont's vitality and how he had to "struggle to relax." This quality enabled the president to find the time and energy to lecture in thirty seminaries across the country, and also to maintain a consistent preaching schedule. Despite a serious illness which required hospitalization, RJL pressed on with his dreams for the Fund as ominous warnings crowded the business landscape. One authority charged:

"The industry fails to understand traditional products are not appropriate to the needs of the typical buyer, nor are they economically viable, nor is the life insurance distribution system financially sound."[27]

While another dolefully predicted intensified competition would cause a "massive shake-out in which at least a third of today's companies will not survive the 1980's."[28]

The unsatisfactory Canadian business was sold for $200,000. A Presidential Study Group examined the Fund's Regional Office System, and was followed by another effort called SPACO (for Strategic Planning for Advancement of Corporate Objectives). SPACO leader Jack B. McElhaney, Jr., former sales coordinator and then vice-president, administration, made it clear that the program came into being because of the president's passion for excellence rather than from financial or management crisis. The thrust of SPACO is marketing for 1984 and beyond. It represents a company determination to not only maintain but improve PMF's historic leadership position for a company its size. "Change" may be "whirling through the life insurance business, converting it to something far different from what it was even five years ago,"[29] but the Fund intends to be ready. Strategies are already formed to meet new objectives including: maintenance of present 3.7 lapse rate; 60 percent increase of first-year premium income; and 8 percent net investment income return.

Psychologist Wittreich discovered something else about the president: "God's scrutiny is the final judgment in his life." This finding is significant as RJL and the Fund face an economic and social environment in which a financial reporter recently stated: "Life insurance companies have to be plenty smart to make money."[30] It means that beyond brains, energy, and work Dr. Lamont resolves the Presbyterian Ministers' Fund will hold fast to its purpose of saving religious professionals from economic disaster, helping them face retirement with dignity, and providing resources for the support of family survivors.

The president and the Board are determined that the company will continue to reflect its Scriptural credo of bountiful sowing and bountiful reaping, and thereby reaffirm a 221-year record as a cornucopia of wealth and a religious horn of plenty.

NOTES

Chapter One

[1] PMF, 175th Anniversary Leaflet, 1934.

[2] *World Book Encyclopedia*, 1952, Vol. 13, p. 6267.

[3] Burt, Struthers, *Philadelphia, Holy Experiment* (N.Y.: Doubleday), 1945, p. 229.

[4] *Ibid.*, p. 143.

[5] Mease, James, M.D., *Pictures of Philadelphia*, p. 355.

[6] Burt, p. 38.

[7] N.Y.: William Norton & Co., Inc., 1978, pp. 31, 32.

[8] "The Oldest Life Insurance Company in America," an address delivered January 27, 1902, at the 143rd meeting of the corporators of Presbyterian Ministers' Fund, p. 3.

[9] Nelli, Humbert O., "A New Look at the History of Personal Insurance," *Journal of the American Society of Chartered Life Underwriters*, Vol. XXXIII, No. 3 (July, 1969), p. 53.

[10] *Ibid.*

[11] Stuart, George H., Jr., *Ibid.*

[12] Mackie, Alexander, *Facile Princeps* (Lancaster, PA.: Lancaster Press, 1956), p. 108.

[13] Stuart, *Ibid.*

[14] "Older Than the General Assembly," *The Presbyterian Tribune*, May 26, 1938, p. 11.

[15] Slosser, Gaius Jackson, "The History of North American Presbyterians," *The Journal of the Presbyterian Historical Society*, Vol. XXXV, March, 1957, No. 1, p. 5.

[16] Presbytery Minutes.

[17] *Ibid.*, Sept. 20, 1710.

[18] *Ibid.*, Sept. 8, 1714.

[19] Hostetter, M. M., *Ibid.*, p. 11.

[20] Presbytery Minutes.

[21] The Synod of Philadelphia, Minutes, Sept. 19, 1717.

[22] Minutes, Sept. 23, 1717.

[23] Minutes, Sept. 18, 1718.

[24] Mackie, Alexander, *Facile Princeps*, p. 66.

[25] Synod Minutes, Sept. 17, 1719.

[26] Mackie, *Ibid.*, p. 16.

[27] Synod Minutes.

[28] Synod Minutes, Sept. 21, 1719.

[29] Synod Minutes, Sept. 23, 1720; Sept. 20, 1721; Sept. 21, 1721.

[30] *Ibid.*, Sept. 17, 1724.

[31] *Ibid.*, Sept. 24, 1726.

[32] Allen, Horace T., "Brief History of Presbyterian Ministers' Fund," an address given at L.O.M.A. Institute Instructor's Seminar, New York, N.Y., October 18-20, 1954.

[33]Synod Minutes.

[34]Armstrong, Maurice W.; Loetscher, Lefferts A.; Anderson, Charles A., *The Presbyterian Enterprise* (Philadelphia: Westminster Press, 1956), p. 21.

[35]Mackie, Alexander, *Facile Princeps*, p. 80.

[36]Black, William, *Pennsylvania Magazine* (1877), Vol. I, p. 412.

[37]Briggs, Charles A., D.D., *American Presbyterianism*, N.Y., 1885, p. 242.

[38]*Ibid.*, p. 242.

[39]Keith, Charles P., *Chronicles of Pennsylvania* (1688-1748), Vol. II, p. 629/630.

[40]Mackie, Alexander, *Facile Princeps*, p. 35.

[41]Synod Minutes, May 23, 1954.

[42]*Ibid.*, May 30, 1755.

[43]*Ibid.*

[44]*Ibid.*, May 25, 1757.

[45]Mackie, Alexander, *Facile Princeps*, p. 80.

[46]Patent Book A, Vol. 20, p. 243.

[47]McAllister, James L. J., "Francis Alison and John Witherspoon, Political Philosophers and Revolutionaries," *Journal of Presbyterian History*, Vol. 54, No. 1 (spring 1976), p. 35.

[48]Tolles, Frederick, B., *Meeting House and Counting House*, (Chapel Hill, N.C.: University of North Carolina Press, 1948), p. 131.

[49]Mackie, Alexander, "Prelude to Life Insurance," *United States Review*, January 10, 1959, p. 3.

[50]"Corporation for Relief of Poor Ministers," *Journal of the Presbyterian Historical Society*, Vol. XXX, No. I (March 1952), pp. 18-21.

[51]Corporation Minutes, December, 1760.

[52]*Ibid.*, April 7, 1761.

[53]*Ibid.*

[54]*Ibid.*, May 25, 1761.

[55]*Ibid.*, Nov. 16, 1762.

[56]*Ibid.*, May 25, 1761.

[57]Mackie, Alexander, *Facile Princeps*, p. 41.

[58]*Ibid.*, p. 44.

Chapter Two

[1]Minutes.

[2]Mackie, Alexander, *Facile Princeps*, pp. 156, 157.

[3]*Ibid.*, p. 189.

[4]Minutes, Oct. 9, 1764.

[5]Minutes, April 28, 1766.

[6]Minutes, May 26, 1763.

[7]Minutes, July 8, 1763.

[8]*Ibid.*

[9]Hostetter, Meyer, "History of the Presbyterian Ministers' Fund to 1789," Company Archives, p. 23.

[10]Fund Minutes.

[11]*Ibid.*

[12]*Ibid.*

[13]Hostetter, p. 22.

[14]Fund Minutes (Taite is not listed, but he was elected this date).

[15]Boston: Little, Brown and Co., 1970, p. 74.

[16]Clough, Wilson O., Editor, *Intellectual Origins of American National Thought*, (N.Y.: Corinth Books, 1955), pp. 244, 245.

[17]Mackie, Alexander, *Facile Princeps*, p. 39.

[18]McAllister, James L. T., "Francis Alison and John Witherspoon, Political Philosophers and Revolutionaries," *Journal of Presbyterian History*, Vol. 54, No. 1 (spring 1976), p. 53/54.

[19]Neel, Gregg L., "History of Insurance in Pennsylvania," January 19, 1945, p. 8.

[20]Mackie, pp. 161, 162.

[21]Hostetter, p. 27.

[22]Minutes.

[23]Minutes, Dec. 21, 1770.

[24]Minutes.

[25]Burt, Struthers, *Philadelphia, Holy Experiment*, (Garden City, N.Y.: Doubleday Doran & Co., 1945), p. 107.

[26]Corporation Minutes, Dec. 19, 1769.

[27]Minutes, May 22, 1771.

[28]*Dictionary of American Biography*, Vol. VI (N.Y.: Charles Scribner's Sons, 1931), p. 237.

[29]Mackie, Alexander, p. 160.

[30]Minutes, Dec. 20, 1773; May 24, 1774; Oct. 17, 1774.

[31]*Ibid*.

[32]"The Rights of the Colonists, 1772," *The Writings of Samuel Adams*, ed. H. A. Cushing (N.Y.: G. P. Putnam's, Vol. II, 1904), p. 350.

[33]The Declaration of Independence, first paragraph.

[34]Miller, Howard, "The Grammar of Liberty: Presbyterian and the First American Constitution," *Journal of Presbyterian History*, Vol. 54, No. 1 (spring 1976), p. 161.

[35]Mackie, Alexander, *Facile Princeps*, p. 35.

[36]Hale, Hayton G., "Adams Smith's Comments on Insurance," *The Spectator*, Vol. 160, No. 3, March 1952, p. 27.

[37]Minutes, June 25, 1760.

[38]Minutes, May 24, 1776.

[39]*Ibid*.

[40]May 27, 1776.

[41]May 28, 1776.

[42]May 24, 1779.

[43]*Dictionary of American Biography*, p. 237.

[44]"Puritan Harvard and Quaker Penn," *The Pennsylvania Gazette*, Nov. 1979, p. 22.

Chapter Three

[1]"In Memory of Rev. James Sproat," unpublished article, Company Records, p. 4.

[2]*Ibid.*, p. 5.

[3]White, William P. and Scott, William H., Editors, *The Presbyterian Church in Philadelphia* (Philadelphia: Allen, Lane and Scott, 1895), p. 8.

[4]Synod Minutes.

[5]VanDoren, Carl, *Benjamin Franklin* (N.Y.: Garden City Publishing Co., Inc., 1941), p. 660.

[6]Corporation Minutes, May 22, 1780.

[7]Mackie, Alexander, *Facile Princeps*, p. 40.

[8]*Ibid.*, p. 189.

[9]Corporation Minutes, May 24, 1779.

[10]*Ibid.*

[11]*Ibid.*

[12]*Minutes of the Presbyterian Church in America 1706-1788*, Klett, Guy S., Editor, Presbyterian Historical Society, Philadelphia, 1976, p. 560.

[13]Konkle, Burton Alva, "The Presbyterian Ministers' Fund," unpublished article, Company Records, p. 22.

[14]Cochran, Thomas C., *Pennsylvania, A History*, (N.Y.: W. W. Norton & Co., Inc., 1978), p. 46.

[15]Klett, *Ibid.*, p. 560.

[16]Thompson, J. Earl, Jr., "Slavery and Presbyterianism in the Revolutionary Era," *Journal of Presbyterian History*, Vol. 54, No. 1 (spring 1976), p. 127.

[17]Weber, Max, *The Protestant Ethic and the Spirit of Capitalism* (N.Y.: Charles Scribners' Sons, 1958), p. 2.

[18]Beadle, E. R., *The Old and the New*, (Philadelphia: J. B. Chandler, 1876).

Chapter Four

[1]Scharf, J. Thomas and Wescott, Thompson, *History of Philadelphia*, Vol. I, 1884, p. 425.

[2]Miller, Howard, "The Grammar of Liberty," *Journal of Presbyterian History*, Vol. 54, No. 1 (spring 1976), p. 151.

[3]Mackie, Alexander, *Facile Princeps*, p. 97.

[4]*Ibid.*, p. 151.

[5]Company Minutes.

[6]Nov. 6, 1780.

[7]Company Minutes.

[8]*Ibid.*

[9]May 17, 1781.

[10]Young, Eleanor, *Forgotten Patriot: Robert Morris*, (N.Y.: MacMillan, 1950), p. 121.

[11]Hostetter, Meyer, "History of the Presbyterian Ministers' Fund to 1789," Company Archives, p. 29.

[12]Mackie, Alexander, p. 18.

[13]Konkle, Burton Alva, *George Bryan and the Constitution of Pennsylvania (1731-1791)*, Philadelphia, 1922, p. 254.

[14]Company Minutes.

[15]Konkle, pp. 281, 282.

[16]*Life of Ashbel Green*, Jones, J. H., Editor, N.Y., 1849, p. 155.

[17]Minutes, May 19, 1785.

[18]Minutes, May 17, 1787.

[19]Mackie, Alexander, *Facile Princeps*, p. 196.

[20]*Ibid.*, May 17, 1787, Minutes.

[21]May 28, 1787.

[22]*The Autobiography of Benjamin Rush*, George W. Corner, Editor, Princeton University Press, 1948, p. 160.

[23]Leybum, James G., "Presbyterian Immigrants and the American Revolution," *Journal of Presbyterian History*, Vol. 54, No. 1 (spring 1976), p. 29.

[24]"History of the Census," U.S. Department of Commerce, Washington, D.C., 1979, p. 1.

[25]Konkle, p. 88.

Chapter Five

[1]Childs, Marquis W., and Cater, Douglas, *Ethics in a Business Society*, (N.Y.: Mentor Books, 1954), p. 55.

[2]Weber, Max, *The Protestant Ethic and the Spirit of Capitalism*, (N.Y.: Charles Scribner's Sons, 1958), p. 175.

[3]*Ibid.*, p. 157.

[4]Mackie, Alexander, p. 166.

[5]*Dictionary of American Biography*, Johnson, Allen, Ed., (N.Y.: Charles Scribner's Sons, 1929), Vol. XV, p. 443.

[6]*Ibid.*

[7]Drinker, Cecil, K., M.D., *Not So Long Ago—A Chronicle of Medicine and Doctors in Colonial Philadelphia*, (N.Y.: Oxford University Press), p. 112.

[8]*Ibid.*, p. 114.

[9]Goodman, Nathan G., *Benjamin Rush—Physician and Citizen—1746-1813*, University of Pennsylvania Press, Philadelphia, 1934, p. 9.

[10]Konkle, Burton Alva, p. 24.

[11]July 14.

[12]Minutes of the Corporation.

[13]The 202nd Annual Report, Presbyterian Ministers' Fund, January 24, 1961, p. 1.

[14]Davies, Benjamin, *Some Account of the City of Philadelphia, The Capital of Pennsylvania*, Philadelphia, 1794, p. 74.

[15]Bigham, Barbara, "Colonial Currency," *Early American Life*, October, 1977, p. 75.

[16]Mackie, Alexander, p. 222.

[17]General Assembly Minutes, May 21, 1793.

[18]Fund Minutes, May 21, 1793.

[19]Mackie, p. 261.

[20]*Ibid.*, p. 141.

[21]*Ibid.*, p. 181.

[22]Corporation Minutes, November 15.

[23]Watson, John F., *Annals of Philadelphia and Pennsylvania in the Olden Time*, Vol. II (Philadelphia: J. M. Stoddart and Co., 1877), p. 382.

Chapter Six

[1]May 22.

[2]Leach, Josiah Granville, *The History of the Girard National Bank of Philadelphia, 1832-1902* (Philadelphia: J. B. Lippincott Company, 1902), p. 86.

[3]General Assembly Minutes.

[4]Finance Committee Minutes.

[5]Mackie, Alexander, p. 251.

[6]Cochran, Thomas C., *Pennsylvania, A Bicentennial History*, p. 67.

[7]*The Bank 1781-1976*, Philadelphia, 1976, p. 47.

[8]*Ibid.*, p. 48.

[9]*The World Book Encyclopedia*, (Chicago: Field Enterprises, 1952, Vol. XVIII), p. 8598.

[10]Mackie, Alexander, p. 241.

[11]Corporation Minutes, May 28.

[12]*Ibid.*

[13]*Ibid.*

[14]Corporation Annual Report, January 24, 1961, p. 1.

[15]Konkle, Burton Alva, p. 32.

[16]Corporation Minutes.

[17]*Ibid.*

[18]Minutes, May 30, 1825.

[19]Nelli, Humbert O., "A New Look at the History of Personal Insurance," *Journal of the American Society of Chartered Life Underwriters*, Vol. XXXIII, No. 3 (July 1969), p. 52, 54.

[20]Corporation Minutes.

[21]*The World Book Encyclopedia*, Vol. IX, p. 3957.

[22]Cochran, Thomas C., p. 81.

[23]Mackie, Alexander, p. 250.

[24]*Ibid.*, p. 256.

[25]*Ibid.*, p. 243.

[26]Jones, Joseph H., *The Life of Ashbel Green* (N.Y.: Carter and Bros., 1849), p. 547.

[27]Baird, Samuel J., *A History of the New School and of the Questions Involved in the Description of the Presbyterian Church in 1838* (Philadelphia: Claxton, Remsen & Haffelfinger, 1868), p. 209.

[28]Mackie, Alexander, p. 258.

[29]Baird, p. 327.

[30]Mackie, p. 260.

[31]Allen, Perry S., "Historical Sketch of the Presbyterian Ministers' Fund for Life Insurance," Published by the Company, Philadelphia, 1929, p. 19.

[32]Corporation Minutes.

[33]Nelli, Humbert O., p. 52.

[34]Corporation Minutes, May 24, 1844.

[35]Minutes, May 17, 1850.

[36]*Life Insurance Fact Book '77*, (N.Y.: American Council of Life Insurance, New York, 1977), p. 110.

NOTES

[37]Johnson, Paul, *Enemies of Society*, (New York: Atheneum, 1977), p. 32.
[38]Minutes, July 2, 1851.
[39]Minutes. Nov. 13. 1851.
[40]"Address" of the Corporation, Philadelphia, 1852, p. 6.
[41]May, Earl Chapin, *The Prudential* (Garden City, N.Y.: Doubleday & Co., Inc., 1950), p. 199.
[42]Corporation Minutes.
[43]Corporation Minutes.
[44]Nelli, Humbert O., p. 56.
[45]Wright, Elizur, *The Bible of Life Insurance* (Chicago: American Conservation Co.), pp. 85, 86.
[46]Minutes, May 17, 1861.

Chapter Seven

[1]Mackie, Alexander, p. 214.
[2]Kane, John K., *Autobiography*, 1848, privately printed, College Offset Press, Philadelphia, PA, 1949, p. 4.
[3]*Ibid.*, p. 5.
[4]Burt, Nathaniel, *The Perennial Philadelphians* (Boston: Little, Brown and Company, 1963), p. 461.
[5]*Ibid.*, p. 331.
[6]Mackie, Alexander, p. 203.
[7]Corporation Minutes, May 24, 1825.
[8]Company Records.
[9]Allen, Horace T., "John Kintzing Kane and His Successors Cling to the Founders' Visions," Company Records, p. 3.
[10]Mackie, p. 220.
[11]Kane, John K., *Autobiography*, p. 55.
[12]Corporation Minutes, February 27.
[13]Mackie, p. 269.
[14]*Ibid.*, p. 217, 218.
[15]*Ibid.*, p. 66.
[16]Wallace, Sarah H. & Gillespie, Frances E. (Editors), *The Journal of Benjamin Moran: 1857-1865* (Chicago, Illinois: University of Chicago Press), p. 156.

Chapter Eight

[1]"Some Reflections on the Writing of Local History," *Pennsylvania History* (Vol. XXI, No. 3), July 1954, p. 239.
[2]*Historical Catalogue of the St. Andrew's Society of Philadelphia*, Philadelphia, 1907, p. 255.
[3]Mackie, Alexander, p. 142.
[4]*Dictionary of American Biography*, Vol. XI, p. 543.
[5]Wolf, Edwin, 2nd., "Origins of Philadelphia's Self-Depreciation," *The Pennsylvania Magazine of History and Biography*, Jan. 1980, p. 63.
[6]Banner, Lois W., "Presbyterians and Voluntarism in the Early Republic," *Journal of Presbyterian History*, Vol. 50, No. 3 (fall 1972), p. 205.

[7]Scharf, J. Thomas and Wescott, Thompson, *History of Philadelphia 1609-1884*, Vol. I, p. 726.

[8]*Ibid.*, p. 746.

[9]*In Memoriam —Charles Macalester* (privately printed, 1873), p. 11.

[10]Corporation Minutes, May 20, 1859.

[11]*Ibid.*, June 13, 1862.

[12]Konkle, Burton A., p. 46.

[13]Minutes, June 19, 1863.

[14]Minutes, Sept. 10, 1863.

[15]St. Andrew's Society Historical Catalogue, p. 257.

[16]Corporation Minutes, May 20, 1864.

[17]Mitchell, Robert B., *From Actuarius to Actuary*, Society of Actuaries, 1974, p. 64.

[18]*Ibid.*, p. 24.

[19]*Ibid.*

[20]Kesslinger, J. M., *Guardian of a Century, 1860-1960* (N.Y.: Guardian Life Insurance Company, 1960), p. 39.

[21]Aspinwall, Marguerite, "Down Through the Years in the Church of the Holy Trinity," Philadelphia, 1964, p. 5.

[22]Corporation Annual Report, January 22, 1963, p. 1.

[23]*Life Insurance Fact Book* '77, New York, 1977, p. 111.

[24]Mitchell, p. 17.

[25]*Ibid.*, p. 19.

[26]Nelli, Humbert O., p. 56.

[27]Corporation Minutes, April 3, 1871.

[28]"Address of 1871," p. 7.

[29]*Ibid.*, p. 13.

[30]Baird, Samuel, J. *History of the New School* (Philadelphia: Claxton, Remsen & Haffelfinger, 1868), p. 2.

[31]*Ibid.*, p. 9.

[32]*Minutes of the General Assembly of the Presbyterian Church in the U.S.A.*, Presbyterian Board of Education, Philadelphia, 1870, New Series, Vol. I, p. 3.

[33]*Presbyterian Reunion: A Memorial Volume 1837-1871* (New York: DeWitt C. Lent & Company, 1870), p. 407.

[34]Gudmundsen, John, *The Great Provider* (South Norwalk, Conn.: Industrial Publication Company, 1959), p. 53.

[35]*In Memorium Charles Macalester*, privately printed, Philadelphia, 1873.

[36]*Ibid.*

Chapter Nine

[1]Vol. XVII, p. 387.

[2]*Ibid.*

[3]*Ibid.*

[4]Mackie, Alexander, p. 234.

[5]J. Wiley & Sons, Inc., N.Y., 1930, p. 143.

[6]Snowden, J. Ross, *Medals of Washington* (Philadelphia: J. B. Lippincott & Co., 1861), p. 197.

[7]Scharf and Wescott, Vol. I, p. 756.

[8]Snowden, J. Ross, p. 185.

[9]*Ibid.*, p. 189.

[10]*Ibid.*, p. 190.

[11]*Ibid.*, p. 192.

[12]Scharf and Wescott, Vol. I, p. 728.

[13]Leach, Frank Willing. "Old Philadelphia Families," *The North American*, Philadelphia, July 14, 1912, p. 7.

[14]*Ibid.*, p. 7.

[15]Nevin, Alfred. *Men of Mark of Cumberland Valley (1776-1786)* (Philadelphia: Fulton Publishing Co., 1876), p. 358.

[16]Scharf and Wescott, Vol. I, p. 788.

[17]Nevin, p. 357.

[18]"Speech of Hon. J. Ross Snowden," Philadelphia, Sept. 17, 1863, privately printed, p. 3.

[19]Nevin, p. 357.

[20]Kemble, Frances Ann. *Further Records 1848-1883, A Science of Letters*, New York, 1891, p. 6.

[21]Corporation Minutes.

[22]Kesslinger, J. M. *Guardian of a Century (1860-1960)*. Guardian Life Insurance Co., New York, 1960, p. 33.

[23]Company Records, April 30, 1874.

[24]*Dictionary of American Biography*, Vol. XVII, p. 387.

[25]Finance Committee Minutes, Oct. 28, 1875.

[26]"Address of the Presbyterian Annuity and Life Insurance Company." Philadelphia, 1875, p. 5.

[27]*Ibid.*, p. 7.

[28]*Ibid.*, p. 8.

[29]*Ibid.*, p. 17.

[30]Boyd, Lois A. "Shall Women Speak?" *Journal of Presbyterian History*, Vol. 56, #4 (winter 1978), p. 287.

[31]Finance Committee Minutes, April 3, 1876.

[32]*Ibid.*

[33]Konkle, Burton A., p. 50.

[34]Corporation Minutes, Oct. 21, 1876.

[35]Directors' Minutes, Jan. 25, 1877.

[36]*Ibid.*, May 10, 1877.

[37]"Address of the Presbyterian Annuity and Life Insurance Company," Philadelphia, 1878, p. 20.

[38]Babcock, Charles A. *Venango County Pennsylvania Her Pioneers and People* (Chicago: J. H. Beers and Company, 1919), Vol. I, p. 109.

Chapter Ten

[1]Minutes of the Board of Directors, May 1, 1880.

[2]Dulles, John Welsh, *Life in India* (Philadelphia: American Sunday School Union, 1855), p. 19.

[3]Trumbull, Henry Clay, *Old Time Student Volunteers* (New York: Fleming H. Revell Company, 1902), p. 187.

[4]*Ibid.*, p. 187.

[5]Dulles, Heatly Cortonne. "Dulles and Related Family Records," Villanova, Pa., 1946, p. 21.

[6]Minutes of the Board of Directors, Jan. 26, 1877.

[7]McGill, Alexander T., Letter to John Welsh Dulles, Princeton, N.J., July 22, 1876.

[8]Family records, courtesy of Miss Julia C. Dulles and Mrs. Anna S. Dulles Buckley.

[9]Minutes of the Board of Directors.

[10]*Ibid.*

[11] Company Advertisement, 133 South 5th Street, Philadelphia, 1878.

[12]Drummond, Andrew Landale. *Edward Irving and His Uncle* (London: James Clarke & Co., Ltd.), p. 73.

[13]Minutes of the Board of Corporators.

[14]Corporators, Jan. 26, 1882.

[15]*Ibid.*

[16]*Ibid.*

[17]*Ibid.*

[18]Kesslinger, J. M. *Guardian of a Century, 1860-1960*, (New York, N.Y.: Guardian Life Insurance Company, 1960), p. 33.

[19]Minutes of the Board of Directors.

[20]*Ibid.*

[21]*Ibid.*

[22]*Ibid.*

[23]*The New York Times*, Vol. XXXIV, p. 1, Nov. 5, 1884.

[24]Minutes of the Corporators, Jan. 24, 1884.

[25]*Life Insurance Fact Book*, American Council of Life Insurance, Washington, D.C., 1979, p. 111.

[26]Scharf, J. Thomas, and Wescott, Thompson, *History of Philadelphia*, Vol. III, 1884, pp. 2126, 2127.

[27]Minutes of the Corporation.

[28]"In Memoriam — Rev. John W. Dulles, D.D." (Philadelphia: Presbyterian Board of Publication, 1887), p. 11.

[29]Miller, J. R., D.D., "The Death of Dr. Dulles," *New York Evangelist*, April 21, 1887, p. 4.

Chapter Eleven

[1]Presbyterian Ministers' Fund, Annual Report, Jan. 27, 1959.

[2]*History of the Presbyterian Ministers' Fund*, unpublished article, 1928, p. 54.

[3]Corporation Minutes.

[4]*Ibid.*, March 20, 1890.

[5]Mitchell, Robert B., *From Actuarius to Actuary*, Society of Actuaries, 1974, p. 26.

[6]Directors' Minutes, Jan. 29, 1891.

[7]Konkle, Burton A., p. 56.

[8]Ferguson, Elizabeth, "The Country Parson," *The Philadelphia Magazines and Their Contributors*, Smyth, Albert H., Philadelphia, Robert M. Lindsay, 1892, p. 130.

NOTES

[9]Letter from the "Committee of Session" signed by James Hewitt, and addressed to Robert P. Field, Directors' Minutes, Nov. 10, 1892.

[10]Tompkins, George, "Report on the Standing of the Presbyterian Ministers' Fund," Philadelphia, 1892, pp. 1, 2.

[11]*Ibid.*, p. 4.

[12]Konkle, p. 58.

[13]Mary Virginia Allen Geyelin, personal interviews with the author, May 25, 1979.

[14]*Who's Who in America*, Volume XIII, Marquis Who's Who, Inc., Chicago, Illinois, 1924-1925.

[15]*The World Book Encyclopedia*, 1952, Vol. 13, p. 6139.

[16]Amory, Cleveland, *The Last Resorts* (New York: Harper and Brothers, 1952), p. 4.

[17]Ellis, David M., Frost, James A., *A Short History of New York State* (Ithaca: Cornell University Press, 1957), p. 618.

[18]*Ibid.*

[19]Chafetz, Henry, *Play the Devil, A History of Gambling in the United States from 1492−1955* (New York: Clarkson N. Potter, Inc., 1960), p. 324.

[20]Mary Virginia Geyelin, personal interview with author, June 1, 1980.

[21]*Minutes of the General Assembly*, Philadelphia, Pennsylvania, 1890, p. 139.

[22]Directors' Minutes, February 9, 1893.

[23]"The Appeal of Life Insurance," *The Insurance Times*, December 1925. "Presbyterian Ministers' Fund, Pioneer Life Insurance Company of America and Oldest in the World," *The Insurance Times*, May 1928.

[24]Directors' Minutes, November 23, 1893.

[25]*Ibid.*

[26]*Ibid.*

[27]Directors' Minutes, Feb. 8, 1894.

[28]Directors' Minutes, March 10, 1894.

[29]Mansfield, Burton, letter dated 3/10/94.

[30]Lowell, James Russell, "A Glance Behind the Curtains," 1843.

[31]Directors' Minutes, January 31, 1895.

[32]*Ibid.*

[33]Directors' Minutes, Aug. 30, 1894, p. 2.

[34]Directors' Minutes, March 1, 1895, p. 1.

[35]*Ibid.*, p. 2.

[36]*Ibid.*, p. 2.

[37]*Ibid.*, p. 4.

[38]Tarbell, E. G., The Equitable Life Assurance Society of the United States, letter dated June 22, 1896.

[39]Allen, Perry S., letter dated Jan. 14, 1896.

[40]Allen, Perry S., letter dated Feb. 20, 1896.

[41]Nicholls, Jr., Shaw, letter dated Dec. 10, 1896.

[42]Allen, Perry S., letter dated Dec. 11, 1896.

[43]Allen, Perry S., letter dated Dec. 19, 1896.

[44]Presbyterian Ministers' Fund, *Annual Report*, Philadelphia, Pa., Jan. 24, 1898, p. 5.

[45]Directors' Minutes, April 11, 1897.

[46]Allen, Perry S., letter dated May 8, 1898.

[47]Allen, Perry S., letter dated July 19, 1898.

[48]Allen, Perry S., letter to Rev. Wm. Fishburn, June 15, 1898.

[49]Allen, Perry S., letter to Rev. W. B. Kennedy, April 25, 1898.

[50]Allen, Perry S., letter to Rev. J. H. Herbener, May 13, 1898.

[51]Allen, Perry S., letter dated April 19, 1898.

[52]Corporation Minutes.

[53]Minutes of the Board of Directors, April 10, 1902.

[54]Allen, Perry S., letter dated August 15, 1895.

[55]Allen, Perry S., letter dated July 3, 1901.

[56]Mitchell, Robert B., *From Actuarius to Actuary*, 1974, p. 35.

[57]Directors' Minutes, June 11, 1908.

[58]"Testimonials," Presbyterian Ministers' Fund, Philadelphia, Pennsylvania, p. 2.

[59]Allen, Perry S., "The Minister's Problem," 1907, p. 1.

[60]Allen, Perry S., "A Word of Explanation," 1907, p. 4.

[61]Allen, Perry S., "The Presbyterian Ministers' Fund and the Problem of Life Insurance," Philadelphia, 1909, p. 9.

[62]*Ibid.*, p. 14.

[63]Armstrong, Loetscher, Anderson, *The Presbyterian Enterprise* (Philadelphia: Westminster, 1956), p. 279.

[64]Directors' Minutes, May 11, 1911.

[65]Allen, Perry S., letter to Morris Williams, Dec. 5, 1910.

[66]Allen, Perry S., letter to Board of Corporators, Philadelphia, February 13, 1915, p. 2.

[67]Executive Committee Minutes.

[68]Konkle, Alva Burton, *History of the Presbyterian Ministers' Fund*, Philadelphia, p. 68.

[69]157th Annual Report, 1916, p. 9.

[70]Directors' Minutes, Jan. 30, 1919.

[71]Directors' Minutes, March 14, 1921.

[72]*The Presbyterian Tribune*, April 19, 1947, and personal interview with Miss Agnes Allen.

[73]Directors' Minutes, April 14, 1921.

[74]Dedication program.

[75]*Ange Pitou*, Vol. I, p. 72.

[76]Corporators' Minutes, Jan. 22.

[77]"Commended by Insurance Department," *The United States Review*, Philadelphia, Pennsylvania, October 18, 1924.

[78]*Ibid.*, March 27, 1926.

[79]Allen, Perry S., "Without Insurance," p. 2.

[80]Allen, Perry S., "Some Life Insurance Paragraphs," p. 1.

[81]Personal interview with the author, June 18, 1979.

[82]165th Annual Report, Jan. 22, 1924, p. 10.

[83]Dedication Program, Jan. 27, 1925, p. 4.

[84]166th Annual Report, Jan. 27, 1925, p. 4.

[85]*Ibid.*, p. 10.

[86]Ward, Quaife M. and Determan, Tedd C., *A Flock of Eagles*, The Million Dollar Round Table, 1977, pp. 41, 42.

[87]*Ibid.*, p. 19.

[88]*Ibid.*, p. 20.

[89]"A Reprint from the Insurance Almanac for 1929." p. 1.

[90]"Town and Country Life," London, 1929.

[91]"The Work of One Man," *United States Review and Southern Underwriter*, Philadelphia, Pennsylvania, October 4, 1930.

[92]Alexander, W., "The Secretary's Memories—No. 9," sent with letter from Arthur H. Reddall, Equitable Life, to Charleton C. Loeble, PMF., Feb. 17, 1941.

[93]*The Evening Bulletin*, November 8, 1930, p. 2E.

[94]Mary Virginia Allen Geyelin, personal interview with the author, June 27, 1980.

Chapter Twelve

[1]Aitken, Hugh, G. J., "Pierre S. du Pont and the Making of the Modern Corporation," *The Pennsylvania Magazine of History and Biography*, Vol. CIV., No. 3, p. 403.

[2]"The American Crisis," No. 1., Dec. 23, 1776.

[3]*U.S. Review and Southern Underwriter*, March 14, 1931.

[4]Mackie, Alexander, unpublished history of the Fund (1929-1958), Philadelphia, 1958, p. 7.

[5]Todd, Galbraith Hall, "A Memorial Minute on the Rev. Alexander Mackie, D.D.," Presbyterian Historical Society, Philadelphia, 1966.

[6]*Ibid.*

[7]Mackie, Alexander, *A Wolf in Sheep's Clothing*, unpublished manuscript, chapter I, p. 4.

[8]Keynes, Geoffrey, *The Letters of Rupert Brooke*, (New York: Harcourt, Brace, and World, Inc., 1968), p. 47.

[9]Mackie, *ibid.*

[10]*Ibid.*, chapter two, p. 6.

[11]*Ibid.* p. 5.

[12]*Ibid.* p. 26.

[13]*The Gift of Tongues, A Study in Pathological Aspects of Christianity*, (N.Y.: George H. Doran Co., 1922), p. 264.

[14]*The Presbyterian*, editorial, May 16, 1929.

[15]*A Wolf in Sheep's Clothing*, pp. 66, 67.

[16]Mrs. Alice Mackie Smullen, personal interview with the author, Sept. 5, 1980.

[17]Letter to Board of Directors, Nov. 13, 1930.

[18]Letters to Rev. Joseph B. C. Mackie, Dec. 27, 1930; Jan. 5, 1930; March 5, 1931.

[19]Letters to the Corporators, Jan. 23, 1931.

[20]Presbyterian Ministers' Fund, *172nd Annual Report*, Philadelphia, 1931, p. 7.

[21]"Suggestions for *Quo Warranto*" Supreme Court of Pennsylvania, Eastern District, January Term, 1932, p. 82.

[22]"Presbyterian Ministers' Fund Elects New President," *United States Review,* May 30, 1931, p. 22.

[23]"The Presbyterian Ministers' Fund," *Christian Observer,* April 29, 1931, p. 3.

[24]Schweitzer, Frederick, "Facts for Consideration of the Policy Holders in the Presbyterian Ministers' Fund for Life Insurance."

[25]Board of Directors' Minutes, pp. 68, 69.

[26]"The Report of the Committee of Seven to the Board of Corporators," p. 61.

[27]Acker, J. Henry R., Letter to Rev. W. O. Garrett, D.D., July 10, 1931, p. 1.

[28]*Ibid.*

[29]Issue of March 5, 1932.

[30]"Last Year the Best of More than 200," March 12, 1932, p. 638.

[31]Feb. 17, 1932.

[32]"How Policyholders were Misled," issued of April 30, 1932.

[33]Directors' Minutes, March 22, 1932, p. 6.

[34]Directors' Minutes, June 9, 1932, p. 1.

[35]Rev. Elliot Field, March 10, 1932.

[36]Rev. Arthur R. McLaughlin, Feb. 17, 1932.

[37]Rev. Harvey C. Travis, March 2, 1932.

[38]Rev. Curtis O. Bowserman, Sept. 13, 1932.

[39]*Ibid.*

[40]Edward Yates Hill, "In Memoriam-President J. Henry Rader Acker," 1933, p. 2.

[41]Presbyterian Ministers' Fund, 174th Annual Report, Jan. 24, 1933, p. 9.

[42]*A Wolf in Sheep's Clothing,* p. 12.

[43]M. S. Johnson, Corporate Secretary, Letter to the Corporators, May 23, 1933.

[44]Letter to Herbert A. Gibbons, March 30, 1933.

[45]*Ibid.*

[46]Bauman, John F., and Coodie, Thomas H., "Depression Report: A New Dealer Tours Eastern Pennsylvania," *The Pennsylvania Magazine of History and Biography,* Vol., CIV., No. 1, Jan. 1980, p. 97.

[47]*Ibid.*

[48]Presbyterian Ministers' Fund, 175th Annual Report, p. 6.

[49]Fund Sales Circular, Feb. 1933.

[50]Fund Sales Circular, August 1933.

[51]*Ibid.*

[52]*Ibid.*

[53]Directors' Minutes, Jan. 25, 1934.

[54]Annual Meeting of the Corporators, Jan. 23, 1934.

[55]Unpublished History of the Fund (1929-1958), p. 97.

[56]Directors' Minutes, Oct. 11, 1934.

[57]Howard, Irving E., *The Christian Alternative to Socialism* (Arlington, Virginia: Better Books, 1966), p. 73.

[58]*Ibid.*

[59]177th Annual Report, p. 6.

[60]*Unpublished History of the Fund* (1929-1958), p. 98.

[61]Directors' Minutes, Aug. 8, 1935.

[62]*United States Review*, Vol. 136, No. 5, p. 1.

[63]*Unpublished History of the Fund*, p. 103.

[64]*A Sheep in Wolf's Clothing*, p. 9.

[65]*Unpublished History*, p. 103.

[66]Life Insurance Application, March 2, 1936.

[67]Directors' Minutes, Dec. 10, 1936.

[68]*Unpublished History*, p. 111.

[69]Directors' Minutes, Oct. 13, 1938.

[70]Directors' Minutes, Jan. 24, 1939.

[71]*Time*, July 26, 1937.

[72]A talk at the City Historical Society of Philadelphia, Oct. 15, 1941.

[73]Directors' Minutes, Dec. 14, 1939.

[74]*Unpublished History*, p. 155.

[75]Jan. 23, 1940.

[76]*Ibid.*

[77]*Ibid.*

[78]Lewis Seymour Mudge, Letter to Harry Lathrop Reed, Jan. 24, 1940.

[79]*Unpublished History*, p. 179.

[80]Corporators' Minutes, May 2, 1940.

[81]*Ibid.*

[82]*Unpublished History*, p. 185.

[83]Memorandum, Oct. 29, 1940.

[84]Jan. 28, 1941.

[85]*Ibid.*

[86]*Ibid.*

[87]*Ibid.*

[88]*Unpublished History*, p. 191.

[89]183rd *Annual Report*, Jan. 27, 1942; 187th *Annual Report*, Jan. 22, 1947.

[90]*Unpublished History*, p. 209.

[91]Jan. 25, 1944.

[92]Memo to all employees from Dr. Mackie.

[93]June 6, 1943.

[94]Nov. 29, 1945.

[95]188th Annual Meeting of the Corporators, Jan. 28, 1947, p. 2.

[96]190th Annual Meeting, Jan. 25, 1949, p. 3.

[97]"The Power of Life Insurance," editorial, *The U.S. Review*, Dec. 28, 1946.

[98]Corporators' Meeting, Jan. 25, 1949.

[99]Letter to Charles E. Fair, May 4, 1948.

[100]Annual Report, Jan. 24, 1950.

[101]Fry, Harrison W. "Big Role in Founding of Nation Played by Merged Churches," *The Evening Bulletin*, March 1949.

[102]Mitchell, Robert B., *From Actuarius to Actuary*, Society of Actuaries, 1974, p. 49.

[103]Correspondence July 19, 1948 — Aug. 4, 1948.

[104]Forty-fifth Annual Meeting, Oct. 3-6, 1950, p. 6.

[105]Office directive from the president.

[106]Letters to Roger W. Sherman, Feb. 13, 1950.

[107]Letter July 9, 1951.

[108]Letter, Oct. 27, 1951.

[109]*The Philadelphia Inquirer*, June 17, 1951.

[110]Souvenir Program.

[111]Souvenir Program.

[112]"Cornerstone for Addition to 'Home Office Building,' " *American Underwriter*, Oct. 20, 1951.

[113]Souvenir Program.

[114]Annual Report, Jan. 27, 1953.

[115]Memorandum to Branch Offices, Nov. 10, 1955.

[116]President's Office Memo, Sept. 27, 1954.

[117]*Newsweek*, June 9, 1952.

[118]"Recent Portraits by Alfred Jonniaux," Arthur U. Newton Galleries, New York, Nov. 6-21, 1953.

[119]"Old Pine Street Church Restoration Fund," campaign brochure.

[120]Annual Meeting Program, Sheraton Hotel, Philadelphia, Oct. 18, 1957.

[121]*The Evening Bulletin*, Philadelphia, Jan. 21, 1966.

[122]*United States Review*, Vol. 172, No. 5, Philadelphia, Pa., Jan. 30, 1954, p. 7.

[123]"Report of the President," 199th Annual Meeting, Jan. 28, 1958.

[124]Annual Report, Jan. 22, 1957.

[125]*Ibid.*, p. 273.

[126]Annual Meeting Minutes, Jan. 27, 1959.

[127]*Ibid.*

[128]"That Is to Say" or "A Preacher Talks About Life Insurance," The Newcomen Society in North America, 1959.

[129]Directors' Meeting, April 9, 1959.

[130]*The Evening Bulletin*, Philadelphia, March 31, 1940.

[131]204th Annual Report, Jan. 22, 1963.

[132]Letter, Jan. 4, 1963.

Chapter Thirteen

[1]Dacey, Norman F., *What's Wrong with Your Life Insurance* (N.Y.: Crowell-Collier Press, 1963), p. 108.

[2]Stone, Mildred F., *A History of Mutual Benefit Life Insurance Co.* (New Brunswick: Rutgers University Press, 1957), p. 1.

[3]*Ibid.*, p. 82.

[4]Dacey, p. 9.

[5]205th Annual Meeting of the Corporators, "Report of the President," Jan. 28, 1964.

[6]"Letter to a Young Clergyman," Jan. 9, 1720, *Bartlett's Familiar Quotations* (Boston: Little Brown & Co., 1968), p. 389.

NOTES

[7]Boss, Harold F., *How Green the Grazing* (Dallas: Taylor Publishing Company, 1978), p. 295.

[8]*Jeanette News-Dispatch*, Jan. 21, 1938.

[9]*The Atlantic Monthly*, Oct. 1938.

[10]"Twelve Sermons on the Apostles' Creed," *Church Management*, Dec. 1943.

[11]Baccalaureate Address, Upper Merion High School, May 27, 1946.

[12]Letter from the Manse, Nov. 11, 1947.

[13]*Ibid.*

[14]Aug. 6, 1948.

[15]"What Makes a Nation Free."

[16]Sept. 20.

[17]Colonial Press, Clinton, Massachusetts, 1960.

[18]President's Office Correspondence, April 25, 1963.

[19]*Ibid.*, March 8, 1963.

[20]June, 1963.

[21]Rev. P. John Acton, July 27, 1963.

[22]Rev. Frederick Tiessen, Nov. 13, 1963.

[23]Sept. 9, 1963.

[24]Directors' Minutes, Oct. 10, 1963.

[25]205th Annual Report, Jan. 28, 1964.

[26]Directors' Minutes, Jan. 28, 1964.

[27]*Ibid.*, Jan. 26, 1965.

[28]"Family Fund News," Vol. I, No. 24.

[29]President's Office Memorandum, Dec. 7, 1965.

[30]*Ibid.*, Nov. 8, 1965.

[31]Directors' Minutes, Sept. 9, 1965.

[32]*Life Insurance News Data*, Vol. XXVI, No. 12, p. 1, Institute of Life Insurance, New York, Jan. 25, 1966.

[33]Directors' Minutes, Oct. 13, 1966.

[34]209th Annual Report of the President, Jan. 23, 1968, p. 1.

[35]*Ibid.*, p. 2.

[36]*Ibid.*

[37]Jan. 1967.

[38]Directors' Minutes, Oct. 10, 1968.

[39]*Ibid.*

[40]Company records, Oct. 1, 1968, p. 1.

[41]*Ibid.*, pp. 2-6.

[42]Report of the President, March 12, 1970.

[43]Directors' Minutes, Oct. 11, 1969.

[44]Annual Meeting, March 12, 1970.

[45]Directors' Minutes, April 9, 1970.

[46]Minutes, Sept. 10, 1970.

[47]Newman, A. Joseph, Jr., *The Evening Bulletin*, March 12, 1971, p. 26B.

[48]*Ibid.*

[49]Schull, Joseph, *The Century of the Sun* (Toronto: MacMillan of Canada, 1971), p. 4.

[50]Jan. 14, 1971.

[51]Article XII, March 21, 1971, p. 7.

[52]"Philadelphia Tradition," *The Philadelphia Inquirer*, April 22, 1980, p. 13-A.

[53]Minutes, p. 5.

[54]March 8, 1973.

[55]*Ibid.*

Chapter Fourteen

[1]*Understanding Your Life Insurance*, American Council of Life Insurance, Washington, D.C., 1979, p. 7.

[2]McKeever, Charles A., "A 20 Year Look at the New Companies & the 1950's," *Best's Review*, March 1979, p. 10.

[3]Interview with the author, April 27, 1979.

[4]Company records.

[5]Numbers 4:30.

[6]"Seven Theological Facets," *Capitalism and Socialism, A Theological Inquiry*, American Enterprise Institute, Washington, D.C., 1979, p. 110.

[7]Moore, Samuel F., M.D., Former President, the Life Insurance Medical Director's Association, Interview with the author, August 30, 1979.

[8]*Analysis and Rating*, 1978.

[9]*The Will to Manage* (N.Y.: McGraw-Hill, 1966), p. 3.

[10]"President's Message," *Fund Family News*, Jan. 1975, p. 1.

[11]1976 Annual Report, March 10, 1977, p. 3.

[12]"How Seven Employees Can Be Made to Do the Work of One," *Fortune*, March 1956, p. 123.

[13]By-Laws, Article III.

[14]Livesay, Harold C., *American Made Men Who Shaped the American Economy* (Boston: Little, Brown and Company, 1979), pp. 209, 291.

[15]*Life Insurance Speaks for Itself* (N.Y.: Harper and Brothers, 1939), p. 39.

[16]Elia, Charles J. "Mushrooming Life Policy Loans Drain Cash," *The Wall Street Journal*, April 28, 1980.

[17]Article VIII (j).

[18]Levinson, Harry, "Criteria for Choosing Chief Executives," *Harvard Business Review*, Vol. 58, No. 4, p. 120.

[19]1978 Annual Report, p. 4.

[20]Hooker, Richard, *Aetna Life Insurance Company*, Hartford, Connecticut, 1956, p. 36.

[21]Rybka, Lawrence S., "Can the Life Insurance Agent Beat Inflation?" *Best's Review*, April 1979, p. 10.

[22]*Time*, Vol. 115, No. 21, May 26, 1980.

[23]Span, Paula, "Oh Noooo, Not Another Life Insurance Article," *Philadelphia Magazine*, June 1980, p. 98.

[24]Epstein, Joseph, "The Virtues of Ambition," *Harpers*, October 1980, p. 54.

[25]216th Annual Meeting of the Corporators, March 13, 1975, p. 3.

[26]"Best's Insurance Management Reports," May 19, 1980.

NOTES

[27]Anderson, James C. H., "Alternative Futures of the Life Insurance Industry," *Insurance Marketing*, Sept. 1977, p. 28.

[28]"The Coming Crunch in Life Insurance," *Business Week*, Dec. 3, 1979, p. 124.

[29]Loomis, Carol J., "Life Isn't What It Used to Be," *Fortune*, July 14, 1980, p. 86.

[30]Saltzman, Cynthia, "Troubled Life Insurance Companies Try Mass-Marketing Tactics to Increase Sales," *The Wall Street Journal*, Dec. 19, 1980, p. 50.

Preface

[1]Essays: First Series, 1841.

[2]Gladfelter, Millard E., interview with author June 8, 1979.

[3]Talk given Oct. 8, 1953, at the 48th Annual Meeting of the American Life Convention (Edgewater Beach Hotel, Chicago).

PERMISSIONS

PERMISSIONS

Permission to quote from Paul Johnson's *Enemies of Society* (copyright ©
1977 by Paul Johnson) is gratefully acknowledged to Atheneum
Publishers, New York.

Excerpts from Barbara Bigham's "Colonial Currency," *Early American Life*
(October 1977) are quoted with permission from the Early American
Society.

Permission to quote from Eleanor Young's *Forgotten Patriot: Robert Morris*
(copyright 1950, by Eleanor Young), and Norman F. Dacey's *What's Wrong
with Your Life Insurance* (copyright © 1963 by Macmillan Publishing Co.) is
gratefully acknowledged to Macmillan Publishing Co., Inc., New York.

Permission to quote from *The Autobiography of Benjamin Rush*, ed. by
George W. Corner (copyright 1948, © 1976 by Princeton University Press)
is gratefully acknowledged. Reprinted by permission of Princeton
University Press.

Permission to quote from Marquis W. Childs' and Douglas Cater's *Ethics
in a Business Society* and Cleveland Amory's *The Last Resorts* is gratefully
acknowledged to Harper & Row Publishers, Inc.

Permission to quote from Cecil K. Drinker's *Not So Long Ago; A Chronicle of
Medicine and Doctors in Colonial Philadelphia* is gratefully acknowledged to
Oxford University Press, New York.

Permission to quote from *The Bank 1781-1976* (1976) is gratefully
acknowledged to the First Pennsylvania Corporation, Philadelphia.

Permission to quote from Earl Chapin May's *The Prudential* (1950) is
gratefully acknowledged to Doubleday & Company, Inc.

Permission to quote from Edwin Wolf II's "Origins of Philadelphia's
Self-Depreciation" (January 1980), Hugh G. J. Aitken's "Pierre S. duPont
and the Making of the Modern Corporation" (Vol. CIV, No. 3), and John
F. Bauman's and Thomas H. Coodie's "Depression Report: A New Dealer
Tours Eastern Pennsylvania" (Vol. CIV, No. 1, January 1980) all in *The
Pennsylvania Magazine of History and Biography*, is gratefully acknowledged to
the Historical Society of Pennsylvania.

Permission to quote from E. Gordon Alderfer's "Some Reflections on the
Writing of Local History," in Pennsylvania History, Vol. XXI, No. 3 (July
1954) is gratefully acknowledged to the Pennsylvania Historical
Association.

Permission to quote from Robert B. Mitchell's *From Actuarius to Actuary*
(1974) is gratefully acknowledged to the Society of Actuaries, Chicago.

Permission to quote from J. M. Kesslinger's *Guardian of a Century 1860-1960* (1960) is gratefully acknowledged to The Guardian Life Insurance Company of America, New York.

Permission to quote from Marguerite Aspinwall's *Down Through the Years in the Church of the Holy Trinity* (1964) is gratefully acknowledged to Holy Trinity Episcopal Church, Philadelphia, Penn.

Permission to quote from David M. Ellis's and James A. Frost's *A Short History of New York State* (1957) is gratefully acknowledged to Cornell University Press.

Permission to quote from Henry Chafetz's *Play the Devil* is gratefully acknowledged to Crown Publishers, Inc., New York.

Excerpts from Quaife M. Ward's and Tedd C. Determan's *A Flock of Eagles* are reprinted with special permission. Copyright 1977, Million Dollar Round Table, 2340 River Road, Des Plaines, IL 60018.

Permission to quote from Geoffrey Keynes' *The Letters of Rupert Brooke* (1968) is gratefully acknowledged to Harcourt Brace Jovanovich, Inc., New York.

Permission to quote from Dan Rottenberg's "Philadelphia Tradition" (Sec. 13A, Tues., April 22, 1980) and "Ten Philadelphia Firms to Be Honored July 2" (June 17, 1951) both in *The Philadelphia Inquirer,* is gratefully acknowledged.

Permission to quote from Alexander Mackie's "That Is to Say" (1959) is gratefully acknowledged to The Newcomen Society in North America.

Permission to quote from Joseph Schull's *The Century of the Sun* (1971) is gratefully acknowledged to Mrs. Horace M. Block.

Permission to quote from Harold F. Boss's *How Green the Grazing* (1978) is gratefully acknowledged to the Fine Books Department, Taylor Publishing Company, Dallas, Texas.

Permission to quote from Lawrence Rybka's "Can the Life Insurance Agent Beat Inflation?" (April 1979) in *Best's Review* and Charles McKeever's "A 20-Year Look at the New Companies and the 1950's" (March 1979) in *Best's Review* and *Best's Insurance Managements Reports* (May 19, 1980) is gratefully acknowledged to A. M. Best Company, Oldwick, N.J.

Excerpts from Marvin Bower's *The Will to Manage,* copyright © 1966 by McGraw-Hill Book Company. Used with the permission of McGraw-Hill Book Company, New York.

PERMISSIONS

BIBLIOGRAPHY

The Bank 1781-1976, A Short History of First Pennsylvania Bank.
Philadelphia: 1976.

Barker, John. *The First Hundred Years.* Pittsfield, Mass.: Berkshire Life
Insurance Company, 1951.

Blamires, Harry. *The Christian Mind.* New York: Harper & Row, 1978.

Boss, Harold F. *How Green the Grazing, 75 Years at Southwestern Life
(1903-1978).* San Angelo, Tex.: Taylor Publishing Company, 1978.

Burns, James MacGregor. *Leadership.* New York: Harper & Row, 1978,

Burt, Struthers. *Philadelphia, Holy Experiment.* New York: Doubleday,
Doran & Company, 1945.

Childs, Marquis, and Cater, Douglas. *Ethics in a Business Society.* New York:
Mentor Books, 1954.

Clough, Wilson O., ed. *Intellectual Origins of American National Thought.*
New York: Corinth Books, 1961.

Cochran, Thomas. *Pennsylvania, a History.* New York: W. W. Norton &
Company, 1978.

Dacey, Norman F. *What's Wrong with Your Life Insurance.* New York: The
Crowell-Collier Press, 1963.

Gudmundson, John. *The Great Provider.* South Norwalk, Conn.: Industrial
Publications Company, 1959.

Hooker, Richard. *Aetna Life, Its First Hundred Years.* Hartford: 1956.

———. *A Century of Service, The Massachusetts Mutual Story.* Springfield,
Mass.: 1951.

James, Marquis. *Biography of a Business 1792-1942.* New York: Bobbs
Merrill Company, 1942.

James, Ollie M. *Splendid Century Centennial History of the Union Central Life
Insurance Company.* Cincinnati: 1967.

Kesslinger, J. M. *Guardian of a Century 1860-1960.* New York: Guardian
Life Insurance Company, 1960.

Lasch, Christopher. *The Culture of Narcissism.* New York: W. W. Norton,
1979.

Leitch, Addison H. *A Layman's Guide to Presbyterian Beliefs.* Grand Rapids:
Zondervan Publishing House, 1967.

Lennox, William G. *The Health and Turnover of Missionaries.* New York:
Methodist Book Concern Press, 1933.

Linton, M. Albert. *Life Insurance Speaks for Itself.* New York: Harper and
Brothers, 1939.

Mackie, Alexander. *A Sheep in Wolf's Clothing.* Unpublished memoir.

———. *Facile Princeps.* Philadelphia: 1956.

———. *That Is to Say.* New York: The Newcomen Society in North
America, 1959.

May, Earl Chapin, and Oursler, Will. *The Prudential, a Story of Human
Security.* Garden City, N.Y.: Doubleday & Co., Inc., 1950.

BIBLIOGRAPHY

Mitchell, Robert B. *From Actuarius to Actuary*. Chicago: The Society of Actuaries, 1974.

Nelli, Humbert O. "A New Look at the History of Personal Insurance." *Journal of the American Society of Chartered Life Underwriters*, Vol. XXXIII, No. 3 (July 1969).

Novak, Michael, ed. *Capitalism and Socialism, a Theological Inquiry*. Washington, D.C.: American Enterprise Institute for Public Policy Research, 1979.

Russell, G. Hugh, and Black, Kenneth, J. *Human Behavior and Life Insurance*. Englewood Cliffs, N.J.: Prentice-Hall, Inc., 1963.

Schull, Joseph. *The Century of the Sun*. Toronto: MacMillan of Canada, 1971.

Smylie, James H., ed. "Presbyterians and the American Revolution." *Journal of Presbyterian History*, Vol. 54, No. 1 (spring 1976).

Spielman, Peter, and Zelman, Aaron. *The Life Insurance Conspiracy*. New York: Simon & Schuster, Inc., 1976.

Stone, Mildred F. *A Calling and Its College*. Homewood, Ill.: Richard F. Irwin, 1963.

———. *Since 1845, a History of the Mutual Benefit Life Insurance Company*. New Brunswick, N.J.: Rutgers University Press, 1957.

Wainwright, Nicholas B. *A Philadelphia Story, the Philadelphia Contributionship*. Philadelphia: William F. Nell Company, 1952.

Wasson, S. Carson. *Eleven O'Clock Sunday Morning*. Clinton, Mass.: Colonial Press, 1960.

CORPORATORS AND BOARD OF DIRECTORS, PRESBYTERIAN MINISTERS' FUND

CORPORATORS
Name and Year Elected

Acker, J. Henry Radey, Esq.
1908 President
Adams, Rev. Arthur M. 1947
Adamson, Charles B. 1903
Agnew, Rev. B. L. 1892
Albright, Rev. Raymond W. 1941
Alexander, Rev. Archibald 1808
Alexander, Walter R. 1952
Alison, Rev. Alexander 1892
Alison, Rev. Francis 1759
(Charter) Secretary
Alison, Rev. Hector 1761
Alison, Rev. Patrick 1775
Alison, Capt. William 1766
Alleman, Rev. Herbert C. 1927
Allen, Andrew 1773
Allen, Francis Olcott 1881
Allen, James 1773
Allen, Rev. Perry S. 1893
Secretary, President
Allen, Rev. R. H. 1870
Allen, Hon. William 1759
(Charter) Treasurer
Anderson, Hurst Robins 1957
Anderson, James M. 1954
Appel, Anthony R. 1965
Appel, John W. 1926
Armstrong, Rev. James F. 1795
Augsburger, Rev. Myron S. 1974
Austin, William L. 1917
Baird, John A., Jr. 1968
Baker, Rev. George D. 1888
Barnes, Rev. Albert 1848
Barnes, Rev. George Emerson
1931
Barr, Rev. W. W. 1891
Barraclough, Henry 1952
Bayard, Andrew 1798
Bayard, Dr. James 1767
Bayard, Col. John 1765

Beaty, Rev. Charles 1760
Bedford, Gunning, Esq. 1793
Benson, Gustavus 1872
Bevan, Matthew L. 1837
President
Biles, Charles H. 1878
Bishop, Dr. Russell H. 1971
Bittner, Silas P. 1957
Black, Israel P. 1896
Blain, Col. Ephraim 1782
Blair, Rev. John Allan 1918
Blair, Rev. John 1760
Blake, Eugene Carson 1953
Blakely, John 1792
Bleakly, John 1759 (Charter)
Boardman, Rev. Henry A. 1848
Bohl, Dr. Robert W. 1980
Bolton, Elmer K. 1952
Bolton, Rev. J. Gray 1905
Book, Edward R. 1981
Boudinot, Dr. Elias 1801
Bourne, Capt. Thomas 1759
(Charter)
Boyd, Rev. James 1795
Bradford, William, Esq. 1782
Brainerd, Rev. Thomas 1853
Breckinridge, Rev. John 1833
Breed, Rev. David R. 1903
Breed, Rev. William Pratt
1869 President
Brown, Christopher G., Esq. 1890
Bryan, Hon. George
1760 President
Burrell, Rev. David J. 1903
Caldwell, Andrew 1773
Caldwell, Rev. Frank H. 1940
Caldwell, John 1798
Caldwell, Samuel 1767
Campbell, Donald K. 1976
Carr, Harold Ford 1954

Chapman, Francis, Esq. 1929
Chapman, S. Spencer, Esq. 1895
Chauncey, Charles, Esq. 1810
Chester, Rev. Carlos T. 1893
  Secretary
Chester, Rev. S. H. 1903
Chevalier, John 1765
Chevalier, Peter, Sr. 1760
Chevalier, Peter 1773
Clark, Robert S. 1851
Cleland, Rev. Thomas H. 1898
Clemmens, William B. 1976
Collingwood, J. Marshall 1890
Colwell, Stephen 1846
Cookenbach, John M. 1967
Cooper, Dr. Lawrence Owen 1972
Cope, Edward 1911
Corson, Bishop Fred Pierce 1949
Cotton, Jarvis M. 1961
Craig, James 1773
Creswell, Robert 1878
Crosby, W. K. 1902
Cross, Rev. Robert 1759
  (Charter) President
Cunningham, Rev. John R. 1933
Cupp, Paul J. 1960
Cuyler, Rev. Cornelius C. 1836
Dales, Rev. John B. 1891
Darling, Rev. Henry 1856
Darling, Rev. Timothy G. 1903
Darrach, Henry 1892
Davidson, Rev. Robert 1782
Davidson, William 1806
Davis, H. L. 1913
Dean, William E. 1935
Dickson, James N. 1851
Dickson, Rev. James Stuart 1890
Distler, Theodore A. 1945
Drummond, Winslow S. 1956
DuBarry, William H. 1955
Dubois, Patterson, Esq. 1890
Dubois, William L. 1871
Dulles, Rev. J. W. 1864
  President
Dunlap, James 1864
Eckles, Rev. Mervin J. 1899
Elliot, Andrew 1759
Engle, James 1818

Engles, Rev. William M. 1833
Evans, Mrs. Colleen Townsend
  1976
Ewalt, Floyd W. 1954
Ewing, Rev. John 1759 President
  and Treasurer
Ewing, Rev. Joseph Lyons 1933
Eyster, Hon. George 1884
Faris, Rev. John T. 1925
Farr, G. W. 1892
Farr, John C. 1873
Faunce, Hon. John E. 1902
Field, Robert Patterson 1887
  Secretarry
Field, Samuel 1881
Finley, Rev. Samuel 1759 (Charter)
Fiske, W. W. 1892
Flemming, Dr. Arthur S. 1970
Forbes, George W. 1856
Fox, Herman C. 1892
Freeland, Thomas M. 1869
Freeman, Rev. Robert 1924
Fullerton, Alexander, Esq. 1849
Fullerton, George 1773
Fulton, David Irvin 1926
Fulton, Rev. Robert H. 1892
Fulton, Rev. William P. 1898
  President
Fulton, Rev. William S. 1899
Furst, William S., Esq. 1905
Gallaudet, Peter W. 1800
Gast, Aaron E. 1962
Gibbons, Henry Johns, Esq. 1906
Gibbons, Rev. Herbert Adams
  1924
Gibbons, Rev. Hughes Oliphant
  1889 President
Gill, John D. 1937
Gladfelter, Millard E. 1956
Glenn, Edwin F. 1892
Goodrich, H. G. 1895
Gordon, William Richard 1965
Graham, Hon. George S. 1889
Graham, Rev. Loyal Young 1889
Graham, Rev. Robert 1892
  President
Green, Rev. Ashbel 1792
  Secretary

Lindquist, Rev. Raymond I. 1947
Lingelbach, Professor William E. 1933
Lingle, Rev. Walter L. 1921
Linn, Rev. John B. 1800
Lippincott, R. Schuyler 1970
Loetscher, Rev. Frederick W. 1908
Loetscher, Rev. Lefferts A. 1952
Luccock, Rev. George N. 1917
Lugg, Ralph G. 1958
Macalester, Charles, Esq. 1849 President
MacBride, Russell H. 1944
MacCallum, Rev. John A. 1911
MacColl, Rev. Alexander 1931
MacIntosh, Rev. John S. 1891
MacKenzie, Dr. Charles S. 1981
Mackie, Rev. Alexander 1924 President
Magee, James F. 1888
Magill, John 1958
March, Rev. Daniel 1869
Marsh, Rev. Daniel L. 1937
Marshall, Thomas 1879
Martien, Alfred 1870
Marvin, Sylvester S. 1899
Mays, Dr. Benjamin E. 1968
McCahan, Professor David 1937
McCall, Dr. Duke K. 1969
McClintock, Rev. J. C. 1891
McClure, Rev. James G. K. 1915
McCord, Dr. James I. 1961
McCormick, Henry B. 1934
McDowell, Rev. Alexander 1760
McDowell, Rev. John 1840
McDowell, Rev. John 1935
McElroy, William J. 1870
McFaden, Rev. F. T. 1904
McIlveine, William 1759 (Charter)
McKay, Dr. Arthur Raymond 1968
McKinney, Rev. W. W. 1895
McMichael, John 1759
McMullin, John 1818
McWhorter, Rev. Alexander 1792
Mears, George W. (as Mease, Fin. Comm. p. 105) 1873
Mease, James 1768

Mease, Capt. John 1759 (Charter)
Mease, John 1768
Millar, Rev. John 1760
Miller, E. Augustus, Esq. 1910
Miller, E. Clarence 1941
Miller, Rev. Rufus W. 1903
Miller, William 1758
Millidoler, Rev. Philip 1804
Minton, Rev. Henry Collins 1902
Mitchel, Dr. Alexander W. 1840 President
Mitchell, J. Henry 1892
Mitchell, Joseph B. 1840
Mitchell, Joseph G. 1870
Monro, Hugh R. 1934
Montgomery, Joseph 1818
Montgomery, Rev. R. Ames 1927
Montgomery, William E. 1951
Moore, Dr. Samuel 1828
Moore, Rev. T. Vernon 1916
Moore, Rev. William E. 1890
Morris, Dr. Arthur N. 1966
Morse, Richard C. 1942
Mudge, Rev. Lewis Seymour 1926
Mueller, Paul A. 1955
Murkland, Rev. W. N. 1891
Mutchmore, Rev. Samuel A. 1890
Neff, Jonathan C. 1921 Treasurer
Neil, Rev. William 1818
Nelson, John Oliver 1954
Nesbitt, Albert J. 1958
Newkirk, Rev. Matthew 1881
Newman, Rev. John Grant 1913
Niccols, Rev. Samuel T. 1878
Nichols, H. S. Prentiss 1927
Nichols, Bishop Roy C. 1974
Nichols, Roy Franklin 1956
Nicholson, John Esq. 1793
Nourse, Joseph 1795
Ogden, Robert C. 1884
Paisley, Harry E. 1926
Parham, Captain T. David 1967
Patterson, Morris 1869
Patterson, Professor Robert M. 1816 Treasurer, Secretary
Patterson, Robert 1785 Treasurer
Patterson, Robert, Esq. 1849 Treasurer

Patterson, T. Elliott 1904
Patton, John W. 1904
Patton, Thomas R. 1910
Paul, Henry N., Jr. 1892
Peacock, James Craig, Esq. 1950
Peale, Dr. Norman Vincent 1939
Pearce, Judge William L. (Pierce)
  1871
Peebles, H. O. 1905
Pendleton, Hon. William W. 1981
Perkins, Abraham R. 1863
Perkins, E. R. 1890
Perkins, Samuel C. 1872
Perkins, Samuel H. 1857
Pettit, Col. Charles 1792
Poling, Rev. Daniel A. 1925
Poling, Rev. Daniel K. 1960
Potter, Hon. William P. 1907
Potts, Rev. George C. 1806
Pugh, Rev. William Barrow 1945
Purveyance, Samuel, Jr. 1767
Raines, Rev. Robert A. 1969
Ralston, Robert 1795 President
Raven, Rev. John H. 1914
Rea, John (Rhea) 1759
Read, Andrew 1760 (Charter)
Read, Joseph, Esq. 1782
Reed, Rev. Harry Lathrop 1934
Reed, Joseph, Esq. 1806
Reed, Rev. Villeroy D. 1874
Redman, Hamilton M. 1967
Redmond, Dr. John 1759
  President
Richards, Rev. George W. 1911
Richards, Dr. J. McDowell 1948
Richter, Richard P. 1977
Ringland, Rev. A. W. 1891
Robbins, Rev. Francis L. 1890
Roberts, Rev. James 1891
Roberts, Rev. William Dayton
  1892
Rodgers, Rev. C. P. 1856
Rodgers, Rev. John 1759
Rogers, Talbot M. 1898
Rollins, Hon. Edward Ashton
  1881
Rush, William 1767
Ruston, Rev. W. O. 1904

Rutgers, Col. Henry 1804
Sargent, Winthrop 1864
Sayre, Francis Bowes, Jr. 1952
Schenk, Rev. Addison V. C. 1891
Schick, Rudolph M. 1891
Schnader, William A., Esq. 1933
Schweitzer, Rev. Frederick 1947
  Secretary
Scott, Hon. John 1887
Scott, John, Jr. 1902
Scott, William H. 1891
Seargeant, Jonathan D. 1782
Sharpe, Rev. J. H. 1893
Sheppard, Franklin L. 1891
Sherrerd, Major Henry D. M.
  1943
Shields, Charles W. 1853
Singmaster, Rev. J. O. 1905
Smith, Rev. John B. 1794
Smith, Col. Jonathan B. 1767
Smith, J. Willison 1935
Smith, Phillip H. 1974
Smith, Rev. Robert. 1759
Smith, Robert (Hatter) 1773
Smith, Robert (Merchant) 1788
Smith, Rev. Sampson 1759
Smith, Samuel 1759
Smith, Rev. Samuel Stanhope 1785
Snowden, Isaac 1785
Snowden, Isaac, Jr. 1798
Snowden, Col. J. Ross 1863
  President
Spaeth, Rev. A. 1902
Sproat, Rev. James 1773
  Secretary
Stair, Mrs. Lois H. 1974
Steele, Rev. David 1902
Steele, Joseph M. 1931
Stewart, Rev. George Black 1910
Stewart, Lee 1918
Stitt, Dr. David L. 1969
Strothman, Raymond O. 1973
Stuart, George H. 1853
Stuart, George H., Jr. 1896
Stuart, George H., 3rd 1923
Stuart, James 1818
Stokes, M. H. 1895
Stone, Rev. John Timothy 1914

CORPORATORS AND DIRECTORS

Strong, Judge William 1871
Sweets, Rev. Henry H. 1910
Taite, Rev. Joseph 1761
Taite, Rev. Richard 1767
Taylor, Rev. James H. 1935
Templeton, John M. 1969
Ten Brook, William E., Esq.
1870 President
Tennent, Rev. Gilbert 1759
(Charter)
Tennent, Rev. William Mackey
1785
Tilden, William T. 1903
Timanus, J. Herbert R. 1944
Tingley, Benjamin W. 1851
Tingley, Clement, Esq. 1846
Treat, Rev. Richard 1759 (Charter)
Tyson, J. B. Millard, Esq. 1959
Upham, Rev. N. L. 1887
Secretary
Van Pelt, Rev. R. H. 1892
Wagner, Rev. James Edgar 1955
Wagner, Paul C., Esq. 1947
Walker, George A. 1918
Wallace, John 1759
Wallace, John C. 1937
Walton, Charles S., Jr. 1943
Warren, G. W., D.D.S. 1923
Wasson, Dr. S. Carson 1951
President

Waters, John B. 1887
Watson, Rev. Charles R. 1903
Webb, Rev. Aquilla 1918
Weir, Silas E. 1825
Wentz, Rev. Abdel Ross 1950
Westbrook, Rev. R. B. 1858
Whallon, Rev. Edward P. 1890
Whallon, Rev. Walter L. 1940
Whyte, Rev. Robert B. 1943
Williams, Morris 1910
Williamson, Dr. Hugh 1767
Wilson, Rev. George P. 1902
Wilson, Rev. George P. 1895
Wilson, Jacob 1891
Wilson, Rev. James P. 1807
Wilson, Rev. J. A. 1901
Wilson, Rev. Robert Dick 1899
Wilson, Rev. Samuel T. 1878
Winchester, Rev. Samuel G. 1833
Wiseman, Dr. William J. 1967
Wishart, Rev. Charles F. 1923
Wolf, Rev. E. J. 1902
Wonacott, Charles N. 1937
Wood, Rev. Charles 1889
Wood, William 1904
Worden, Rev. James A. 1907
Wylie, Rev. Theodore W. 1858
Wynkoop, William 1890
Wynn, G. W. 1891
Young, James T. 1878

313

DIRECTORS

INDEX

INDEX

317